A Key to American Literature

A Home Education Program in American Literature

with Explanatory Comments, Questions and Answers,

including a Biographical Encyclopedia of Authors,

Glossaries of Literary Terms, and Comprehensive

Indexes to the Reader's Bookshelf of American Literature

PREPARED EXCLUSIVELY

FOR THE SPECIAL EDITION

BY

WILLIAM VAN O'CONNOR

AND

THE EDITORS OF THOMAS Y. CROWELL COMPANY

PUBLISHED BY

Thomas Y. Crowell Company

NEW YORK

PREFACE

American literature is among the world's youngest literatures. In some ways it is an offshoot of English literature, but it has its own unique qualities and characteristics. The London *Times Literary Supplement* devoted a large issue to it a few years ago, entitled "American Literature — Its Independence and Vigor."

In the seventeenth and eighteenth centuries the United States produced only a few significant writers. In the nineteenth century the number increased greatly, and in the twentieth there have been many many excellent writers. Some scholars claim that twentieth-century American literature is pre-eminent among world literatures.

How should one read and study this literature? Attentively and carefully, to be sure. But one should not be intimidated by great writing, be frightened or awed by it. Usually a great work of literature wears an air of simplicity — its point can be grasped. Grasping the point of a poem or short story or play is the reader's initial duty. Most of the questions in this Study Guide are designed to help him grasp it. Other questions are designed to help him develop a fuller sense of chronology, historical and biographical data. Yet others involve answers of a more literary or formal kind, relating to the writer's skill and artistry.

One American critic has said that in reading a truly original and significant work of literature one experiences a sense of intellectual and emotional growth. The editor of this Study Guide hopes that each reader can and will experience such growth.

WILLIAM VAN O'CONNOR

University of Minnesota

HOW TO USE
A Key to American Literature

As you examine the Table of Contents on the following pages, you notice that there are eight separate tools in this volume, carefully designed and integrated. They will enable you to use the other five volumes of *The Reader's Bookshelf* with maximum efficiency so that you can acquire complete familiarity with American literature. These tools are:

Biographies of the Editors   *Tool No. 1*

28-Week Reading Course   *Tool No. 2*

This reading course is mapped out to require a minimum of twenty-eight consecutive weeks, reading about twenty minutes a day — or several hours a week. The material is arranged topically (as The American West, Henry James, etc.) and in historic progression (that is, beginning with the seventeenth century and ending with the present). The amount of reading each week tends to increase as the 28-Week Reading Course progresses, for your skill and reading rate should improve, too. In fact the time budgets for each selection are shown in the column at the extreme right. The volume in which you will find the selection (P, for *American Poetry;* E, for *American Literary Essays,* etc.) is indicated at the extreme left. Also the page numbers within that volume are shown immediately to the right of the selection title. Now the inside column of page numbers (to the left of the time budget column) refers to the relevant questions in the Systematic Study Guide, thus integrating the 28-Week Reading Course with the Systematic Study Guide. Simply look on the page referred to and your eye will pick up the relevant question or questions to the selection you have just read.

Alphabetical Index by Author   *Tool No. 3*

Here all of the authors contained in *The Reader's Bookshelf* are arranged alphabetically, next to them their works, then the volume in which each work is contained, and the page therein. This Index has special usefulness for you as a review check list.

Significant Background Facts and Dates   *Tool No. 4*

This table places literary facts in juxtaposition with the events of history, thus giving the reader a clear picture of American Literature from the standpoint of time and history.

Systematic Study Guide   *Tool No. 5*

The contents of this important tool are:
      questions covering the material in each volume
      sample answers to the questions
      a section of Special Aids for Further Understanding of American
          Literature
      questions and exercises covering the special aids
      sample answers to these questions
      four glossaries of terms that you will need:

1. Literary Glossary
2. Fiction Glossary
3. Poetry Glossary
4. Drama Glossary

The Systematic Study Guide differs in plan from the 28-Week Reading Course in that it is arranged volume by volume. There are six main parts: one for each of the five volumes in the bookshelf, and a sixth part containing special aids. Thus Part 1 deals with *American Literary Essays,* and the questions thereunder are divided into batches under topics. There are questions on the *Introduction,* questions under the topic *Possibilities,* the topic *People.* Then follow sample answers. Thereafter are questions under the topics *Poetry, Prose, Fiction* and *Prospects;* again sample answers given topic by topic. With respect to the other four volumes the questions on all the selections are first given; then followed by all the sample answers. Under Part 6 — Special Aids — you will find special questions and exercises, followed by sample answers or suggestions.

You will find the four glossaries conveniently placed before each section to which it pertains. (Note that there is a single glossary, *Fiction Glossary,* pertaining to both *American Short Novels* and *American Short Stories.*)

The remaining five tools are reference tools to enable you to answer the questions that occur to you and help you find easily what you are looking for. They are:

Biographical Encyclopedia of American Authors   *Tool No. 6*

This is a complete encyclopedia of every author included in *The Reader's Bookshelf,* with portraits of many of them. This enables you to look at every author not from the standpoint of a single selection which you may have read, but from within the context of his whole life and work.

Index to First Lines of Poems   *Tool No. 7*

Frequently people can recall the first few words of a poem, rather than the title. This index will enable you to locate poems in *The Reader's Bookshelf* easily and quickly.

Dictionary-Index to The Reader's Bookshelf of American Literature   *Tool No. 8*

Finally there is this special dictionary-index. Here you will find:
    every author, with pertinent dates
    his works, listed thereunder
    every work in the set, in this single index, with its date
    all characters that appear: like Ahab, or Wingate
    places: like Africa, Texas, etc.
    literary allusions, with explanations and dates: like Aeschylus
    other allusions, explained: like Breughel, Shays' Rebellion, etc.

In supplying you with these eight tools, the editors have given you the means for achieving a complete coverage of American literature, the means of exploring the fascinating byways that this reading will open, and the means of answering the questions and pinning down the facts that you encounter.

TABLE OF CONTENTS

BIOGRAPHIES OF THE EDITORS

Each of the five volumes of the *Reader's Bookshelf of American Literature* is devoted to a particular American literary field: the essay, poetry, the drama, the short story, and the novel. The contents of each volume have been selected by a distinguished expert in that field. Together, the five volumes serve as a rich representation of American literature from the Colonial period to the present. Or, individually, any volume can be used by a reader wanting to pursue an interest in that particular field.

This collection is marked by three purposes.

First, the five volumes reflect faithfully the historical range of American literature: our initial conformity to British patterns and our struggle to emancipate ourselves; a century and a half of tension between the Jeffersonian and the Hamiltonian traditions; the development of regional and racial strains in our national life; the special problems presented to the artist by a culture without fixed literary traditions of its own; the attraction and color of the ever-open West; and our constant examination of the democratic tradition. Reflecting this historical range are, for example, four poems of the seventeenth-century New England poetess Anne Bradstreet, a portion of Franklin's *Autobiography,* the first play by a United States citizen to be produced here, our first truly distinguished short stories (by Hawthorne, Poe, Irving) as well as our contemporary classics (by Faulkner, Hemingway, Katherine Anne Porter, Eudora Welty, Steinbeck). Here are our Concord Transcendentalists, our Boston Brahmins, our developing symbolists and realists; here are Lincoln's *Gettysburg Address,* Faulkner's Nobel Prize Acceptance Speech, and Stephen Vincent Benét's poem "American Names."

A second purpose is to show the variety of achievement of American writers. The classic writers are here: Poe, Melville, Whitman, Twain, Henry James, Frost, Eliot. James is represented by his short novel *Washington Square,* an essay, and two short stories; Poe by seventeen lyrics, two short stories, and a critical essay; Twain by his short novel *The Man That Corrupted Hadleyburg,* a short story, and his hilarious dissection of "Fenimore Cooper's Literary Offenses." Here are twenty-three lyrics of Emily Dickinson. Our revolutionaries, such as H. L. Mencken, Ezra Pound, and Hart Crane, are represented; and so are our realists, such as Stephen Crane and Theodore Dreiser. You will find our great contemporary experimenters, such as Gertrude Stein, E. E. Cummings, and William Carlos Williams (whose *The Great American Novel* is published here for the first time in the United States); and our penetrating academic critics, such as Trilling, Blackmur, and Tate. Here, also, is a cross section of American writers writing about other American writers: Chapman on Emerson, Blackmur on Melville, Melville on Hawthorne, Thoreau on Whitman, Whitman on Poe, Lowell on Thoreau, Tate on Dickinson.

A third purpose of the *Reader's Bookshelf* is to reflect American writers' attempts for two centuries to understand, in William Van O'Connor's words, "in what ways American literature is different from other literatures, in its various subject matters, its aspirations, its persistent myths." *American Literary Essays* is directly concerned with this quest. Examples of classic devastation are H. L. Mencken's "American Culture" and "Poetry in America." The fact that this quest continues today, with humor, verve, and provocativeness, is illustrated by John A. Kouwenhoven's recent essay, "What Is American About America?" In it he lists a dozen artifacts, from the Manhattan skyline and jazz to chewing gum and Whitman's *Leaves of Grass*—all recognizably American though apparently without any relation to one another—and shows how all of the twelve have one thing in common which is characteristic of American life—"a concern with process rather than with product."

The general editor of the *Reader's Bookshelf of American literature*, William Van O'Connor, is Professor of English at the University of Minnesota, where he has been director of graduate studies for a number of years. Following several years of wartime services, he was a Rockefeller Foundation Fellow in Humanities. He has been a Fulbright lecturer at the University of Liége, a participant in the American Studies program at Cambridge, England, Berg Professor of English and American Literature at New York University; and he has taught in summer sessions at various universities, including Southern California, Duke, and Columbia. He is listed in *Who's Who, Twentieth Century Authors, The Authors' and Writers' Who's Who,* and other reference works. He has published hundreds of articles and reviews in a large number of magazines, including *The New York Times Book Review, The Saturday Review, Poetry, College English, Sewanee Review,* and *Kenyon Review.* His books include *The New Woman of the Renaissance, Climates of Tragedy, Sense and Sensibility in Modern Poetry, The Shaping Spirit: A Study of Wallace Stevens, An Age of Criticism: 1900-1950, The Tangled Fire of William Faulkner,* and a book of short stories, *Campus on the River.* With Robert Penn Warren and Allen Tate, he is an editor of the University of Minnesota pamphlet on American writers. Among the volumes he has edited are *Forms of Modern Fiction: Essays Collected in Honor of Joseph Warren Beach, Twentieth Century Literature* (with Frederick Hoffman), *Modern Prose,* and *A Casebook on Ezra Pound* (with Edward Stone). He has served as advisory editor and as a contributor to several encyclopedias, including the Britannica, Grolier, and Collier's. He is also the general editor of a series of casebooks on literary subjects for Thomas Y. Crowell Company.

Richard P. Blackmur, editor of *American Short Novels,* is Professor of English at Princeton and one of the most admired of American literary critics. For some years he was a free-lance critic and poet and an editor, with Marianne Moore and Kenneth Burke, of the *Dial,* one of the most important literary magazines in twentieth-century America. On three occasions he has held Guggenheim Fellowships. For three years he was a member of the Institute for Advanced Study at Princeton. He has lectured in various parts of the world for the State Department, and is a Fellow of the Library of Congress in American literature. He is also a member of the National Institute of Arts and Letters. His books include *The Double Agent, From Jordan's Delight, The Expense of Greatness, The Second World, The Good European, Language as Gesture,* and *The Lion and the Honeycomb.* For many years Mr. Blackmur has been acknowledged as a foremost student of the theory of fiction. In 1941 he edited *The Art of the Novel: the Critical Prefaces of Henry James* (James being our foremost theoretician on the structure of fiction, including the short novel). He has also edited many of the novels of Henry James.

Alan Downer, Professor of English at Princeton, has established himself as one of the foremost critics and historians of the English and American drama. He is also a student of Shakespearean drama and teaches the advanced Shakespeare course at Princeton. In 1951, he published *Fifty Years of American Drama,* which has sold widely both in hard covers and in a paper-covered edition. He has lectured on American drama in various parts of Europe, sponsored by the Fulbright commission, and has taught American drama at the Harvard-sponsored Salzburg Seminar in Austria. He has written *The British Drama,* contributed articles on the drama to *Hudson Review* and many other periodicals, and has edited *Twenty-Five Modern Plays.*

Karl Shapiro is one of the best-known American poets of this generation. Born in Baltimore, he attended the University of Virginia and Johns Hopkins. He was among the first boatload of American GI's to reach Australia during World War II. His first book, *Person, Place and Thing,* was published while he was en route to Australia. He served with medical units in New Guinea, Biak, and other islands. (It was in New Guinea that he and the general editor, William Van O'Connor, first met.) During the war Shapiro published *V-Letter,* which won the Pulitzer Prize for Poetry, and *Essay on Rime.* After the war he taught at Johns Hopkins, leaving there to serve for several years as editor of *Poetry, a Magazine of Verse,* in Chicago. He is a Fellow of the Library of Congress, held a Guggenheim Fellowship, and has won many poetry awards. His books include *Trial of a Poet, Bibliography of Modern Prosody, Poems 1940-53, Poems of a Jew,* and *Beyond Criticism.* For the past few years he has been Professor of English at the University of Nebraska and editor of *Prairie Schooner.*

Ray West, now Professor of English at San Francisco State University, took his Ph.D. in American literature at the University of Iowa. After a short period at Kansas State, he returned to Iowa to teach writing, with Paul Engel, in the Iowa School of Letters. A number of his own stories have been included in *The O. Henry Awards* and *The Best Short Stories of the Year.* About ten years ago he published *The Rise of Short Fiction, 1900-1950,* still widely used as a critical guide to the American short story. He has taught literature and writing courses at various summer sessions and writers' conferences. For many years he edited *The Western Review*.

Lewis Leary, editor of *American Literary Essays,* is Professor of English at Columbia University. He took his B.S. at the University of Vermont and his Ph.D. at Columbia. He is the author of *That Rascal Freneau: A Study in Literary Failure* and *The Literary Life of Nathaniel Tucker*, and the editor of *Articles on American Literature: 1900-1950, The Last Poems of Philip Freneau, The Unity of Knowledge, Motive and Method in the Cantos of Ezra Pound, Selected Essays of Henry David Thoreau,* and *Contemporary Literary Scholarship: A Critical Review*. From 1941 to 1945 he was a Special Assistant in the Office of Strategic Services, working in Washington and Cairo. During 1957-1958 Leary was Visiting Professor, sponsored by the Fulbright commission, at the University of Amsterdam. He is a member of the Editorial Board of *American Literature,* and has contributed articles to *American Literature, New England Quarterly, Virginia Quarterly Review, The Saturday Review, The Nation,* and other periodicals.

28-WEEK READING COURSE IN
AMERICAN LITERATURE

28 weeks averaging only 20 minutes a day

To enable you to get the most out of *The Reader's Bookshelf of American Literature* the entire five volumes have been programmed for a 28-week course requiring on an average about 20 minutes a day reading time. Thus, in seven months you can enjoy and learn the whole sweep of American novels, stories, essays, dramas and poems from the earliest times to the present.

Furthermore we have provided for your convenience time budgets so that you can use your time most efficiently. These have been set up at a reading rate of 240 words per minute, which is slightly higher than the national average reading speed.

The five volumes are keyed as follows:

E   American Essays

N   American Novels

S   American Short Stories

P   American Poems

D   American Drama

Thus in the program list below, the letter at the left will tell you instantly what volume is referred to. The figure at the right will tell you how many minutes you should budget for each selection. Also, we have provided check-back periods to go with the shorter assignments. We suggest that in these check-back periods you go back over the ground you have covered to strengthen the continuity of your reading.

Even more important, however, is this: PLEASE BUDGET TEN MINUTES TO RIFFLE THROUGH THE PAGES AND PREVIEW EACH WEEK'S WORK BEFORE YOU BEGIN READING IT.

And now ... *good reading to you!*

1
THE 17TH CENTURY

8
WHITMAN

9
EMILY DICKINSON AND SOME OTHER POETS

10
THE AMERICAN WEST

11
HENRY JAMES

12-13
HENRY JAMES

		Relevant Page Reference in the Study Guide	Time Budget Reading Time in Minutes
	Preview		[10]
N	James, "Washington Square" (pp. 134-235)..................	76-77	4 hours 10
	Preview		[10]

14-15
REALISM

	Preview		[10]
E	Holmes, "Realism in Literature" (p. 233)......................		2
E	Howells, "Art and Democracy" (p. 38).........................	48	2
E	Howells, "Subjects for American Fiction" (p. 236)........	57	8
E	Garland, "Local Color in Art" (p. 244)..........................	57	8
D	Introduction (pp. 6-8)	130	8
D	Herne, "Shore Acres" (pp. 48-105).................................	131-132	2 hours 23
D	Moody, "The Great Divide" (pp. 106-139)...................	132	1 hour 20

16
STEPHEN CRANE

	Preview		[10]
N	Crane, "Maggie: A Girl of the Streets" (pp. 97-133)....	68-69	1 hour 30
S	Crane, "The Blue Hotel" (pp. 143-161).........................	81	45
S	Crane, "The Upturned Face" (pp. 161-163)...................	81	8
P	Crane (pp. 143-145)	101	33

17
REALISM AND CRITICISM

	Preview		[10]
S	Dreiser, "The Lost Phoebe" (pp. 163-173).....................	81	25
E	Farrell, "Social Themes in American Realism" (p. 264)	57	15
E	Norris, "The Novel with a Purpose" (p. 247)...............	57	7
E	Mencken, "American Culture" (p. 39)..........................	48	9
S	Anderson, "I Want to Know Why" (pp. 173-179)........	81	15
E	Smith, "The Prospects of Literature" (p. 298).............	58	5

18
THE NEW POETRY

	Preview		[10]
P	Introduction (pp. 6-8).......................................	93	7
P	Quotation from Rodman (pp. 234-235)..........................	111	2
E	Amy Lowell, "The Poet's Trade" (p. 195)..................	56	2

THE NEW POETRY (Cont.)

		Relevant Page Reference in the Study Guide	Time Budget Reading Time in Minutes
P	Masters (pp. 136-139)	101	7
P	Robinson (pp. 139-143)	101	10
P	Quotations from Frost (p. 236)	111	1
E	Frost, "The Figure a Poem Makes" (p. 204)	56	5
P	Frost (pp. 145-156)	101-102	28
P	Sandburg (pp. 156-157)	102	3
P	Stevens (pp. 158-162)	102-103	15
P	Lindsay (pp. 163-167)	103	10
P	Quotation from Pound (p. 236)	111	1½
P	Pound (pp. 170-173)	104	9
E	Eliot, "Tradition and the Individual Talent" (p. 199)	56	12
P	Eliot (pp. 182-185)	105	9
P	Aiken (pp. 185-186)	106	2
P	Millay (pp. 186-187)	106	2
P	Hart Crane (pp. 195-205)	107	25
E	Mencken, "Poetry in America" (p. 196)	56	7

19
THE NEW DRAMA

	Preview		[10]
D	Introduction (pp. 8-12)	130	12
D	O'Neill, "The Hairy Ape" (pp. 140-166)	133	1 hour 5

20-21-22
NEW DIRECTIONS IN FICTION

	Preview		[10]
P	Wylie (pp. 169-170)	103-104	2
N	Wylie, "The Venetian Glass Nephew" (pp. 344-396)	71	2 hours 10
P	William Carlos Williams (pp. 167-169)	103	5
N	William Carlos Williams, "The Great American Novel" (pp. 307-343)	70-71	1 hour 30
N	Stein, "Melanctha" (pp. 236-306)	69-70	2 hours 55
S	Hemingway, "The Capital of the World" (pp. 179-186)	82	18

23
THE THIRTIES: POETRY AND DRAMA

	Preview		[10]
P	Fletcher (pp. 173-175)	104	5
P	Jeffers (pp. 175-178)	104	8
P	MacLeish (pp. 187-190)	106	8
P	Benét (pp. 194-195)	107	2
P	Tate (pp. 205-207)	108	5
P	Fearing (pp. 207-208)	108	2
D	Wilder, "The Long Christmas Dinner" (pp. 210-221)	134	27

24
A DEPRESSION DRAMA

		Relevant Page Reference in the Study Guide	Time Budget Reading Time in Minutes
	Preview		[10]
D	Sherwood, "The Petrified Forest" (pp. 167-209) 133-134		1 hour 45

25
THE THIRTIES: FICTION AND CRITICISM

	Preview		[10]
S	Steinbeck, "The Chrysanthemums" (pp. 218-225)	82	18
S	Faulkner, "A Rose for Emily" (pp. 186-192)	82	15
S	Faulkner, "Wash" (pp. 192-200)	82	20
S	Porter, "The Grave" (pp. 200-204)	82	10
S	Warren, "Blackberry Winter" (pp. 204-218)	82	35
P	Warren (pp. 210-212)	109	8
E	Brooks, "On Literature Today" (p. 301)		16
E	Rourke, "Humor in America" (p. 42)	48	8

26
POST-WAR POETRY

	Preview		[10]
P	Quotations from Jarrell and Dupee (p. 235)	111	1
E	White, "Poetry" (p. 206)	56	3
E	Hall, "The New Poetry" (p. 215)	56	27
P	Moore (pp. 178-179)	105	2
P	Ransom (pp. 179-182)	105	7
P	Eberhart (pp. 208-210)	109	5
P	Shapiro (pp. 217-221)	110	10
P	Schwartz (pp. 221-223)	110	5
P	Jarrell (pp. 223-225)	110	4
P	Berryman (pp. 225-228)	110	8
P	Viereck (pp. 229-230)	111	1
P	Robert Lowell (pp. 230-231)	111	2

27
POST-WAR FICTION AND DRAMA

	Preview		[10]
S	Welty, "The Hitch-Hikers" (pp. 225-234)	82	21
S	Clark, "The Wind and the Snow of Winter" (pp. 234-242)	82	20
D	Tennessee Williams, "The Glass Menagerie" (pp. 222-260) 134-135		1 hour 32

28
YESTERDAY, TODAY, AND TOMORROW

		Relevant Page Reference in the Study Guide	*Time Budget Reading Time in Minutes*
	Preview		[10]
E	William Van O'Connor, "Traditions in American Literature" (p. 50)......................................	48	17
S	Powers, "The Valiant Woman" (pp. 242-248).............	82	13
S	Cassill, "Larchmoor Is Not the World" (pp. 248-258)..	82	27
S	Flannery O'Connor, "The Life You Save May Be Your Own" (pp. 258-265)......................................	82	18
P	Roethke (pp. 212-215).....................................	109	8
P	Bishop (pp. 216-217).......................................	109	5
P	Ciardi (pp. 228-229)	110	3
P	Wilbur (pp. 231-232)	111	2
E	Faulkner, "The Stockholm Address" (p. 312)..............	58	2
E	Faulkner, "To the Youth of Japan" (p. 313).................	58	3
E	Barrett, "We're on the Road" (p. 307)........................	58	13

ALPHABETICAL INDEX BY AUTHOR

*Numbers on the Dickinson poems are those of the Johnson edition.

SIGNIFICANT BACKGROUND FACTS AND DATES

1572 St. Bartholomew's Day Massacre of 10,000 Huguenots.

1603 Shakespeare's *Hamlet* printed.

1609 Jamestown settled.

1620 Signing of Mayflower Compact.

1642 Civil War in England after Charles I tried to impeach and imprison five members of House of Commons.

1650 Anne Bradstreet's *Tenth Muse Lately Sprung Up in America*.

1660 Restoration brought Charles II to English throne.

1662 Act of Uniformity in England sends many dissenting clergymen to America. Founding of Royal Society.

1667 *Paradise Lost* published. Treaty of Breda gives all Dutch colonies in America to the English, and Acadia (Nova Scotia) to the French.

1688 Glorious Revolution; bloodless, it brings William and Mary to English throne.

1692 Special court appointed to investigate witchcraft in village of Salem, Massachusetts.

1701 Yale College founded.

1718 New Orleans founded.

1732 First issue of *Poor Richard's Almanac*.

1748 Montesquieu's *Esprit des lois*, a treatise that influenced the American constitution.

1752 First regular theatrical troupe visits colonies.

1756 Beginning of Seven Years' War, called French and Indian War in America.

1762 Rousseau's *Social Contract*.

1765 Riots follow *Stamp Act*.

1771 First spinning mill established by Samuel Arkwright in Derbyshire, England.

1774 Edmund Burke's *Speech on American Taxation*, an example of Whig support of American claims.

1776 Declaration of Independence.

1781 Kant's *Critique of Pure Reason*.

1782 Crèvecoeur's *Letters from An American Farmer*.

1783 Treaty of Paris, and recognition of American independence.

1789 Washington's *First Inaugural*.

1798 Wordsworth & Coleridge, *Lyrical Ballads*.

1802 Ohio admitted as seventeenth state.

1810 Population census shows there are more than seven million people in the United States.

1815 Napoleon defeated at Waterloo.

1818 Birth of Marx.

1819 Birth of Victoria.

1826 Cooper's *Last of the Mohicans*.

1828 Hawthorne's first novel, *Fanshawe*. Birth of Tolstoy. Birth of Ibsen.

1832 English Reform Bill. Death of Goethe.

1833 Balzac's *Eugénie Grandet* published.

1834 Death of Coleridge.

1835 Poe begins contributions to *Southern Literary Messenger*.

1837 Second of serious business depressions in Europe, adding to discontent of working classes.

1838 Atlantic crossed by steamships.
Publication of *Oliver Twist*.

1840 Birth of Zola.

1844 Emerson's *Essays* (Second Series).

1845 Annexation of Texas and Florida to the U.S.

1847 Birth of Hardy.

1848 Irish potato famine, leading to mass emigration to U.S.A.
Louis Napoleon elected president of France.
Beginning of Hapsburg reign.
Wisconsin admitted as thirtieth state.

1849 Thoreau's "Civil Disobedience" published.

1850 Compromise of 1850: admission of California, thirty-first state, free.
Tennyson made Poet Laureate.

1855 Longfellow's *Hiawatha*.

1859 Publication of *Origin of Species*.

1860 Abraham Lincoln becomes President.
South Carolina secedes from the Union.

1861 Russian serfs freed.

1863 Battle of Gettysburg.

1864 Newman's *Apologia pro Vita Sua*.

1865 Lee surrenders.
Mark Twain's "Celebrated Jumping Frog of Calaveras County."
Whitman's *Drum Taps*.

1867 Alaska purchased from Russia.
Parliament Buildings in London completed.

1870 Population census shows there are almost forty million Americans.
Rome occupied by Victor Emmanuel. Italy unified.

1871 Germany, after defeating the French, takes the provinces of Alsace and Lorraine.

1872 Secret ballot introduced in England.
Charles Lutwidge Dodgson (Lewis Carroll) writes "Jabberwocky."

1877 Henry James' *The American*.

1883 Matthew Arnold goes to America to lecture.

1889 North Dakota, South Dakota, Montana and Washington enter the Union.

1892 Wilde's *Lady Windemere's Fan* produced in London.

1893 Stephen Crane's *Maggie: A Girl of the Streets*.

1894 R. L. Stevenson dies in Samoa.

1899 Veblen's *The Theory of the Leisure Class*.

1900 Conrad's *Lord Jim*.

1901 Victoria dies.

1914 Frost's *North of Boston*.
World War I begins in Europe.

1915 Sinking of Lusitania.

1917 Czar Nicholas of Russia abdicates.
U.S. enters the War.

1919   Treaty of Versailles signed by Allies, to end World War I.

1920   League of Nations established, but U. S. declines to join.

1922   Eliot's *The Waste Land* published in *The Dial*.
       Mussolini and Fascists take power in Italy.

1923   Hitler's "Beer-hall Putsch" fails.
       Stevens' *Harmonium*.

1924   Lenin dies. Stalin emerges as new Russian leader.

1925   Fitzgerald's *The Great Gatsby*.
       Sinclair Lewis' *Arrowsmith*. Faulkner goes to Europe on walking tour. Publisher has ms. of his first novel, *Sartoris*.

1928   First Russian Five Year Plan.

1929   Stock market crash. Beginning of the Great Depression.
       Hemingway's *A Farewell to Arms*.

1931   Alfonso of Spain forced to abdicate. Republic proclaimed.

1932   America protests Japanese occupation of Manchuria.

1933   Hitler becomes Chancellor of Germany.

1935   Italy invades Ethiopia.

1936   Spanish Civil War begins.

1939   Germany attacks Poland. England and France declare war.
       Roosevelt declares national emergency.
       Steinbeck's *The Grapes of Wrath*.

1940   Churchill replaces Chamberlain as English Prime Minister.

1941   Germany scraps treaty with Russia and invades her borders.
       Japan attacks Pearl Harbor. Germany and Italy also declare war on U.S.

1944   Shapiro's *V-Letter* wins Pulitzer Prize for Poetry.

1945   Germany surrenders unconditionally.
       President Roosevelt dies.
       Ezra Pound arrested in Italy by American Army.
       Atomic bomb dropped on Hiroshima.

1946   Nuremberg trials of Nazi war criminals begins.
       First assembly of the United Nations meets in London.
       Warren's *All the King's Men*.

1947   Communists oppose Marshall Plan designed to help European countries regain economic strength.

1948   Americans establish airlift for Berlin after Russians blockade city.
       Chinese Nationalist Government under Chiang Kai-shek is defeated by Chinese Reds; National Chinese flee to Formosa.
       Harry Truman elected to full term as President.

1950   Mao Tse-tung of China signs mutual defense treaty with Stalin.
       India and Pakistan win independence.
       Truman orders General McArthur to oppose North Ko-

rean troops aided by Chinese Communists.

Theodore Roethke's *The Waking* wins Pulitzer Prize.

1953　Stalin dies. Three-man committee takes over. Nikita Khrushchev emerges as most powerful of group.

1954　Hemingway wins Nobel Award for Literature.

1956　Dwight Eisenhower for the second time defeats Adlai Stevenson for the Presidency.

1958　Boris Pasternak wins Nobel Award for novel, *Dr. Zhivago.* Declines Award under pressure from the Russian government.

De Gaulle comes to power in France; formation of the Fifth Republic.

Russians put a satellite, Sputnik I, into orbit. Soon after, they launch a much larger satellite, Sputnik II, containing a live dog.

1959　U. S. puts satellite in orbit. Post Master General bans Lawrence's *Lady Chatterly's Lover* from U.S. mails but is over-ruled by U.S. District Court.

1960　Khrushchev breaks up "Summit Conference" in Paris.

Faulkner publishes *The Mansion,* third and final volume of the Snopes trilogy.

Kennedy nominated in Los Angeles as Democratic candidate for Presidency; Nixon as Republican candidate, in Chicago.

1961　Russians put second astronaut into orbit. Circles globe seventeen times.

Hemingway dies, July 3, of self-inflicted shotgun wound. Steinbeck's *Winter of Our Discontent* published.

Exercise:

Prepare a chronology of American literary events, using whatever dates, information and events you can find in the five volumes of *Reader's Bookshelf of American Literature.* See pages 30, 31, 32, 33.

Nathaniel Hawthorne
Concord, Massachusetts

William Cullen Bryant
Roslyn, Long Island, New York

HOMES OF AMERICAN AUTHORS

James Fenimore Cooper
Otsego Hall
Cooperstown, New York

James Russell Lowell
Elmwood
Cambridge, Massachusetts

Henry W. Longfellow
Craigie House
Cambridge, Massachusetts

George Bancroft
Round Hill
Northampton, Massachusetts

Washington Irving
Sunnyside
Irvington-on-Hudson, New York

Ralph Waldo Emerson
Concord, Massachusetts

A Systematic
Study Guide

to

American Literature

BY

WILLIAM VAN O'CONNOR

AND

THE EDITORS OF THOMAS Y. CROWELL COMPANY

Literary Glossary

(All page numbers refer to pages in this volume.)

Abstract. See page 89.

Advance-guard. See page 128.

Allegory. See page 65.

Archetype. A term frequently used in connection with mythic interpretations of literature. First used by C. G. Jung, who says certain images and symbols and story patterns recur in the dreams, myths, fantasies, and religions of all peoples, at all times and in all places. There are journeys under the sea, over mountains, through deserts; there is the roguish Male Hero, there are devil types, with death and rebirth themes, etc. Archetypal characters can be found, for example, in Herman Melville's and in William Faulkner's work.

Aside. See page 128.

Atmosphere. See page 65.

Attitude. See page 89.

Ballad. Narrative poem presumably of communal origin. Folk ballads usually deal with common people; depend on dialogue and incremental repetition. Metrically, they usually have long seven-stress lines, printed as two lines of four and three stresses each. American folk ballads include war ballads ("Yankee Doodle"), racial group ballads ("John Henry," Negro), and desperado ballads ("Jesse James"). Carl Sandburg collected many ballads in *American Ballads and Songs* (1927).

Blank verse. See page 89.

Bucolic. From the Greek word for *herdsmen*, it is poetry about country matters. Robert Frost is sometimes called a "bucolic poet."

Cacophony. See page 89.

Caesura. See page 89.

36

Character. See page 65.

Chorus. See page 128.

Climax. See page 65.

Closet drama. See page 128.

Coincidence. See page 128.

Comedy. See page 128.

Commonwealth period. End of Civil War in England, 1649 to the Restoration in 1660. Also called the *Puritan Period.* England was ruled by Parliament, under the control of Oliver Cromwell. Theaters were closed. It was a period of great religious controversy, and the writing of many tracts. John Milton was among the tract writers. In America there were similar religious and political controversies, and the country saw the multiplication of religious sects.

Conceit. See page 89.

Convention. Any accepted literary device. A room on a stage is represented by three walls, a table and a chair; a battle by the roll of drums, the clash of metal, and the darkening of the sky. In a play, a character may confide to the audience (a soliloquy). In Southern fiction, it is a convention to stress decay, alcoholic "aristocrats" caught up in the new industrial order, befuddled old maiden ladies, etc. Hemingway created the two-fisted, tight-lipped hero, and the type has frequently been imitated, especially in detective stories. There is also the young man in the gray flannel suit, the tweedy, absent-minded professor, or the Negro running wildly through the cemetery, and many other stereotypes. A convention is useful when it helps to dramatize a subject. But conventions can lose their vigor and become empty, meaningless expressions.

Cosmic irony. See pages 89-91.

Couplet. See page 89.

Criticism. The examination, description, and evaluation of literary works. Plato wanted literature to be subservient to the state. Aristotle described its nature, especially poetry and tragedy, and its effect on audiences. In the late Renaissance, in Italy and France, criticism tended to be concerned with rules. Literary criticism in all periods concerns itself with the way the work reflects (imitation) or distorts the real world, with the author, and with the audience of the work of literature. In the Middle Ages and even later, critics tended to find moral truths and moralistic dicta in literature. In the eighteenth century (the Age of Neo-Classicism) there were many attempts to rediscover the laws or rules believed to be sacred to the ancients. In the nineteenth century there was considerable concern with the author and the nature of genius, but also with *organic form* (Coleridge) as opposed to *mechanical* or *pre-determined form.* James developed this theory in relation to fiction; Coleridge had concerned himself mostly with drama and poetry. In the 1890's, in England and America (*e.g.,* James G. Huneker), there developed an art-for-art's sake movement, borrowed from the French. The French, incidentally, had taken the doctrine from Edgar Allan Poe. It minimized or ridiculed the didactic use of literature. Modern literature and criticism — T. S. Eliot, Ezra Pound, Wallace Stevens, E. E. Cummings, and many others — are greatly indebted to this movement, art-for-art's sake. *The New Criticism* (see pages 147-151) is, in part, an art-for-art's sake movement. Criticism in each period has been influenced by the various theories and intellectual movements of that period. In Darwin's period, critics tried to find analogies with *evolution.* When scientific methods have been dominant, many critics have tried to reduce literary discussions to formulas. Thus the literary work has been held to be the inevitable product of its milieu and the race that produced it, for example, the Elizabethan Age plus the Anglo-Saxon-Celtic people gave the world *Hamlet, Prince of Denmark.* Reactions against science produced subjective or *impressionistic* criticism, which respected the uniqueness and very special nature of each literary work. American critics have included Poe, Henry James, and James Russell Lowell in this line. In the twentieth century there have been Marxist critics, New Humanists (see page 42), sociological critics, and the New Critics (see page 147). The twentieth century has been called An Age of Criticism.

Dactyl. See page 89.

Decadence. Characteristic of literature associated with the 1890's, with Oscar Wilde, Aubrey Beardsley, Ernest Dowson, and *The Yellow Book*. In America there was a magazine, *Mlle New York*, comparable to *The Yellow Book*, and such writers as James Gibbons Huneker and Edgar Saltus. The decadent movement in the United States seems, in retrospect, at once more extravagant and artificial than its counterpart in England.

Denotation. See page 89.

Denouement. See pages 65, 128.

Deus ex machina. See page 128.

Diction. See page 90.

Didacticism. See page 90.

Double plots. Common to Elizabethan drama. They create a sense of multiple levels, allowing for contrasts and complementary actions. In modern fiction the double, even triple, plot has been used by Faulkner and Warren.

Drama. See page 129.

Enjambment. See page 90.

Enlightenment. Term associated with eighteenth-century rationalism, faith in an orderly universe, and in man's capacity to solve his political, social and psychological problems. Thomas Jefferson had great faith in the Enlightenment, and it is commonly said that the American political system is a product of the Enlightenment. Lionel Trilling's criticism in *The Liberal Imagination* discusses literature in relation to the Enlightenment. Robert Penn Warren's *Brother to Dragons*, a long poem, can be called anti-Enlightenment, or critical of certain Enlightenment doctrines.

Episode. See page 65.

Episodic. See page 65.

Expressionism. A movement that began in Germany before World War I. A revolt against realism by distorting objects, exaggerating, breaking up time sequences. It is less concerned with objective fact than with the external world as it appears to a troubled, sick or abnormal mind of a character. Eliot's poem, *The Waste Land,* has been called expressionistic, but the term is usually applied to works in the theater. The theater has resources of lighting, stage design, symbols and stylized acting to exploit. *The Hairy Ape* and *The Emperor Jones,* by Eugene O'Neill, and *The Adding Machine,* by Elmer Rice, are expressionistic plays. They use memory and dream sequences, shifts in time, etc. Arthur Miller's *Death of a Salesman,* among latter-day stage plays, uses some of these devices.

Farce. See page 129.

Feminine ending. See page 90.

Foreshadowing. See page 65.

Freudianism. In literature, Freudianism is associated with stream-of-consciousness in writing, miltiple meanings in words, latent meaning in symbols, dream-like structure in poetry, the mind as a metaphor-creating organ. In criticism, Freudians have emphasized the Oedipus complex, traumatic experiences that give rise to an author's preoccupation with a certain subject, and the importance of sex in human motivation and conduct.

Genteel Tradition. Term coined by George Santayana in "The Genteel Tradition in American Philosophy" (1913). America, Santayana said, was a new country, with a new mentality, a fast-developing industrial order, great cities, various racial groups, etc., but in philosophy and literature it was living off its New England past. No philosophy, he said, can be vital if it is not developed from actual social, economic and political conditions. Thus he favored the new American philosophy of pragmatism. The wisdom of the genteel tradition, he said, seems "thin and verbal," unrelated to the actual life of America. It had left a part of the American mind floating "gently in the backwater, while along-side, in invention and industry and social organization the other half of the mind was leaping down a sort of Niagara Rapids." The nineteenth century literary mind, especially in the latter part of the century, and on into the twentieth, was dominated by the genteel tradition. It avoided frank discussion of sex, the language of the everyday world, and tried to elevate and spiritualize all experience, at least in literature. There are genteel aspects to Longfellow, Lowell, Howells, even James and Twain. Bayard Taylor is a gen-teel poet. Lesser genteel critics are Bliss Perry, George Edward Woodberry, and W. C. Brownell. In the 1920's and earlier, realistic writers attacked the genteel tradition. When Sinclair Lewis was awarded the Nobel Prize he devoted his talk to saying the award to him meant the end of the dominance of the genteel tradition in America. Stephen Crane, Theodore Dreiser, Frank Norris, Sherwood Anderson, and H. L. Mencken were among those who attempted to destroy the genteel tradition.

Heptameter. See page 90.

Iamb. See page 90.

Imagery. See page 90.

Imagist. See page 90.

Impressionism. Impressionism in criticism finds its center in "the impres-sions of the individual in his isolation, each mind keeping as a solitary prisoner its own dream of a world" (Walter Pater, *Studies in the History of the Renaissance*). Anatole France, skeptical of all systems and fixed values, said the critic "relates the adventures of his soul among master-pieces." The impressionist is keenly aware of the way each object, under temporary conditions, reflects impressions that are flickering and inconstant. American impressionist critics were James Huneker, Lewis Gates, Edgar Saltus, who was also a novelist, Vance Thompson, Joseph Percival Pollard, Carl Van Vechten, also a novelist, H. L Mencken, whose early work was indebted to Huneker) James Branch Cabell, the novelist, and Paul Rosenfeld. The

American impressionists were influenced by their reading of Nietzsche and Schopenhauer.

In medias res. A term used by Horace, meaning the action begins at a late point in its chronology or sequence. Earlier actions and motivations are then explored. Sometimes there are flashbacks. Method allows for a greater intensity in the action.

Internal rhyme. See page 91.

Intrigue comedy. See page 129.

Irony. See page 91.

Light verse. A tone of badinage rather than of severity. Modern writers of light verse are W. H. Auden, Ogden Nash, Morris Bishop, Dorothy Parker, Phyllis McGinley, and Mrs. Helen Bevington.

Melodrama. See page 129.

Metaphor. See page 91.

Myth. Man responds to symbols (e.g., to the flag, the Statue of Liberty, Lincoln's log cabin, Monticello, etc.), whether political, religious, or social. They have to do with his convictions about love and marriage, his moral, religious and political commitments, with the role he sees himself playing in society, or in the universe. Myths include stories, songs, traditions, rituals. In modern criticism we refer to the Faulkner Myth of Yoknapatawpha County, the Puritan world of Hawthorne, or the innocent wilderness of James Fenimore Cooper.

Naturalism. See page 65.

New Humanism. From 1910 into the 1930's, Irving Babbitt, Paul Elmer More, and Norman Foerster argued for a return to an ethical emphasis in the study of literature. The New Humanists were opposed to such doctrines as environment as a determining factor in conduct, or the obligation of the state or society to support the individual. They believed it was the duty of each human being to be righteous, dedicated and hard-working. George Santayana said the sixteenth century humanists were tolerant and inclined to accept relativistic doctrines, but that the New Humanists were preaching the doctrines of John Calvin and John Knox.

Onomatopoeia. See page 91.

Paradox. See page 91.

Pentameter. See page 91.

Peripety. See page 129.

Petrarchan. See page 91.

Plot. See page 65.

Poetic drama. See page 129.

Point of view. See page 66.

Portmanteau word. Term coined by Lewis Carroll, author of *Alice in Wonderland.* Two words, such as "lithe and slimy," are joined together,—thus "slithy." Joyce used portmanteau words. So, on occasion, do William Faulkner and E. E. Cummings.

Proletarian literature. Term applied to writers who contend that society and literature are consequences of economic factors, and these factors are only understandable in terms of Marxist theory. In earlier American literature, Marxist critics find forerunners in Emerson, Thoreau, Whitman, who attacked society, in H. B. Fuller, Edwin Markham, Hamlin Garland, Robert Herrick, D. G. Phillips, Jack London, Upton Sinclair, and others. Contemporary authors at one time or another considered proletarian are such novelists as James Farrell, Waldo Frank, Robert Cantwell, and Grace Lumpkin. Among the Marxist critics were Granville Hicks, Michael Gold, and Joseph Freeman. *The Masses* was the leading journal of Marxist writing.

Protagonist. The chief figure, or "hero." When he is pitted against another character in the action the latter is called the *antagonist*. Thus, in "Billy Budd," Billy is the protagonist and Claggert his antagonist.

Purple patch. Term from Horace, meaning a rich passage of writing; heightened style, or highly figurative language which make the passage stand out in its context.

Quatrain. See page 91.

Realism. See page 66.

Romantic. See page 91.

Satire. Type of writing which evokes scorn, contempt, amusement at the expense of foolish or stupid persons or actions. *Comedy,* as such, is less concerned to deride than is satire. Horatian satire (derived from Horace, the Latin poet) is urbane, tolerant, amused at human folly. Horace was well known to eighteenth and nineteenth century American writers. Juvenalian satire (from Juvenal, the Latin poet) is more intensely moralist, indignant, denunciatory. Juvenal was more influential in English than in American poetry. Among recent American satiric poets one would include E. E. Cummings, Kenneth Fearing, and Karl Shapiro. In fiction, the most notable American satirist has been Sinclair Lewis. He derided the culture of small town America in the 1920's, and lampooned Babbitt, the unself-critical booster and joiner. Younger fiction writers in the satirical mode are Randall Jarrell *(Pictures from an Institution)* and Mary McCarthy *(The Groves of Academe). The New Yorker* Magazine frequently publishes satiric articles and stories.

Sentimentality. See page 66.

Simile. See page 91.

Slant rhymes. See page 91.

Sonnet. See page 92.

Spondee. See page 92.

Stock response. See page 66.

Stream of See page 66.
consciousness.

Subjective. See page 92.

Symbol. See page 66.

Theme. See page 66.

Tone. See page 66.

Tradition. A heritage. There is the tradition of the tall tale and folk humor, used by Mark Twain and William Faulkner. There is the tradition of the western story, with the cowboy as hero, the prairies, and the individual taking the law as he finds it. We speak of the Puritan tradition, or heritage, as a way of life and a set of values. Or the Southern heritage, also a way of life and a set of values. There is the classical tradition, the use various generations have made of the art, laws, and customs common to Greece and Rome. There is the Christian tradition. There are traditions in architecture, painting, and in literary conventions, for example, the picaresque novel, the sonnet sequence, the pastoral, or the heroic couplet. T. S. Eliot, in "Tradition and the Individual Talent" (1917) attempted to systematize an understanding of tradition for the western writer. Allen Tate, Lewis Mumford, and Van Wyck Brooks have written essays on the American's search for, or his indifference to tradition.

Tragedy. See page 129.

Trochee. See page 92.

Understatement. See page 92.

Unity. See page 92.

Unity of action. Aristotle said a plot is unified when all the parts are "so closely connected that the transposal or withdrawal of

any one of them will disjoint and dislocate the whole."
Samuel Taylor Coleridge and Henry James, with their
doctrine of *organic form,* insisted on unity of action. The
three unities, of time, of place, and action, were a creation
of Renaissance critics. In American drama only the Aris-
totelian *unity of action* has been a matter of critical discussion or preoccupation.

Verse. See page 92.

Wit. Originally meant knowledge, good sense, quickness of
mind. In the seventeenth century the Metaphysical poets
(like the American Taylor) were called witty because of
their use of paradox and combination of ideas. Eighteenth
century critics called Metaphysical wit *false wit.* Today
wit most often means a clever twist of words and meaning. In poetry, sometimes wit tends to be epigrammatic.
Robert Frost occosionally employs the epigrammatic style.

Part I: AMERICAN LITERARY ESSAYS
EDITED BY LEWIS LEARY

QUESTIONS —

Introduction (pages 1-10)
(See Sample Answers to Questions, p. 50)

NOTE: Page references are to *American Literary Essays,* except where in italic, as above, *"See Sample Answers to Questions, p. 50,"* which refer to pages in this volume.

1. Leary says one of the characteristics of the essay is that it is "personal" (page 1). Explain.

2. The essay, Leary also says, shifts as the age shifts (page 2). Illustrate.

3. Who are some of our early American essayists (pages 4-5)? What are the titles of their more important works?

4. Emerson, Thoreau, and Whitman, Leary implies, have certain themes in common (pages 7-8). What are these themes?

5. Leary discusses the stylistic possibilities of language and characterizes certain tendencies and abuses (pages 8-9). Refer to certain writers, books, or periodicals from your own reading experiences that illustrate his observations.

Possibilities (pages 13-68)
(See Sample Answers to Questions, pp. 51, 52, 53)

1. Americans have looked upon themselves as a new people in a new country. Summarize Crèvecoeur's thesis (pages 13-16).

2. American literature, in part, is an off-shoot of English literature. English readers have sometimes tended to be supercilious about American literary efforts and Americans, in turn, have sometimes been belligerent and extravagant in the claims made for American literature. Characterize Washington Irving's views on this subject (pages 16-21).

3. What are the differences between Paulding's notions about nationalism in literature (pages 33-35) and Poe's (pages 35-36)?

4. Emerson and Whitman had great faith in the promise of American literature. What was the basis for Emerson's hope (pages 21-33) and Whitman's (pages 36-37)?

5. Henry James said the American scene lacks many social and cultural phenomena that Europe, or England, has (pages 37-38). List these. Yet he implies that the American writer has other advantages. What might some of these advantages be?

6. Howells believed there was an inevitable connection between American art and democracy (pages 38-39). Explain.

7. Mencken was an acute critic of shortcomings in American life and literature. What does he see as difficulties the American writer faces (pages 39-42)?

8. One sometimes hears comments on "American humor." Does Miss Rourke believe there is a unified, single type of American humor (pages 42-45)?

9. Trilling, in part, bases his descriptions of "reality" as conceived by Americans on Parrington's *Main Currents in American Thought* (pages 45-50). Summarize what he says about Parrington's views.

10. O'Connor uses three terms — "innocence," "horror," and "experience" — in his brief survey of American literature (pages 50-57). Explain the meaning of each term, referring whenever possible to specific authors and works.

11. Kouwenhoven says that American literary forms exhibit the same principles of organization to be found in American jazz, architecture, movies, and fine arts (pages 57-68). What are these principles? To what authors does Kouwenhoven refer in discussing these principles?

12. In the preceding essays (pages 13-68) the terms "American" and "Literary form" have been employed frequently. Write an essay (six hundred to one thousand words) entitled "Characteristics of American Literature."

People (pages 71-158)
(*See Sample Answers to Questions, pp. 53, 54, 55*)

1. In the headnote to "Portion of an Autobiography," Leary comments on the simplicity of Franklin's style (page 71). Select three or four of Franklin's sentences, then rewrite them in a more ornate and formal style. Discuss and evaluate the differences in the two styles.

2. Franklin is sometimes called a "sententious writer." What does this mean? Illustrate.

3. Twain employed much of his characteristic humor in poking fun at James Fenimore Cooper (pages 80-88). Point out several witty devices. Is Twain merely using Cooper's novels as the occasion for humorous comments, or is he seriously criticizing Cooper's weaknesses as a novelist?

4. Whitman admitted that Poe's view of the universe was very different from his own (pages 88-90). In what ways, according to Whitman, were their views unlike?

5. Melville was fascinated by the power of "blackness" in Hawthorne's writing (pages 90-92). Explain. Refer, in your answer, to "Traditions in American Literature" (pages 50-57).

6. Chapman says that one of Emerson's important messages was his advice to beware the "tyranny of democracy" (pages 92-96). Explain.

7. Melville was clearly in sympathy with Hawthorne. Would you say that Lowell is clearly and wholly in sympathy with Thoreau (pages 96-102)? Write a short essay (250 to 350 words) entitled "Lowell on Thoreau."

8. Blackmur implies that Melville is a sufficiently great writer to be able to stand up against negative criticism and, even, that negative criticism can help to illuminate the nature of his greatness (pages 102-115). Explain.

9. Write an essay (400 to 500 words) entitled "Two Views of Whitman: Thoreau and Lanier" (pages 115-117).

10. Tate's thesis is that Emily Dickinson's power as a poet is to be accounted for, in part, by her appearance on the literary scene while New England was undergoing a significant cultural shift (pages 117-126). Explain.

11. Thoreau said that when it came time for him to die he did not want to discover "that I had not lived" (pages 127-135). Remaining unencumbered, he implies, is essential to living fully. What does he mean?

12. Emerson often stressed man's need to realize himself as an individual. In "New England Reformers" (pages 135-147) he presents man in relation to society. How, according to Emerson, should a man conduct himself as a social being?

13. What does Holmes mean by "the Brahmin Caste of New England" (pages 147-150)? Is he critical of it?

14. What does Henry Adams mean in saying the New Englander has a heritage of resistance (pages 150-153)? What is the effect of Adams' writing about himself in the third person?

15. Rahv says James moved through a "maze of contradictions," that his treatment of them is his great strength as a novelist (pages 154-158). Explain.

SAMPLE ANSWERS TO QUESTIONS* —

Introduction

1. By "personal" Leary means that the essayist can indulge or pursue his own interests or whims, also that the nature of his writing or style is likely to express the uniqueness of his mind and character.

2. The essay, despite being personal, necessarily reflects its age. Seventeenth century essayists were likely to be intensely involved in religious controversies, whereas eighteenth century essayists, for example, were preoccupied with elegance, decorum, and a rational ordering of their experiences.

3. Benjamin Franklin, Thomas Paine, John Adams, Alexander Hamilton, Philip Freneau, Benjamin Rush, John Trumbull, Noah Webster, Joseph Dennie, Washington Irving, *et al.*

4. All three are concerned with the life of the human spirit, of man in society and man in relation to nature.

5. Acuteness of mind and an ability to use language precisely and effectively make original and significant writing possible. But

---

Because of the limitations of space, the answers given here tend to be succinct, even elliptical. In giving your answers you can afford to be more expansive, to refer to more specific details, and to give illustrations.

certain magazines and many popular writers sacrifice subtlety and qualifications, preferring simple slogans and emotional responses to genuine thought. . . .

Possibilities

1. In Europe, according to Crèvecoeur, the Church, royalty, inherited wealth, etc. served to put a great distance between the rich and the poor. In America no one was excessively rich and no one excessively poor. The land lay open, giving everyone who wished it a fresh opportunity. In the Church and in government too one could begin afresh, without having to revolt against thoroughly entrenched vested interests.

2. Irving concerns himself with the misrepresentations of American life that was to be found in the English press of the time. He blamed this on the fact that few or no philosophical or speculative Englishmen visited America. Instead the visitors tended to be merchants and adventurers, men not especially suited to be disinterested observers. Toward the end of his essay, Irving says that America necessarily imitates England, in her political heritage, manners, culture, etc. Generally, he says, the English heritage is a great one, and American writers should not, out of hurt feelings, allow themselves to ridicule that heritage or turn their backs on it.

3. Paulding says America had not achieved greatness in literature, despite her resources, because her writers were servile imitators. But the American spirit had moved ahead in other respects, and therefore it was only a matter of time before her literary achievements were equally significant. Poe says there has been a lot of confusion about what a "national" literature means. He seems to fear the possibility that writers will become politically minded. Then he turns his attention to the situation or plight of the American writers: he is not protected by international copyright, the British inundate America with their publications, and the American writer is badly treated by the British critics, and unfortunately American readers accept these judgments as just.

4. Emerson says "We have listened too long to the courtly muses of Europe." The American must free himself from timidity, from imitation, and from the temptations of money, avarice, indulgence. He must see the world not as writers in the past have seen it, not, that is, from a study of their books, he must look at the world anew because he believes himself "inspired by the Divine Soul which inspires all men." Whitman says "The United States themselves are essentially the greatest poem." The strength of the U.S., he says, is in the common people. "It awaits the gigantic and generous treatment worthy of it."

5. The American novelist, unlike the English novelist, according to James, could not write about royalty, aristocracy, country gentlemen, palaces, castles, manor houses, parsonages, thatched cottages, public schools (Eton, Harrow, etc.), etc., etc. James implies that despite the absence of such things in American life that there are other matters that might engage the American writer. For example, he could watch the building of new cities, westward expansion, the development of a national character, man confronting nature, etc.

6. Like Whitman, Howells saw the future strength of American literature as lying in an awareness of the common man.

7. Mencken deplores the absence of an aristocracy in the U.S. An artistocracy, he implies, owes its position to its strength, intellectually and culturally, not to mere privilege. America had the beginnings of one with Jefferson, Washington, *et al.*, but the promise was never fulfilled. Consequently there is a fine field for demagogues, appealing to prejudices of all kinds. In place of an aristocracy we have a plutocracy, monied people, who are vulgar and also subject to prejudice; it is opposed to the inquiring spirit.

8. Miss Rourke believes "the American character is split and many sided," but that "a shadowy outline has been drawn by the many ventures into comedy." There are, she says, two lines in American humor, the low key, understatement, refined and subtle humor, and also a rhapsodic line, common to orators, certain story tellers, and cartoons.

9. Parrington, according to Trilling, believed in social and economic determinism. He believed that man, as a subjective mind, had to adjust himself to an objective world in which things were fixed and orderly; *reality* was the objective world, subjectivity was the turning away from it or a romanticizing of it. Reality, in Parrington's view, tends to be grim, sober. Parrington is attracted to what he calls "romanticism," but feels he should not give in to it.

10. Innocence connotes open-heartedness, optimism, hopefulness, virtue, generosity, but also ingenuousness and lack of shrewdness. Almost all of the writers referred to in the article are aware of innocence in one or more of these connotations. The literature of *horror* implies a threatening or meaningless universe. C. B. Brown, Poe, Melville, Hawthorne, Faulkner, Warren, *et al.*, are in this tradition. The literature of *experience* examines innocence or horror, seeing to what extent either is justified; it also

takes the world of society on a kind of day-to-day basis, avoiding any large philosophical or metaphysical decisions about its ultimate nature. Robert Frost, Ransom, Anne Bradstreet, Marianne Moore, *et al.*, are in this tradition.

11. The key to American literature and art, Kouwenhoven says, is not subject matter, it is style. Twain and Whitman, like the architects of sky scrapers, and like jazz musicians, use simple units (episodes or meter) and repeat them according to a varying rhythm.

12. The essay you are asked to write might include references to American literature as imitative and original. How is it imitative (see Washington Irving) and how original (see James, Crevecoeur, O'Connor, Kouwenhoven)? Or you may choose to organize your paper according to some other plan.

People

1. Franklin's first sentence (page 71) begins, "From a child I was fond . . ." One might rewrite it thus: "The sun had witnessed my advent into, and presence in, the world for a mere several years before it was clearly evident that each bit of gold or silver upon which I could lay an eager hand was spent for reading matter, theological, historical, biographical, polemical, etc. . . ." The imitation of Franklin is pompous and pretentious. One tends not to believe what the author is saying; one does believe Franklin.

2. Sententiousness is giving advice in a solemn manner. See page 74, on which Franklin quotes Pope.

3. Twain's opening sentence (page 80) is tongue-in-cheek. Secondly, he undercuts Cooper's dignity by calling Chingachgook, Chicago. Thirdly, he parodies Cooper's method of telling a story. Cooper can hardly be as bad a novelist as Twain says. On the other hand, Twain put his finger on many weaknesses in Cooper. Twain, as a professional writer, was deploring many of the unprofessional qualities in Cooper's work.

4. Poe, according to Whitman, was a demonic writer. He saw the universe as malevolent. Nineteenth century poetry, he says, is preoccupied with morbidity and sickness. He would prefer poetry to deal with health, the earth, the sea, democracy, etc.

5. Melville disliked writers who were filled with "sweetness and light," and had no sense of what he called, referring to Hawthorne, "roaring Niagaras." In "Traditions in American Literature" there is a list of writers similar to Hawthorne.

6. It is easy to praise democracy since it is concerned with the rights of all men. It is unpopular to criticize it. But, according to Emerson, men in the mass can be rude, undiscriminating and, by the simple fact of having a majority, repressive. Especially they can ridicule and repress distinction in mind, in achievement. Democracy must not allow the lowest common denominator in society to dictate that achievement must not be allowed to rise to the levels open or possible to the more gifted members of the society. This message, Chapman says, was among the most important Emerson preached.

7. Obviously Lowell did not wholly admire Thoreau. His essay makes the points that Thoreau was conceited, self-centered, unoriginal, without humor, without logic, sentimentalized nature — but, and, here Lowell changes his tune abruptly, he rebuked, following Emerson, America's preoccupation with things, and in his narrow range was a master of English. In writing your paper, you might want to consider several or more of these points.

8. Blackmur says or implies that Melville was a great master of words, but not a great novelist. He is frequently intoxicated by his cadences and rhythms, and, beautiful though they are, they lead him away from the reality he is attempting to probe in his fiction. Melville, also, according to Blackmur, refuses at times to accept the limitations the craft of fiction forces on a novelist. In other terms, he tries to make words in and by themselves serve in lieu of a fictional structure.

9. Thoreau: Some of Whitman's poems are merely sensual and do not show a proper respect for the proprieties; but the sensuality does remind us of experiences we know to be human experiences; sometimes he seems overly hearty, and offers great expectation of illumination—and sometimes he follows this promise by rude and ineffectual remarks; yet the general effect is of primitive greatness. Lanier: In its ruggedness, gracelessness, etc., Whitman's poetry tries to imitate democracy itself; democracy itself doesn't concern itself with the poetry; Lanier is more impressed with weak-eyed office workers than with Whitman's muscle-types; he thinks we ought to repudiate muscle superiority and emphasize other forms of distinction; Whitman dislikes dandyism, as typified by Tennyson, but is Whitman's pose as a man of the open road not equally a gesture, a stance? You might consider some of these points in comparing the two views of Whitman.

10. Tate says that New England in Miss Dickinson's day was a different culture from what it had been in the seventeenth century and later. Theocracy was on the decline, and industry was on the increase. The older pieties were not entirely dead, but Miss Dickinson, while participating in them to some extent, brings a skeptical mind to her thinking about them.

11. Emerson said of his and Thoreau's age, "Things are in the saddle." He meant that people pursued material things, houses, furnishings, property of various sorts. The irony of this sort of success is that things can become a burden to their owner, and far from freeing him to enjoy freedom, take his freedom from him. Thoreau discusses man naked, to speak figuratively, in the world, and the ways in which this enables him to experience the world, its seasons, its beauties, its joys.

12. Emerson says one is often tempted to be publicly critical of this or that social enterprise. But that we should be content with self-reform, self-improvement. Only, he says, "by obedience to his genius, only by the freest activity in the way constitutional to him, does an angel seem to arise before a man and lead him by the hand out of all the wards of the prison."

13. By the "Brahmin caste" in New England, Holmes meant not a monied aristocracy but a cultural and intellectual aristocracy. A member of this aristocracy or caste is a scholar and probably the son and grandson of a scholar. Rather frequently there are marriages between families in this caste, and the breed thereby is improved. Far from being critical of this caste, Holmes admires it greatly.

14. New England, Adams says, bred resistance into one's bones. His ancestors had viewed nature as something to be reformed. The universe was filled with evil which one had to resist. Writing about himself in the third person, rather than the first person, enabled Adams to achieve an air of objectivity, as though he were writing a biography rather than an autobiography. Certain readers strongly object to a first-person narrator. On the other hand, what might have seemed a warm, intense struggle, if told in the first person, takes on a rather chilly quality, adding to Adams' own insistent sense of irony, when told in the third.

15. Rahv says that there is a tension or doubleness in all of James' best fiction: the world is corrupt, and yet one must experience and in a sense best it; innocence asks for experience, and yet having it one has lost something irretrievable; Europe is excitement, civilization, reality, yet the life of the spirit lives vitally in America. The play of these oppositions gives him his subjects, his irony, his humor.

QUESTIONS —

Poetry (pages 161-225)
(See Sample Answers to Questions, pp. 58, 59 60)

1. Emerson sees the poet as a great seer (pages 161-174). Point to one or more passages that might have been written by Whitman, or, at least, passages of which Whitman would have approved. Emerson is an exclamatory writer. Illustrate.

2. Poe, in denying poetry the right to be didactic, was quarreling with a basic assumption of his age (pages 174-176). Summarize his position.

3. Whitman says he sang or chanted his age but that without the age, which made his work possible, he would not exist as a poet (pages 177-180). Explain.

4. The poet, according to Santayana, creates sensuous beauty and music, is imaginative, and understands the ideal (pages 181-195). Outline the points made in this essay.

5. In commenting on Miss Lowell's "The Poet's Trade" (page 196), Leary refers to her "Poe-like remarks on the poet's trade." In what ways are her remarks like Poe's?

6. Mencken was often a belligerent and vituperative critic, but his "Poetry in America" (pages 196-199) calls for an escapist or sentimental view of poetry. Explain.

7. Eliot says a poet does not express his personality in writing — he escapes from it (pages 199-204). And in creating a poem, Eliot adds, he modifies the existing literary tradition. Explain.

8. Frost implies that a poem is a matter of *discovery* (pages 205-206). Explain.

9. White discusses types of obscurity in poetry and various reasons for them (pages 207-208). Does his essay make any points in common with Frost's?

10. Auden is concerned with differences between English and American poetry (pages 208-215). What are these differences?

11. List the "young poets" Hall discusses or mentions in "The New Poetry" (pages 215-225). Summarize briefly his comments on Lowell, Roethke, Shapiro, and Wilbur.

Prose Fiction (pages 229-315)
(See Sample Answers to Questions, pp. 60, 61, 62, 63)

1. It is commonly said that Poe in "The Tale Proper" has stated the theory of the modern short story (pages 229-230). Apply Poe's theory to two or more stories in Ray West's *American Short Stories.*

2. Early and late in American criticism there have been a number of attempts to distinguish the romance from the novel. What points do Simms (page 231), Hawthorne (pages 231-233), and Chase (pages 270-279) share in common?

3. What distinction does Twain make between the humorous and the witty story (pages 234-235)? Write an essay (200 to 300 words) developing Twain's comments on the art of narrative (page 235). Does Twain seem committed to the idea of the regional novel or the national novel (pages 235-236)? Is there, or can there be, such a thing as "the great American novel?" What would Twain presumably say on the subject?

4. Howells is sometimes presented as a novelist and critic who helped make the realistic novel possible in America, and he is sometimes seen as a genteel prude who refused to face human life in its entirety. On the evidence of "Subjects for American Fiction" (pages 236-239), which characterization seems to you the more accurate?

5. Summarize the points Harte makes about the western short story (pages 240-244).

6. Are the points Garland makes about "local color" (pages 245-247) identical with those Twain made about regionalism (pages 235-236)?

7. In "The Novel with a Purpose" (pages 248-250), Norris says there are three types of fiction. Under each heading list four or five novels that you have read. Justify your listing them as you do.

8. James (pages 250-264) makes two very important points about fiction, one, that reality wears different guises, two, that content and form are inseparable. Explain each point in some detail, using illustrations.

9. Make a list of the writers (and their works) that Farrell places in the realistic line (pages 264-270). Are there other types of realism (see James, pages 250-264)?

10. Make a list of critical observations you have read in this section, Prose Fiction (pages 229-315), which you believe you would find useful in reading short stories or novels.

Prospects (pages 283-315)
(See Sample Answers to Questions, pp. 63, 64)

1. Write an essay (200 to 300 words) summarizing Emerson's doctrine of self-reliance (pages 283-298). Can you see any dangers in the kind of individualism he advocates?

2. Lincoln's "The Gettysburg Address" (page 298) is justly acclaimed a great and simple statement about the dignity of man. Rewrite the address in a more round-about, evasive kind of language. What is lost?

3. Smith says (page 299), quoting Trollope, that early success is a misfortune. What does he mean?

4. Barrett says (page 311) that American history from the beginning has been "a curious dialogue with the land." Explain.

5. Faulkner's "The Stockholm Address" (pages 312-313) has been widely acclaimed, especially because Faulkner insists that the writer ought to treat "the human heart in conflict with itself." Explain. Can you list other American writers who have been awarded the Nobel Prize for literature?

6. Faulkner says (pages 313-315) that writing thrives on adversity. Explain.

SAMPLE ANSWERS TO QUESTIONS —

Poetry

1. The passage on page 163 beginning, "For it is not metres, but a metre-making argument that makes a poem" and ending with "for the world seems always waiting for its poet." Many critics would take this statement as a description of *Leaves of Grass* and the manner in which Whitman wrote. On page 165, the sentence "The Universe is the externalization of the soul." This too is Whitman doctrine. Emerson as an exlamatory writer: on page 173, he writes, "Doubt not, O poet, but persist." And on the same page, "O poet! a new mobility is conferred in groves and pastures, and not in castles or by the sword blade any longer."

2. Nineteenth century poets for the most part were deliberately and explicitly didactic. Poe was not. Intellect, he says, concerns itself with truth, the moral sense concerns itself with duty, but an immortal instinct concerns itself with beauty. Poetry, he adds, is the rhythmical creation of beauty. If precepts about duty or honor are introduced into a poem they are dependent upon beauty.

3. On page 173 Whitman says in effect that the United States, its history, its people, and its future are his subject and his poem. Without them he would not have written, at least not in the form he employed. Thereafter he shows some of the ways in which the poetry and art of the Old World differs from those of the New World.

4. The following are some of the points Santayana makes in his essay: Poetry depends upon metrics, or measure, it is sensuous, employing euphony (he downgrades Pope because he lacks euphony or sensuousness), and it draws upon disparate objects and experience that arouse emotions. The poet's organization or vision of the world differs from the scientist's because the scientist's system is abstract and lacks "sensation." Poetry at its highest level is concerned with the ideal, with ordering man's aspirations, hopes and moral capacities. It is closely related to religion.

5. Miss Lowell compares the beauty of trees to the beauty of poems — and we do not ask trees to teach us moral lessons.

6. On page 197 Mencken says poetry is an enemy of the intellect. "Its purpose is not to establish facts, but to evade and deny them. What it essays to do is to make life more bearable in an intolerable world by concealing and obliterating all the harsher realities."

7. Eliot's impersonal nature of poetry doctrine reverses the traditional nineteenth century emphasis that a poet expressed his personality in verse and it was his personality or character that one experienced in reading the poetry. Eliot says the poem wants to be anonymous, to live its own life apart from its creator. The more successful the poem or play, he implies, the clearer it is that the poet or the dramatist has managed to transform his personal feelings and attitudes into the substance of the poem or play. Tradition: Eliot believes that a good poet is aware of all the important literature in the tradition he participates in. His poem is a part of that tradition. If his new poem is in some way original then the tradition itself is partly modified.

8. In the opening paragraph Frost says that sound, meters, rhythms are half of the delight one feels in a poem, but that without insight,

perception on which the sound and rhythms can play (and vice versa) one has only half a poem.

9. There are various types of obscure poetry: that written by mad poets, that by poets wishing to appear mad, that created by poets who write vaguely and are unable to express themselves clearly and precisely, and that which results when a poet gets so involved with the lyric possibilities of certain sounds that he is no longer very sure what he wanted to say. There is another kind that Mr. White ignores, the obscurity that is the result of concentration and complication and which reveals its meaning if studied carefully.

10. Among the differences Auden cites are these: differences in pitch and rhythm; the American can more easily conceive of a world without human beings; democracy invites constant experimentation; American poets contemporary with each other will be very different from each other, whereas British contemporaries will tend to be much alike.

11. The younger poets: Robert Lowell, Randall Jarrell, Karl Shapiro, Theodore Roethke, J. V. Cunningham, John Ciardi, John Frederick Nims, Richard Wilbur, James Merrill, Barbara Howes, William Jay Smith, Anthony Hecht, Louis Simpson, Andrienne Cecile Rich, Cecil Hemley, W. S. Merwin, Isabella Gardner, James Wright, Edgar Bowers, Philip Booth, Elizabeth Bishop, Jean Garrique, Peter Viereck, E. L. Mayo, Hyman Putzik, Daniel Hoffman, Howard Nemerov. Hall says Lowell is very aware of his Puritan ancestry and the forces of rigidity, sin and cruelty, and he searches for liberation from capitalist-Protestant New England. Roethke, he says, is preoccupied with our biological and physical nature, and is a very accomplished poet outside of strictly conventional forms. Shapiro's earlier work, he says, was exhuberant, concerned with jukeboxes, Buicks, gim-crackery, but his later poetry is more strictly intellectual. Wilbur he sees as a poet of great elegance, intellectual refinement, cleverness, and decorum.

Prose Fiction

1. Poe said the short tale was a preferable art form to the novel because in it, unlike the novel, one could achieve a *totality*, a unified effect, that the novel, because of its nature and also because it cannot be read at a sitting, cannot achieve. The poet, he says, is concerned to create beauty, whereas the short story writer is concerned not merely with beauty but with truth. Crane's "The Blue Hotel" is a good example of a unified effect. The descriptions and the actions of the characters create an air of

hallucination and unreality, and this is maintained until the last lines of the story when what has actually happened is explained. Clark's "The Wind and the Snow of Winter" is also a good example. The cold, the wind, the darkness, the passage of time, and so on seem of a piece with the old man's loss of memory, his old age, and approaching death.

2. Simms says the romance is closer to poetry than is the novel, and it does not confine itself to what is known or even to what is probable. Simms says the romance is a child of the epic. In the epic the marvelous (that which transcended verisimilitude) was a frequent component. Hawthorne says the marvelous should be or is a part of the romance, but that the author ought not to indulge his liking for it too freely. The romance, Hawthorne also said, seeks out the shadow, antiquity, mystery, the picturesque, and gloomy wrongs. Chase presumably agrees with all of the above. He sees the English novel, except for occasional works such as *Wuthering Heights,* concerned with a close-up view of reality, with people involved in the everyday business of life; it involves a close knowledge of motivation, and of social class. By contrast, the romance is free "to render reality in less volume and detail" — it "encounters less resistance from reality." As romances he includes Brown's *Wieland, The Scarlet Letter, The Blithdale Romance, Moby Dick, Pierre, The Confidence Man, Huckleberry Finn, McTeague,* etc.

3. The humorous story, Twain says, had been told orally, and requires great art. The narrator's method is grave, and he does not indicate he sees anything humorous or funny in the story. It has a "nub," but the listener has to be wary or he may miss it. The comic and witty story do not depend upon the manner of telling but on the substance or the "nub," and usually, Twain says, an exclamation point is put after it. Art of narrative: Twain's thesis is that there is no law of narration, but he wants a narrative to go briskly, to be constantly in movement. In writing your paper, you may want to refer to stories that satisfy Twain's requirements, and some that don't. Twain thinks the regional novel will participate in the national characteristics, but he believes a national novel as such is an abstract conception and cannot be written. There is no such thing as a "great American novel" because American life is too complex and no single aspect of it can speak for the remaining parts of it. Twain would probably agree with this statement.

4. Howells argues that the American novelists don't write about the sort of thing that Flaubert and Zola were free to write about because their manners along with American manners generally were improving! Their function, he says, is like the function of the priest and the physician. In certain essays Howells was less genteel in his demands than he is

here, but here certainly he is on the side of the genteel and therefore unwilling to look at any aspect of human life.

5. Harte says that the movement of people engendered by the Civil War made American literary men aware of the people in various parts of the country and aware of the variety of regions and their characteristics. Humor got into the stories, thanks to the tradition of humor developed in the western press. Such writers as himself, Harris, Cable, Twain, *et al.*, began to treat subjects characteristic of American life, with a knowledge of its peculiarities, avoiding fastidiousness, and aware of the inchoate poetry in many seemingly unlikely situations.

6. Garland's local color doctrine seems not very different from Twain's comments on regionalism, but Twain implies or says more clearly than Garland does that the national significance or universal significance is there despite the regional differences.

7. The novel that tells something: *Tarzan, Celia Garth, The Virginian,* and *Riders of the Purple Sage.* Such books have pace, movement and interesting description but no significant inner life. Novels that show something: E. M. Forster's *Howard's End* and *The Longest Journey* show the workings of the inner life and the lives of those who are callous and indifferent to the needs of sensitive people. Joyce Cary's *Charlie Is My Darling* and *The Horse's Mouth* show two types in action, the former a group of delinquent children and the latter an artist who is concerned only with creating his art. Norris' third group is novels that prove something: Faulkner's *Intruder in the Dust* tries to prove that the South must solve the race problem on its own. Farrell's *Studs Lonigan* tries to show that environment can be a very destructive force. H. G. Wells in *Tono Bungay* tries to prove that one should have faith in science and technology. Crane, in *Maggie,* like Farrell, tries to show that a child's environment can be a destructive force. Norris believes the third class of fiction is the more significant. But most critics nowadays would probably say that class two, as a class, is more likely to produce significant fiction.

8. Reality: James says that all fiction of any importance gives off an air of reality, but reality is varied and takes many forms. Cervantes, Chaucer, Shakespeare, Jane Austen, and William Faulkner, for example, give one a sense of their dealing with reality, but each is very different from the others. All the writer can do is to try to achieve a sense of it. He cannot say there is only a single formula for achieving a sense of it. Content and form: James says the story (content) cannot be separated from its form (technique or treatment). The diction in which it is told, the characterizations, the pace, the suspense, etc., are all a part of what the story itself finally becomes or is.

9. Writers in Farrell's line of realism: Dreiser, Frank Norris, Sherwood Anderson, Sinclair Lewis, Richard Wright, and presumably Farrell himself. James would appear to have a more catholic, larger conception of realism, in that he would be more willing to think of fantasy or highly personal and subjective studies as being in the line of realism.

10. Critical observations: (1.) Importance of unified effect in short fiction. (2.) There are a number of distinctions between the "novel" and the "romance." (3.) The particularized descriptions on a regional novel do not rule out the possibility of universal significance. (4.) The American writer ought to be aware of what is indigenous, peculiar to the world he is describing. (5.) Fiction has different ends, methods, and purposes. (6.) There are many forms of realism. (7.) The *way* in which a story is told is an integral part of *what* the story is.

Prospects

1. These are some of the points Emerson makes: Nothing can reach you except through the agency of yourself, what you are. You must trust yourself. You must also be a nonconformist. There is no need for consistency. It is a profanation to seek aids or interventions in reaching for God; one should approach him directly. Etc. Emerson's critics have occasionally said that his stress on the uniqueness and the glories of the individual invites arrogance, self-preoccupation, and ignores the needs man has for intervention in his behalf and props of various kinds.

2. Here is the first sentence of "The Gettysburg Address" written in a more round-about style: "Eighty odd years or so ago, our ancestors, from various parts of the civilized world, came up with a theory that all men are equal — it had not been tried before — at least as equal before the law." This sentence lacks dignity, is evasive, and carries no conviction. Rewrite the rest of the speech in similar language.

3. Trollope, the English novelist, said that early success frequently causes the decay or disintegration of talent. It destroys ambition, and takes away the previous need to improve and grow. Smith says that our journalistic situation is such that a young writer who does something noteworthy is lionized and made much of, and that this is not good for him, except in small doses. Publishers too, he says, want to exploit his talent, and do by making him repeat successes and write too quickly and rapidly, thereby denying him time to allow himself and his stories to mature.

4. Presumably Barrett means something like this. America is different from other countries in that there are no dim and mythy reaches in her pre-history. She suddenly became a nation, full-blown. As Americans we are self-conscious about our identity. We seem to ask the land itself for answers. We leave it by going to Europe as exiles or to Greenwich Village, but we return to it, as though in search of our own roots. However critical writers are there is an implied promise that they are searching for health, personal and national, and ultimately have faith in their own and their country's future.

5. Some of the literature in our time has stressed the way in which forces control human destiny (environment, heredity, etc.), but Faulkner insists that greatness, in action or in literature, comes only from personal struggle, our better, more decent impulses in conflict with our baser instincts. Writers who have won the Nobel Prize: Sinclair Lewis, Eugene O'Neill, Pearl Buck, T. S. Eliot, and Ernest Hemingway.

6. Faulkner sees man as a creature of struggle and effort, out of which come his achievements. If he is not confronted by the need to struggle he is less likely to achieve anything of moment. The South, he says, faced adversity, and out of it came a significant literature. Japan, he adds, has also faced adversity, and he expects that an important literature may be written in response to it.

Part II: AMERICAN SHORT NOVELS

EDITED BY R. P. BLACKMUR

Fiction Glossary

Allegory. The kind of story in which the characters are not taken as "real" but as standing for a system of ideas, item by item.

Atmosphere. The special world of the action (of sunshine, gloom, barren landscape, treacherous waves, rich cornfields, harsh neighborhood, etc.).

Character. An actor in a narrative. Sometimes he represents an ethical position. His thought, speech, and action establish what he is. Certain characters are referred to as *flat, one-dimensional,* and more complicated characters as *round.* But in fiction, as compared with actual life, most characters are flat, that is, they have fewer characteristics and complications than actual people.

Climax. Point at which action reaches highest or most intense point of conflict.

Conflict. All stories are based on conflict, as man against environment, a complication of forces, or against something in himself.

Denouement. The final resolution, or untying of the action, the point at which the reader knows what finally happened.

Episode. One action in a larger action or series of actions.
Episodic. So called when episode follows episode without any strong causal reason or connection.

Foreshadowing. Intimations of events to follow.

Impressionism. A method of rendering scenes and experiences; depends on sense impressions; frequent use of metaphor, analogy, color, etc.

Irony. Various forms of simulation, saying one thing and implying another; illuminating contrasts.

Naturalism. Characters are controlled by forces beyond their power to control or, usually, even to understand.

65

Plot. Outline of the action; what happened.

Point of View. The method of narration: first person, who is either involved in the action or who tells his own story; a narrator telling what objectively happened, with no great attempt to get inside the characters' heads; or he may go inside their heads; the narrator may limit the information he employs or, relatively, be omniscient.

Realism. Having a strong sense of actuality. (Refer to James' "The Art of Fiction")

Sentimentality. Emotional response in excess of the object, occasion, or justification.

Stock response. Conventional, uncritical response to a symbol or situation.

Stream of consciousness. Order dictated by writer's associations, not by logic.

Symbol. An object, situation or event that stands for something else.

Theme. The point, or meaning, of a story; the insight or perception of the author which gives significance to the action, thus lifting it above an inert, meaningless series of episodes.

Tone. Attitude of author towards his material: humorous, flip, biting, sympathetic, etc.

QUESTIONS —

Introduction (pages 1-17)

(See Sample Answers to Questions, p. 73)

NOTE: Page references are to *American Short Novels,* except where in italic, as above, *"See Sample Answers to Questions, p. 73,"* which refer to pages in this volume.

1. What do you understand Blackmur to mean by the "symbolic imagination" (page 1) and allegory (pages 1-3)?

2. Re-read Chase's "The Broken Circuit: Romance and the American Novel" (*American Literary Essays,* pages 270-279). Is his thesis about American fiction in any way similar to Blackmur's?

3. Blackmur (page 3) says that James' method was such that "a very little life could be very greatly felt." What does he mean?

4. Blackmur says (page 17) that American writers are drawn toward allegory* — "allegory is germane to their sensibility and appropriate to the culture they represent." What reasons can you give for this situation? Can you think of any American writers, not represented in this volume, who write in a similar allegorical fashion? Refer to specific works.

Billy Budd (pages 18-67)
(See Sample Answers to Questions, pp. 73-74)

1. In "Billy Budd" (pages 18-67), Captain Vere distinguishes between absolute justice and the poor "justice" that grows out of practical necessity. Explain.

2. In another of his novels, *Pierre,* Melville speaks of the conflict between absolute idealism and expediency or compromise. "A virtuous expediency, then, seems the highest desirable or attainable excellence for the mass of men, and is the only earthly excellence that their Creator intended for them." Is this doctrine applicable to "Billy Budd"?

3. Certain critics have said that "Billy Budd" is Melville's *Tempest* or *Winter's Tale,* his reconciliation with the world, with suffering and injustice. An occasional critic disagrees, saying Melville is being grimly ironic in "Billy Budd." Which view would you defend? Why? Are other views possible?

---

* See page 65, Fiction Glossary

4. Is it likely that a 20th century author, in England or America, would approve of Captain Vere's actions at all or to the same extent that a 19th century author might approve? Why?

5. What is the significance of the vessel's name, *Rights of Man?*

The Man That Corrupted Hadleyburg   (pages 69-96)
(See Sample Answers to Questions, pp. 74-75)

1. Would it be fair to say that Twain in "The Man That Corrupted Hadleyburg," despite his humor, is more soldily and persistently pessimistic than the Melville who wrote "Billy Budd"?

2. Are the characters in Twain's story "flat" or "round"? What relationship does the nature of them have to do with allegory?

3. What immediate differences are observable between the style of "Billy Budd" and "The Man That Corrupted Hadleyburg"? How do you account for these differences (author's attitude, subject, etc.)?

4. Certain stories emphasize plot, or character, or atmosphere, or theme. Which does Twain emphasize here?

5. What is the "point of view" in "The Man That Corrupted Hadleyburg"?

6. Remembering Blackmur's use of "allegory," does "The Man That Corrupted Hadleyburg" seem more, or less obviously, allegorical than "Billy Budd"?

Maggie: A Girl of the Streets   (pages 97-133)
(See Sample Answers to Questions, pp. 75-76)

1. What evidence is there in "Maggie: A Girl of the Streets" that Crane was contemptuous of the "genteel tradition"?

2. One of the doctrines of Naturalism was that environment determined character. Explain the use Crane made of this doctrine.

3. Crane used many impressionistic phrases and metaphors. Illustrate.

4. In section 17 (pages 128-130), Crane leaves certain inferences up to the reader. Is this more effective than a more explicit treatment might have been?

5. In the question on "The Blue Hotel," you were asked to comment on fear as a motivating factor. Does fear help to account for the actions of Maggie?

6. Does Crane in any way appear to condemn Maggie?

7. There are notable instances of irony in this story. Point out several.

8. Is Norris' "The Novel With a Purpose" (*American Literary Essays,* pages 248-250) applicable to "Maggie: A Girl of the Streets"?

Washington Square (pages 134-235)
(See Sample Answers to Questions, pp. 76, 77)

1. What is the nature of the victory Catherine wins? If she had married Morris, knowing as much as she now does about his motives, could she also have won a Jamesian sort of victory? Explain.

2. If you were to rewrite "Washington Square" as a three-act play, indicate the subject matter of each act. Justify your divisions. Are the various characters good or poor dramatic types?

3. Write an essay (350 to 400 words) analyzing the relationship between Catherine and her father.

4. Is this a realistic or naturalistic story. Justify your answer.

5. Is this emphasis in the story on theme, plot, character, atmosphere, or on all of them equally?

6. From what "point of view" is the story told?

Melanctha (pages 236-306)
(See Sample Answers to Questions, p. 77)

1. In *Composition As Explanation* (1925) Gertrude Stein said that in "Melanctha" there was "a constant recurring and beginning

there was a marked direction in the direction of being in the present although naturally I had become accustomed to past present and future, and why, because the composition forming around me was a prolonged present." Indicate instances of Miss Stein's use of the "prolonged present."

2. Donald Sutherland, in *Gertrude Stein: A Biography of Her Work* (1951), says of the language employed in "Melanctha," ". . . the work had to have not its romantic or literary meaning but the immediate meaning it had to the contemporary using it, a literal axiomatic meaning confined to the simple situations of the average life." With the situation of Melanctha's life, background, and temperament in mind, comment on her use of language.

3. Miss Stein uses repetition (1) to force the reader's consciousness to concentrate on the identity of the object or situation being described, and (2) to provide the avenue along which change and movement can occur. Point out examples of such uses of repetition.

4. In *Lectures in America*, Miss Stein said she objected to punctuation because it interfered with the "going-on." A comma for example, "by helping you along holding your coat for you putting on your shoes keeps you from living your life as actively as you should lead it." Comment on her analogies.

5. Would you place "Melanctha" in the same tradition as "Maggie: A Girl of the Streets" or with "Washington Square." Justify your answer.

The Great American Novel (pages 307-343)
(See Sample Answers to Questions, p. 78)

1. What did Twain (see *American Literary Essays*, pages 235-236) think about the possibility of the great American novel? Does William Carlos Williams believe in the possibility? If so, what, according to him, should it be or represent or catch about America?

2. Blackmur has also said that "The Great American Novel" has no plot and has been called an "impressionistic essay." What appears to be the theme of the essay?

3. In his introduction (pages 12-15), Blackmur says that Williams and Miss Stein have a good deal in common. What is it they share?

4. "The Great American Novel" was written early in the 1920's. Does the date of its composition help to account for its subject and its manner?

The Venetian Glass Nephew   (pages 344-396)
(See Sample Answers to Questions, pp. 78, 79)

1. The setting and action of "The Venetian Glass Nephew" is an amalgam or mixture of the 18th century, the artificiality and decadence of Oscar Wilde's *Dorian Gray,* and a never-never land. Explain and illustrate.

2. Blackmur says (page 16) that Rosalba is a victim of "romantic love." What does he mean?

3. We sometimes aspire to create an exquisite art, free from and above the pain and problems of life. Exquisite creations, however, may seem a little sad, and evoke a sense of pathos. Can these comments be related to "The Venetian Glass Nephew"?

4. Blackmur also says (page 15) that Williams would disapprove of "The Venetian Glass Nephew." Why?

*   *   *   *   *

(See Sample Answers to Questions, p. 79)

1. In what way does the typical structure of a short story differ from the short novel? And how does the short novel differ from the long or full length novel? Write an essay (500 to 600 words) on this subject, using as examples some of the short stories and short novels you have read.

2. Write a dialogue in which Melville, Twain, Crane, James, Gertrude Stein, Williams and Elinor Wylie comment on their own and each other's stories.

A LIST OF ADDITIONAL SHORT NOVELS:

SAUL BELLOW	*Seize the Day*
WILLA CATHER	*A Lost Lady* *Neighbor Rosicky*
STEPHEN CRANE	*The Monster* *The Red Badge of Courage*
WILLIAM FAULKNER	*The Bear* *Old Man* *The Wild Palms*
F. SCOTT FITZGERALD	*The Rich Boy*
HENRY JAMES	*The Beast in the Jungle* *The Pupil* *Daisy Miller* *Madame de Mauve* *The Bench of Desolation* *The Turn of the Screw*
HERMAN MELVILLE	*Benito Cereno*
KATHERINE ANNE PORTER	*Old Mortality* *Pale Horse, Pale Rider* *The Leaning Tower*
GERTRUDE STEIN	*The Good Anna* *Lena*
JOHN STEINBECK	*The Pearl* *Red Pony*
ROBERT PENN WARREN	*The Circus in the Attic*

SAMPLE ANSWERS TO QUESTIONS —

Introduction

1. The fiction writer may use his imagination in inventing characters, episodes, in telling a story that wears the guise of realism (houses that look like ordinary houses, and characters that talk like one's neighbors), or he may employ symbolic figures, standing for certain virtues or certain vices or certain attributes of a culture or a people. Blackmur says the American fiction writer inclines toward the use of the symbolic imagination, and toward allegory. An allegory is an extended story in which the characters are not taken as representing the real so much as representing ideas.

2. Chase says that the writer of the romance is freer to "render reality in less volume and detail," is less concerned with a close-up view of reality in its daily forms. There is a greater sense of ideas in motion unobstructed by the details of reality. Blackmur implies that the American allegorist is a romantic writer in this sense, more the creator of romances than of novels.

3. Certain writers can present a great many details—the design in a dress, the color of the wallpaper, the style of furniture, etc.—without giving a vivid sense of what is being described. James could take a few details and give them resonance, make them radiate significance. James was interested in theme, in meaning, and he selected realistic details that fed meaning or on which meaning could feed.

4. Chase, in his essay on romance, implies that American life is less complicated socially than English or French life. The novel has always been seen as the genre or form in which man's social life could be studied and discussed. The American novel has been more concerned with man in nature and man in terms of future hopes than with his immediate social situation. Therefore just as the American writer is drawn toward romance he is drawn toward allegory.

Billy Budd

1. There is the absolute justice of law books and of abstract discussion. If one does certain things, according to abstract justice, one should be punished in this or that fashion and to this or that degree. But human beings break the law, and they do it for different reasons, under

different pressures, some coldly and deliberately, others in sudden anger, some because of poverty, some because of twisted and perverse needs of their own. And the dispensers of justice, also being human, do the best they can, or should. They are subject to poor judgment, prejudice, etc.

2. In *Pierre* Melville implies that man is a weak creature and can achieve only partial virtues and should not try for more than that. Those who try for absolute virtue are destroyed. This is not the precise issue in *Billy Budd*. Billy accepts his limitations, his inability to understand what has happened to him. In a sense, this puts him on the side of those who see themselves as weak and accept his weakness as inevitable and not to be changed. He even achieves peace of mind in recognizing this.

3. In *The Tempest* and *The Winter's Tale* Shakespeare sees beyond conflict and difficulty, even though he sees them. He sees man as a part of a long history and process, and he is detached from the anguish of his struggles. This is one view of Melville in Billy Budd, namely, that Melville is accepting the injustices of the world, submitting his neck to them. Other critics say he is grimly ironic that a young man like Billy would thus submit, and is contemptuous of the "superior" or "higher" justice of the court, above immediate human needs. Another view: Melville might have been doing a kind of "anthropological" study, saying the big world, society, the courts, civilization feed on the young, offering them up in wars, or throwing their helpless bodies to the vultures, to the society that is nurtured by their sacrifice.

4. A nineteenth century audience was more likely to appeal to the rights of society than to the rights of the individual. Thus in England a man could be sent to jail for years for a petty theft. The twentieth century is more preoccupied with the rights of the individual. Therefore we are less likely to listen sympathetically to Vere's speeches.

5. The name of the vessel is ironic.

The Man That Corrupted Hadleyburg

1. Probably it is right to say that Twain seems more deeply pessimistic in this story than Melville is in his. Melville is speculating about human (and "inhuman") justice, whereas Twain seems obsessed by the venality, the openness to corruption of the human being. Melville sees a noble side. Twain does not.

2. Twain's characters are barely described. Mostly they are names and sometimes they have jobs, but mostly they are forces representing self-aggrandizement. Therefore they are flat characters. As flat characters they serve the allegorical nature of the story more directly.

3. Melville's style has a greater variety of tone, shifts in movement and pace. His subject is larger and has within it a great philosophical tension — and it is altogether appropriate that the style be varied. Twain's style is almost uniform in tone, is deadpan and serious, intent on the final "nub" as he called it, that would make his intention clear beyond any doubt.

4. Twain does not emphasize character or atmosphere, and he emphasizes plot only insofar as it enables him to make his point. Therefore he must be said to emphasize theme.

5. The narrator is omniscient. He presents himself as someone who knows everything that relates to the town and the stranger.

6. Twain's story is more deliberately allegorical than Melville's. Melville, for example, presents characters that tend to be round, not as round certainly as characters can be, but certainly not as flat as Twain's are.

Maggie: A Girl of the Streets

1. See Crane's account of a genteel drama, pages 112-113.

2. Crane presents a world of ignorance, violence, and intolerance that sink a pretty, well-intentioned girl. She is a victim of her mother, her seducer, and her neighborhood.

3. See opening paragraphs of each section, 1 through 9.

4. Probably. The Greeks did their murders offstage, and it is commonly believed that the imagination, given certain aids, can do more than explicit description can.

5. Maggie has tried to rise out of a situation of indignity and degradation. She fails. She foresees further and more ignominious defeats, and seeing no possible solution she kills herself.

6. Outside of the story, in his critical comments, Crane spoke in sympathetic terms about girls like Maggie. In the story he remains detached, allowing the reader to draw his own inferences.

7. One of the most notable ironies is the cry of Maggie's mother at the end, "Oh, yes, I'll forgive her! I'll forgive her!"

8. Obviously Crane's story is a "novel with a purpose." Its purpose is to awaken indifferent, unaware or calloused persons to the suffering, disease and crime that such neighborhoods as Maggie's encourage or make inevitable.

Washington Square

1. James likes his characters to win spiritual victories that involve repressing or denying what he saw as their baser natures. Catherine certainly could have had a kind of happiness as the wife of Morris, but she refused to accept him on the terms he had offered her. She found them humiliating. Another writer, with a different view-point from James, might have caused her to swallow her pride and settle for a relatively happy life as Morris' wife. This would have been a very different story, and not one that James could have written.

2. The first act might end not after Catherine falls in love with Morris, but after Dr. Sloper, her father, is convinced he should not allow the marriage. End of section 14. The second act includes Catherine's determination to marry Morris, his delaying tactics and finally his leaving. End of section 29. Act three would include the later years of her life, what she makes of her days, and Morris' return, and her refusal to marry him. End of section 35. Characters: The main characters are good dramatic types. The stiff, domineering father. The opportunistic, handsome lover, Morris. The plain girl of simple virtue and stern, uncompromising self-respect, even when it costs her a romantic love affair.

3. This would involve an account of the doctor's marriage, his wife, his expectations in life, her death, his frustrations, a plain daughter, etc. One might speculate a bit on the psychological implications, even though James does not.

4. It is a realistic, not a naturalistic story. In naturalistic fiction forces control people's destinies. In this story character controls the action.

5. The plot is well worked out; it is dramatic. The atmosphere of lower New York City, Washington Square, is excellently evoked. But probably the emphasis may be said to be on theme and character, the former dramatizing the later and the later making the former possible.

6. It is an omniscient point of view, and there are occasion asides to the reader, in the nineteenth century manner.

Melanctha

1. The first two or three pages (pages 236-238) of the story show this recurring present. Over and over again Miss Stein says pretty much the same thing about her characters, extending our awareness of them slightly each time she circles them again.

2. The story of Melanctha would not, at first thought, seem very promising as a fictional subject. The language is the language one might hear on the street or on a bus as people, in whatever city or whatever part of the world, talked about their problems. For example, on page 247, there is this: "Melanctha's father during these last years did not come very often to the house where his wife lived and Melanctha. Melanctha was not sure that her father was any longer here in Bridgepoint. It was Melanctha who was very good now to her mother. It was always Melanctha's way to be good to anyone in trouble."

3. An episode with this sort of writing begins on page 244, bottom of the second column, "Melanctha Herbert was sixteen when she first met Jane Harden," and ending on page 247, top of the left hand column, "Jane out in any of her trouble, and later, when Jane really went to pieces, Melanctha always did all that she could to help her."

4. There is something to what Miss Stein says about punctuation interfering with the free flow of a sentence. Perhaps a minimum of punctuation is a good rule, especially in fiction, but if one does not employ punctuation carefully a reader is frequently at a loss to know precisely what the writer meant.

5. Melanctha is certainly influenced by her environment, and one is half aware usually that this is so. But the dominant interest is not in the way environment is influencing her but in Melanctha herself and the strange, seemingly inexplicable workings of her mind and emotions.

The Great American Novel

1. Twain said the diversity of America, the many racial groups, religious groups, the various regions, made it impossible to write *the* American novel. In the 1920's, however, when Williams wrote his short novel there was a great deal of discussion of the possibility of a novel that would catch what Americans were, what America was. At the center of Williams' doctrine is an objection to trying to impose European culture as a complex and achieved entity onto the American continent. America was itself, its own sort of society, changing, striving, trying to find itself. Williams too tries always for the scene, the accent, the situation, the nuance that strikes him as "truly American."

2. Blackmur, on pages 14-15, discusses this work at some length, saying what Williams was trying to do and putting it in its historical context.

3. The 1920's was an age of ferment and experiment. World War I marked the end of the Victorian world, and writers consciously and sometimes belligerently attacked the Victorian world. There was a brave new world ahead. Experimentation in the arts was a part of it. Gertrude Stein, like Hemingway, Pound and Eliot, experimented with language and so did Dr. Williams. Cummings, for example, seemed to fragment the traditional English sentence, and to want to start again to rebuild it. Stein and Williams are a part of this experimentation.

4. See answer to #3.

The Venetian Glass Nephew

1. Oscar Wilde, Aubrey Beardsley and others in the 1890's created stories with a cut-glass artistry. Their characters and the settings seemed something out of art, not out of life. Miss Wylie's characters and setting are in this cut-glass tradition. She has also employed the Rome of the 18th century, but removing it from its flesh and blood actuality into a kind of never-never land.

2. Love, like all ideals and aspirations, has to make its way in the world, and the world makes claims and counter-claims on us and on our emotions. It asks for compromises, and there are many forces that pull against or deny the possibility of pure love. Rosalba refuses to allow the counter-claims.

3. Many critics and poets have said that if there were no such thing as death there would not be anything similar to what we know as beauty. Pain, suffering, and the passage of time, by contrast, make us appreciate sunsets, the laughter of small children, and the vigor of youth. Art apart from these facts of human life has no significance. The chief characters in Miss Wylie's story are removed from life, and the pathos inheres in that.

4. He would see its cut-glass artistry as too formal, too Europeanized, too un-American.

✻   ✻   ✻   ✻   ✻   ✻

1. Perhaps the short novel can be compared to a convex mirror at the far end of a long room. It refracts everything in the room. The short story would have taken a small part of the room, say two persons sitting on a settee in a corner, concentrating on them. The novel would do what the short novel does, and more— would look minutely into the history of the room and the history and states of mind of all persons in it. It would, in short, indulge in more meanderings.

2. You might, to simplify matters, have Melville talk to Crane and James, Twain to Elinor Wylie, and Gertrude Stein to Williams.

Part III: AMERICAN SHORT STORIES

EDITED BY RAY WEST

QUESTIONS —

Introduction (pages 1-11)
(See Sample Answers to Questions, pp. 83, 84)

NOTE: Page references are to *American Short Stories*, except where in italic, as above, *"See Sample Answers to Questions, pp. 83, 84,"* which refer to pages in this volume.

1. West (page 2) says Irving was a "forerunner" rather than a "founder" of the American short story. Explain.

2. Why does West group Hawthorne, Poe, Melville, and James (pages 2-3)? What do they have in common?

3. West (page 4) speaks of the American "voice" or style in the short story. What contributed to its special quality?

4. What are some of the ways in which American writers responded to the Romantic doctrine that "nature" was benevolent (pages 5-6)?

5. Crane, West says (page 7), is a transitional figure from the nineteenth century to the modern story. Explain.

6. Hemingway is indebted (page 8) to Twain and Crane. Explain.

7. What are some of the themes developed by such Southern writers as Faulkner, Katherine Anne Porter, Warren, Eudora Welty, and Flannery O'Connor (pages 9-10)?

8. Make a list of fifteen or more eminent American short story writers, listing at least one volume of short stories for each of them.

American Short Stories
(See Sample Answers to Questions, pp. 84, 85, 86, 87, 88)

1. Is "The Legend of Sleepy Hollow" (pages 12-30) a story in which *theme* is the essential factor, *plot*, or *tone?* Characterize Irving's humor. (See Twain on difference between humor and wit, Leary, pages 234-235.)

2. What, according to Hawthorne's interpretation of Ethan Brand (pages 31-41), is the Unpardonable Sin? What is the meaning of the symbolism of the heart? Is this an inexcusable offense against realism? (See Hawthorne on romance, Leary, pages 231-233.)

3. What is the *theme* of "Young Goodman Brown" (pages 41-49)?

4. Poe in "Ligeia" (pages 49-58) employs romantic, far-away settings and characters very remote from our everyday world. Does this make the credibility of the action easier or harder to accept? Refer to Poe's "The Tale Proper" (Leary, pages 229-230). Does he seem to you faithful to his own critical doctrine?

5. "The Facts in the Case of M. Valdemar" (pages 58-64) might, on first reading, seem merely morbid melodrama. Can it be said to have greater significance than this? In other words, is Poe merely or solely an eerie story-teller or do his tales seem to be telling us something about human psychology?

6. What is the theme of "Bartleby the Scrivener" (pages 64-87)?

7. "The Real Thing" is a parable about the artist or writer trying to use actuality in drawing, painting, or in fiction. Explain. (Refer to James' "The Art of Fiction," Leary, pages 251-264.) Does art *mirror* life, *refract* it, *distort* it? Explain.

8. Is "Mrs. Medwin" (pages 103-115) the sort of story more likely to have had a European than an American setting? Why? (Refer to James' "Absent Things in American Life," Leary, pages 37-38.)

9. Characterize the *tone* of "The £1,000,000 Bank-Note" (pages 116-127). Is the story loosely episodic?

10. In what ways can "Mliss" (pages 128-143) be said to be a "local color" story? (Refer to "The Rise of the Short Story," Leary, pages 240-246, and "Local Color in Art," Leary, pages 244-246.)

11. It is often said that Crane's subject was fear. Is this true of "The Blue Hotel" (pages 143-161)? Crane used color not only impressionistically but symbolically. Explain.

12. "The Upturned Face" (pages 161-163) is a story that could have influenced Hemingway. Explain.

13. Is "The Lost Phoebe" (pages 163-173) a sentimental or a movingly realistic story? Justify your answer.

14. "I Want to Know Why" (pages 173-179) treats of lost innocence, a boy's introduction into the world of adult evil. What are the symbols of innocence in the story? Is the image of the red-headed woman sitting on Jerry Tilford's lap a powerful image of evil? Justify your answer.

15. "The Capital of the World" (pages 179-186) is also concerned with innocence confronting evil. Explain. Is Hemingway's *tone* flip or essentially serious? Justify your answer.

16. Does the theme of "A Rose for Emily" (pages 187-192) depend upon the story having a southern setting?

17. "Wash" (pages 192-200) makes very effective use of *atmosphere*. Explain. At least two crucial actions in the story are suggested or implied, not explicitly stated. What are these, and what effect does this method have on the story?

18. "The Grave" (pages 200-204), like "I Want to Know Why," shows innocence confronting death, evil, horror. Which is the more effective story? Why?

19. There are several symbols of evil in "Blackberry Winter" (pages 205-218). What are they, and how do they function?

20. In "The Chrysanthemums" (pages 218-225) the significance of the story resides in the nature of the betrayed Elisa's experience. Explain.

21. Characterize the *tone* of "The Hitch-Hikers" (pages 225-234).

22. "The Wind and the Snow of Winter" (pages 234-242) has a great deal in common with "The Lost Phoebe." Explain. The closing paragraph of the story, by implication, recapitulates the entire story. Explain.

23. West, in the introductory note to "The Valiant Woman" (pages 242-248), says many of Powers' stories treat of the conflicting claims of religion and life. Relate this comment to the present story.

24. "Larchmoor Is Not the World" (pages 248-258) is a story about trying to escape from reality. What is its point?

25. Mr. Shiftlet, in "The Life You Save May Be Your Own" (pages 259-265), says of himself, "I'm a man . . . even if I ain't a whole one." What significance does this have for the story?

26. Write an essay (600 to 700 words) entitled The American Short Story Since Crane.

SAMPLE ANSWERS TO QUESTIONS —

Introduction

1. The short story or tale had been written in all times and places, and Irving's tales were in part borrowed from older literatures. He did however bring to them his own or perhaps it should be called an American humor.

2. Hawthorne, Poe, Melville and James looked upon the short story, and the practice of writing it, as a serious art and commitment. They were very much aware of the formal problems involved in short fiction.

3. Cooper treated the Indians as "noble savages," and Emerson treated nature as idyllic. And Thoreau believed nature would provide man with all his necessities if man would submit to its benevolent demands.

4. Crane is indebted to Twain, or at least writes a prose that is not unlike Twain's, and is also indebted to nineteenth century impressionism. But he broke with the "genteel tradition" and saw himself as writing in the new realistic line of Garland, Dreiser, London, *et al.*

5. In Twain and in Crane one often sees an innocent, well-intentioned young man confronting evil, in nature, in society, in himself, and he is shocked, affronted, "wounded." He responds to this by developing a "code," rules of conduct. He tries not to lie to himself, to be courageous, not to be taken in by humbug, and he speaks a crisp, laconic, understated, ironic language.

6. Southern writers tend to be preoccupied with nineteenth century manners and ideals and the twentieth century repudiation or modification of them. Faulkner is haunted by the ante-bellum world, its glories and its viciousness; and he shows how actions in that world carry over and influence his own world. Katherine Anne Porter writes mostly about the conflict between the romantic aura that can be put about one's actions or the actions of those dear to us and the unromantic actuality that frequently lies beneath them. Eudora Welty sees the middle class and lower middle class Mississippi world as comic, and pathetic. She laughs at them, but sympathetically. Warren brings the old evangelical sense of evil, or original sin, into the modern world, with its psychology, sociology, in conflict. Flannery O'Connor, a Georgia writer, is a Roman Catholic. She sees her characters searching for religious belief in a society that lacks the forms

or traditions or beliefs that would enable them to understand what it was they are in search of.

7. Hawthorne, *Tale of My Native Land, Twice Told Tales, Mosses from an Old Manse, The Snow Image and Other Twice Told Tales.* Poe, *Tales of the Grotesque and Arabesque, The Murders in the Rue Morgue, Tales.* Melville, *Piazza Tales, Billy Budd and Other Prose Pieces.* James, *A Passionate Pilgrim and Other Tales, The Madonna of the Future and Other Tales, Tales of Three Cities, Stories Revived, The Real Thing and Other Tales.* Etc.

1. Irving is not much interested in theme. He is interested in a comic tale, and therefore in plot and the manner of its telling. Twain says the teller of the humorous story does his best to conceal the fact that he is even dimly aware that there is anything funny in what he relates. Irving obviously is aware that he is telling a funny story. In Twain's terms then, he is a comic writer, not a humorous one. The nub, as Twain calls it, of the story is the wild ride. Irving builds up to it, and stresses its importance in the story.

2. The unpardonable sin, as Ethan Brand says, is intellectual pride and separation from other people. The marble heart is an inhuman heart, stone rather than flesh and blood. Hawthorne's doctrine of romance would make such symbolism justified. Furthermore he gives it a basis in reality, putting the man's heart into the lime kiln.

3. Goodman Brown is predisposed to see wickedness in those about him. He "sees" it in his young wife Faith, and consequently darkens the rest of his life and the lives of those about him.

4. Poe's stories exist on two levels, as sheer horror stories, and tales that hint at sinister psychological meanings. We don't expect them, in their guise as the former, to be realistic. And being what they are probably makes it easier for us to think of them as a kind of psychological allegory. Poe's doctrine: Ligeia is unified in tone, atmosphere, and total effect.

5. Poe was preoccupied with sadism, masochism, the death wish, and other psychological phenomena. In this story, he is concerned with mesmerism, and with the power it enables one human being to exert over another. More specifically, he is concerned with the way in which it interferes with the normal process of death.

6. Bartleby symbolizes those who refuse to accept the rules of everyday society. He withdraws or in effect "resigns" from society. Bartleby's separation has an aura of dedication to it. He refuses, with dig-

nity, to participate in the successful, bureaucratic, workaday world. His own inner life presumably becomes the object of his contemplation. He is a madman, a clown and a kind of savior.

7. Life is life and art is art, and the two while related are not the same. Art is life selected and stylized. It tries to achieve certain aesthetic and emotional effects. It employs exaggeration and distortion, it heightens certain things and minimizes others. James' story shows how this works for a book illustrator; it works in a similar way for fiction writers.

8. Europeans live in a more tightly organized society than do Americans. Europeans draw more numerous social lines between groups, depending on money, profession, and prestige. The sort of situation James describes could take place in the U.S. but would be much more likely in Europe.

9. The situation Twain describes is nearly wholly incredible but it is told in something approaching a deadpan style. The tone therefore is humorous. Episodic: The story is episodic. Events seem to happen rather than be caused; that is, one event does not lead inevitably to the next event.

10. Much of the description — notice the opening paragraphs — describes the California mountains and the mining camp atmosphere. The dialect and misspellings of Mliss, for example, are out of the Old West and Southwestern tradition of humor.

11. Each person in the story who is involved in the card game or later in the murder is motivated by fear. The Swede had a great fear of the lawless West. Johnnie is afraid to admit he cheated at cards. The Easterner is afraid to admit he knows Johnnie cheated. The gangster, a slight man, is afraid of the Swede, and when he is attacked uses a knife to defend himself. Impressionism: The first three paragraphs of the story exhibit Crane's talent for impressionistic writing. See also the first four paragraphs in section 8 (pages 157-158).

12. "The Upturned Face" could be a Hemingway story. First, the scene is from a war. A soldier has been killed and his friends, still under fire, want to bury him. They do not have the proper tools and they have neither a casket nor box to bury him in. The reader sees them torn by mixed emotions, wanting to bury him properly and wanting to save themselves. The realism of the dirt striking the dead man's face is like Hemingway. There is also innocence confronting evil in a shocking form. And the style employs understatement. There is nothing flowery or rhetorical about the writing.

13. The story is very sad, but it is not sentimental. It would be sentimental if one were asked to respond emotionally without any good justification. In the old man and his quest there is justification. He is senile and not wholly responsible for what he does. He has lost his wife, and she represented the love, the beauty and the warmth of human experience that are now lost to him. He searches for them, for Phoebe, and the reader knows he will never find them.

14. The symbols of innocence are the world of the race track, the horses, and the colored men. It is a boy's world. The red-headed woman typifies evil, and Jerry Tilford, in being drawn to her, is the adult world committing itself to evil. Tilford's sitting in the woman's lap is not a very vivid symbol of evil. Anderson might have found others, in disease, in death, or elsewhere, that would be more striking and more moving.

15. Paco works in the hotel, and seems to be protected by the very institution itself. He admires the work of the bullring, and plays at being a bullfighter. But the very play has in it such elements of danger that Paco meets his death, suddenly, unexpectedly. Tone: Hemingway may at first seem to be flip, but there is a seriousness underneath the tone.

16. There is no doubt that much of the charm and appeal of the story is in the descriptions that are Southern. Miss Emily is a Southern lady and her lover was a Yankee. Possibly something can be made of their opposition and struggle. But essentially the story is that of a frustrated woman, whose father refused her the normal outlets for her desires and affections and who, consequently, sought abnormal outlets. It is a psychological story.

17. The past glories of the war are caused to play on the present scenes of poverty and degradation, somehow elevating them, giving Wash's life and the life of his granddaughter some degree of dignity and hopefulness. The two realms, the present and Sutpen in the war, are frequently juxtaposed. The poverty of Wash, for example, is caught in the vivid descriptions of the shed he lives in. Suggested actions: The three deaths, Sutpen's (page 198), Milly's (page 199) and Wash's (page 200) are not described. The reader is left to infer what happened. The effect is like a murder offstage, it is a little more awe inspiring, a little more terrifying.

18. Miss Porter's story recalls a child's first awareness of birth and death, and then the various scenes and experience in later life that renew her impressions. It is a more vivid confrontation of evil because more universal and more significant than the symbolism of the red-haired woman.

19. The land itself during the storm is a symbol of evil, the cabins are similarly symbols of poverty and struggle, and the tramp himself, perhaps most clearly of all, is a symbol of something irremediable in the human situation. There is an excellent contrast between his world and the world of the boy's father on page 217.

20. Elisa is a sensitive and sympathetic woman. She needs the association of people who feel the same way she does about flowers. The man who talked with her about the flowers, and about growing them, was simply an opportunist; he had no interest in the flowers. When she sees the flowers on the road, where he had thrown them, she is deeply frustrated and hurt.

21. In a general sense the tone of this story is comic. There is something grotesque in the action, especially in the murder. All of the characters seem somehow bemused, as though their controlling forces were emotions they experienced but could not understand and do not question. It is therefore both sad and eerie.

22. Clark's story has to do with senility, with the loss of memory of an aged man, with the way lost past events merge in his mind with recent events. He has fought or struggled with nature and for a time seemed to have bested it, but finally nature takes hold of him, as it were, and shows him she has him in her control. The situation in "The Lost Phoebe" is very similar. Final paragraph: The shadows, the dim light, the eerie movement of the shadows in the light all recapitulate what the story as a whole says.

23. Frequently in thinking about idealistic conduct or ways of life, such as the ministry, we think of them as somehow apart from ordinary life, and therefore free of everyday annoyances. Someone had referred to ministers as "walking Sundays." But the most idealistic, the most dedicated men suffer annoyances. Because they feel less free to indulge their weaknesses the annoyances take on a comic air. This is the situation in Powers' story.

24. The teacher in this story appears to feel that he can suffer the inanities of life in a girl's school because it frees him from many of the problems he would face in the outside world. But suddenly, on the eve of a holiday, when the school should be at its most peaceful, the problems of a girl intrude themselves on his life. He becomes involved, in such an intense way that he loses his job, and is forced back into the world.

25. Mr. Shiftlet is a kind of marginal hero. He is a villain, but he refuses to be used and he persists in believing or at least hoping

that what he calls the slime of the world can be cleansed. He says that certain people see the world only as matter and fail to be aware of the spiritual needs of man.

26. These are some of the topics you might consider in your paper: (1) Crane as a transitional figure. (2) Nature in Crane. (3) Impressionism. (4) Debt to Twain. (5) Hemingway's debt to Crane. (6) Comparison with Dreiser. (7) Anderson's relationship to Hemingway. (8) Southern writers: Faulkner, Porter, Warren, Welty. (9) Recent writers: Clark, Powers, Cassill, O'Connor. (10) Short story as work of art (Poe, James).

A LIST OF ADDITIONAL SHORT STORY VOLUMES:

SHERWOOD ANDERSON	*Death in the Woods and Other Stories.*
WILLA CATHER	*Youth and the Bright Medusa.*
STEPHEN CRANE	*Twenty Stories.*
WALTER VAN TILBURG CLARK	*The Watchful Gods and Other Stories.*
WILLIAM FAULKNER	*Collected Stories.*
F. SCOTT FITZGERALD	*Taps at Reveille.*
ELLEN GLASGOW	*The Shadowy Third.*
CAROLINE GORDON	*The Forest of the South.*
NATHANIEL HAWTHORNE	*Twice Told Tales.*
ERNEST HEMINGWAY	*Men Without Women.*
HENRY JAMES	*The Short Stories of Henry James.*
HERMAN MELVILLE	*The Piazza Tales.*
EDGAR ALLAN POE	*Tales of the Grotesque and Arabesque.*
KATHERINE ANNE PORTER	*Flowering Judas.*
J. F. POWERS	*The Prince of Darkness and Other Stories.*
JOHN STEINBECK	*The Long Valley.*
PETER TAYLOR	*A Long Fourth and Other Stories.*
R. P. WARREN	*The Circus in the Attic.*
EUDORA WELTY	*A Curtain of Green.*

See also the annual *The O. Henry Awards* and *The Best Short Stories of the Year.*

Part IV: AMERICAN POETRY
EDITED BY KARL SHAPIRO

Poetry Glossary

Abstract. General statements are called abstract. Poetry, even more than other literary forms, depends upon the *concrete*, the *particular*, on *images* and *metaphors*.

Alliteration. The repetition or frequent recurrence of the same consonants, especially initial consonants, as in "the rivers that restlessly roll."

Allusion. Reference to some event or person of historical or literary significance.

Ambiguity. Multiple meanings, or a complex of meanings in a given word or phrase.

Anapest. Metrical foot consisting of two unaccented syllables followed by an accented syllable.

Assonance. Identical or similar vowel sounds (scream and beach; his and hither.

Attitude. The author's way of regarding his material, causing him to be playful, ironic, sympathetic, to use a certain kind of diction, etc., thus effecting the *tone* of a poem.

Blank verse. Unrhymed iambic pentameter.

Cacophony. Harsh, or dissonant sounds.

Caesura. The main pause in a line of verse.

Conceit. A comparison of the dissimilar, frequently an extended comparison.

Cosmic irony. See *Irony.*

Couplet. Two consecutive lines of verse, rhymed.

Dactyl. An accented foot followed by two unaccented feet.

Denotation. The specific, or primary, meaning of a word. *Tiger* is one of a class of carnivorous animals, has stripes, etc. The *connotations,* implied meanings, include slinkiness, sudden leaps, power, violence, etc.

Diction. Choice of words. Eliot is likely to use a different diction from Tennyson, or Cummings from Stevens.

Didacticism. Attempt to point a moral; preachy.

Enjambment. Run-on lines; not end-stopped lines.

Feminine endings. Unaccented last foot in rhyme. Masculine rhymes: *marsh, harsh.* Feminine: *regretfully, hopefully.*

Free verse. No observable metrical pattern.

Heptameter. A line of seven feet.

Iamb. A metrical foot consisting of an unaccented syllable followed by an accented syllable.

Imagery. Language appealing to the senses; metaphor, simile, symbol.

Imagist. Group of poets prior to World War I who attempted to re-emphasize certain poetic practices:

1. Use ordinary language; exact or precise word; avoid decoration.

2. Create new rhythms. Employ "free verse" but not rely on it as sole form.

3. Allow freedom of subject matter.

4. Employ images; avoid vague generalities.

5. Produce poetry that is hard and clear; never blurred.

6. Concentration is the essence of poetry.

Imagism was in revolt against the *didacticism* of Victorian poetry. Pound, Amy Lowell, "H.D.," and Fletcher were among early Imagists. The doctrine influenced Wallace Stevens, William Carlos Williams, Marianne Moore, Eliot, and other modern poets.

Internal rhyme. Rhyme occurring within a line of verse.

Irony. Language employing simulation, saying one thing and meaning another.

Cosmic irony, exhibiting human actions against the timeless backdrop of eternity and the immensity of the universe. (See Stephen Crane.)

Paradox, a statement which at first seems untrue, but which, upon closer examination, can be seen to contain an element of truth, often profound truth. (T. S. Eliot: "Liberty is a different kind of pain from prison." Wallace Stevens: "A duchess is not a duchess one hundred yards from her carriage.")

Understatement, exhibiting a discrepancy between what is actually said and what justifiably could be said. (See Robert Frost.)

Metaphor. An implied comparison. "My lovely rose and I were wed."

Onomatopoeia. Words that imitate the sound they designate. *Slurp, slap, slam, bang,* etc.

Paradox. See *Irony*.

Pentameter. A line consisting of five feet.

Petrarchan. A convention in the sonnet of representing the beloved as more than humanly beautiful, with eyes like rich dark jewels, teeth like pearls, lips like rubies, skin white as alabaster, etc.

Quatrain. A stanza of four lines. (See John Banister Tabb.)

Romantic. A period in English and American literary history, late eighteenth and early nineteenth century. Qualities: remote, exotic, exaggerated, bizarre, highly subjective, emotional.

Simile. A comparison employing *like* or *as*. "My love is like a red, red rose."

Slant rhymes. Partial rhymes: *top/tap, beat/bite.*

Sonnet. Fourteen-line poem, with discernible metric pattern and rhyme scheme.

Italian sonnet, iambic pentameter, rhyming *a b b a a b b a c d e c d e.* First eight lines are called the *octave.* Second six lines are called the *sestet.*

Shakespearean sonnet, iambic pentameter, rhyming *a b a b c d c d e f e f g g.* Usually develops its theme in three quatrains, and concludes it, or gives it a twist, with the couplet.

Irregular sonnets, variations on the Italian and Shakespearean sonnets.

Spondee. Two stressed syllables, making a foot. *Dear heart; drop dead!*

Subjective. Emphasis is on personal response to object or situation, not on the object or the situation itself. *Classical* poetry usually is held to be *objective* in emphasis, *romantic* poetry *subjective* in emphasis.

Tone. See *Attitude.*

Trochee. A foot of verse made up of an accented syllable followed by an unaccented syllable.

Understatement. See *Irony.*

Unity. Relationship of all parts of the poem: theme, metrical pattern, imagery, diction, etc., creating a sense of wholeness.

Verse. A single line of a poem. Synonym for poetry.

QUESTIONS —

Introduction (pages 1-8)
(See Sample Answers to Questions, p. 112)

NOTE: Page references are to *American Poetry*, except where in italic, as above, *"See Sample Answers to Questions, p. 112,"* which refer to pages in this volume.

1. Shapiro attempts to differentiate American poetry from English poetry. What evidence does he provide that there are differences?

2. Which poets illustrate Shapiro's statement (page 3) that our seventeenth century poetry "is a theology-centered literature" and our eighteenth century poetry "a politics-centered literature"?

3. Shapiro says (pages 5-6) that Poe and Whitman represent opposite poles in American poetry. Explain.

4. What poets does Shapiro place (pages 6-7) in the Pound-Eliot line? Which in the Whitman line?

Anne Bradstreet (pages 9-12)
(See Sample Answers to Questions, p. 112)

1. Who were some of Anne Bradstreet's contemporaries in America, in England?

2. Is there anything peculiarly American about her poetry?

3. Is her diction the sort a twentieth century poet would use?

4. Characterize the attitude * (tone) Anne Bradstreet brought to the subject matter of her poems.

Edward Taylor (pages 12-14)
(See Sample Answers to Questions, p. 113)

1. Taylor employs an extended conceit in "Huswifery," showing how the spinning of cloth can exhibit a series of analogies with the service of God. Write a paraphrase of this poem.

---
* See page 89, Poetry Glossary

2. Does Taylor stay with his conceit throughout "Upon a Spider Catching a Fly"? Is this a witty poem? If so, does the wit interfere with the piety of a religious poem? Are there any internal rhymes?

3. Does the conceit employed in "Meditation Eight" seem more far-fetched and labored than those in the two preceding poems? If so, why?

4. Samuel Johnson, the great eighteenth century English poet and critic, was the first critic to characterize the sort of poetry that Taylor and others wrote. He calls it "metaphysical poetry." In his "Life of Abraham Cowley," he wrote: "But wit, abstracted from its effects upon the hearer may be more rigorously and philosophically considered as a kind of *discordia concors,* a combination of dissimilar images, or discovery of occult resemblances in things apparently unlike." Does Taylor's poetic practice fit this definition? Explain.

5. A famous metaphysical poem is John Donne's "A Valediction Forbidding Mourning":

As virtuous men pass mildly away,
    And whisper to their souls to go,
While some of their sad friends do say,
    The breath goes now, and some say, no:
So let us melt, and make no noise,
    No tear-floods, no sigh-tempests move,
T'were profanation of our joys
    To tell the laity our love.
Moving of the earth brings harms and fears,
    Men reckon what it did and meant;
But trepidation of the spheres,
    Though greater far, is innocent.
Dull sublunary lovers' love
    (Whose soul is sense) cannot admit
Absence, because it doth remove
    Those things which elemented it.
But we by love, so much refin'd,
    That ourselves know not what it is,
Inter-assured of the mind,
    Care less, eyes, lips, and hands to miss.
Our two souls therefore, which are one,
    Though I must go, endure not yet
A breach, but an expansion,
    Like gold to airy thinness beat.
If they be two, they are two so
    As twin stiff compasses are two,

Thy soul the fixt foot, makes no show
    To move, but doth, if th' other do.
And though it in the center sit,
    Yet when the other far doth roam,
It leans, and harkens after it,
    And grows erect, as that comes home.
Such wilt thou be to me, who must
    Like th' other foot, obliquely run;
Thy firmness makes my circle just,
    And makes me end, where I begun.

Comment on the analogies Donne employs, referring them to Johnson's discussion of the metaphysical poem. Which poet, Taylor or Donne, seems the more expert? Justify your answer.

Philip Freneau (pages 14-17)
(See Sample Answers to Questions, p. 113)

1. Freneau belonged to the eighteenth century, although he lived thirty-two years into the nineteenth as well. The eighteenth century is sometimes called the Neoclassical age. Its ideals about literature were that it should exhibit restraint, decorum, polish, wit, brilliance, clarity, logic, "correctness," and "good taste." There was a good deal of didactic writing. The most successfully employed verse form was the couplet—because it was suitable to epigrammatic barbs and neat summaries:

    The relish of the muse consists in rhyme:
    One verse must meet another like a chime.

After several careful readings of Freneau's poems, write an essay (350 to 400 words) on the Neoclassical elements in his poetry.

2. Does there seem to be a pull, or tension, in Freneau's mind between the rationalist, the admirer of objective fact and logic, and the romantic, who is drawn toward the strange and mysterious? (Refer to the biographical note, page 240.)

William Cullen Bryant (pages 17-25)
(See Sample Answers to Questions, p. 113)

1. Is the doctrine expressed in "Thanatopsis" different from that expressed in Freneau's "On the Universality and Other Attributes of the God of Nature" (page 16)?

2. The soothing effects of nature, as in "Inscription for the Entrance to a Wood," is a persistent one in American literature. Can you indicate other poems or stories that employ it?

3. Is "To a Waterfowl" a didactic poem?

4. Bryant frequently refers to the great American wildernesses. What did they represent to him?

5. Compare Bryant's poem on Lincoln with Walt Whitman's (pages 113-118), and Robinson's ("The Master," pages 139-140). What common views of Lincoln do they express?

Ralph Waldo Emerson (pages 25-34)
(See Sample Answers to Questions, pp. 113, 114)

1. Bryant and Emerson appear to share certain attitudes and themes in common. What are they?

2. Is Emerson employing irony of any kind in "Earth Song" (page 30)?

3. In "Ode" (page 31), lines 50-51, Emerson says "Things are in the saddle, And ride mankind." Write an essay (400 words) on this subject.

Henry Wadsworth Longfellow (pages 34-40)
(See Sample Answers to Questions, p. 114)

1. What allusions does Longfellow employ in "The Jewish Cemetery at Newport" (pages 34-35)?

2. In "Hymn to the Night" the images are closely related to each other. Explain.

3. During the period between World War I and World War II, when Longfellow's reputation was under attack, he was sometimes called a sentimental poet. Is there any evidence of this in the poems reprinted in *American Poetry*?

John Greenleaf Whittier (pages 40-42)
(See Sample Answers to Questions, p. 114)

1. The rhythms of Whittier's poems are on the blatant rather than on the subtle side. Compare the rhythms (and the tone) of one of his poems with one by Longfellow, and with one by Oliver Wendell Homes (pages 62-65).

2. Is Whittier a didactic poet?

3. If Whittier is one of the New England graybeard poets, who are the others? (See the biographical notes in *American Poetry*.)

Edgar Allan Poe (pages 42-62)
(See Sample Answers to Questions, p. 114)

1. Re-read "The Heresy of the Didactic" (*American Literary Essays,* pages 174-176). Apply the doctrines expressed there to "Tamerlane," "The Lake: To———," and "Evening Star."

2. What is the nature of Poe's quarrel with science in "Sonnet—To Science"? What sonnet form is employed?

3. Poe, in poetry as well as in fiction, is adept at creating *atmosphere*. Describe the atmosphere in "Al Aaraaf" and explain the devices by which Poe achieved it (the diction, symbols, vagueness, exotic names, etc.).

4. In "To Helen," Poe employs alliteration and assonance. Illustrate.

5. Images of night and stillness are common to Poe's poetry. Point out examples.

6. Which of Poe's poems, reprinted in *American Poetry*, have almost identical themes and subject matter?

Oliver Wendell Holmes (pages 62-65)
(See Sample Answers to Questions, p. 115)

1. Compare Holmes' humor with Whittier's.

2. Rewrite stanza one of "The Deacon's Masterpiece," employing blank verse. Then compare the tone of your version with the original. What are the differences?

Jones Very (pages 65-66)
(See Sample Answers to Questions, p. 115)

1. Is Jones Very a metaphysical poet, in Samuel Johnson's sense?

2. Compare the final lines of "The Latter Rain" with the final lines of "The Created." Which are the more effective? Why?

Henry David Thoreau (pages 67-69)
(See Sample Answers to Questions, p. 115)

1. Thoreau travelled very little, feeling it was essential to rediscover the orginal relationship of man and nature, and that this could be done at home, in Concord, Massachusetts, and its countryside. Are "The Inward Morning," "The Summer Rain," and "The Fall of the Leaf" statements of his doctrine? Explain.

2. Thoreau said of *Walden,* "I do not propose to write an ode to dejection, but to brag as lustily as chanticleer in the morning, standing on his roof, if only to wake my neighbors up." Are Thoreau's poems "lusty"? If not, how would you characterize them?

Walt Whitman (pages 69-121)
(See Sample Answers to Questions, pp. 115, 116)

1. Does Whitman's celebration of himself in "Song of Myself" seem arrogant, egotistical, or a justifiable acceptance of himself and the world he found himself in?

2. Is "Song of Myself" a celebration of life or of death, or of process and change?

3. One can find words in "Song of Myself" that one would not expect a finished, careful poet to use. Make a list of them, and comment on them.

4. Can you find passages in "Song of Myself" that Emerson might have liked?

5. Write an essay (300 to 350 words) explaining what you understand "The Sleepers" to mean.

6. What does Whitman mean by the word "adhesiveness" (line 22) in "So Long" (pages 111-113)?

7. "When Lilacs Last in the Dooryard Bloom'd" is one of Whitman's most carefully constructed poems. What are some of the recurrent symbols?

8. Which of the poems on pages 118-121 seem to you the most, or the least, skillfully done? (Consider the imagery; the diction, the theme, tone, etc.)

9. Of what importance, relative to other aspects of Whitman's poetry, would an analysis of his use of meter be in evaluating this poet's work?

Herman Melville (pages 121-122)
(See Sample Answers to Questions, p. 116)

1. What differences in attitude, tone, and theme are there between Whitman's Civil War poems (pages 118-121) and Melville's (page 121)?

2. Can "The Maldive Shark" be read as an allegory? Explain.

3. Is "The Berg" merely a literal account of an iceberg destroying a vessel? Why does Melville call it "A Dream"?

4. Do you feel there are any significant similarities between Melville the poet and the Melville who wrote "Billy Budd" (*American Short Novels,* pages 18-67) or "Bartleby the Scrivener" (*American Short Stories,* pages 64-87)?

Bayard Taylor (pages 122-124)
(See Sample Answers to Questions, p. 116)

1. Taylor is typical of certain writers in the nineteenth century whose work has been called "genteel." They mistrusted science, materialism, realism, naturalism, etc., and made an effort to spiritualize nature, human love, and ideals. Write an analysis of "Kilimandjaro" (200 words) saying why it can be characterized as "genteel."

2. Discuss the tone of "Bedouin Song."

Henry Timrod (pages 124-126)
(See Sample Answers to Questions, p. 116)

1. Comment on the final line of "I Know Not Why, but All This Weary Day."

2. There is a preoccupation with death in Timrod's poetry. Illustrate.

Emily Dickinson (pages 126-131)
(See Sample Answers to Questions, pp. 116, 117)

1. Poem no. 67 is based on a paradox. Explain.

2. Discuss the diction employed in several of Miss Dickinson's poems.

3. Discuss the imagery employed in no. 303.

4. Write a paraphrase of no. 609.

5. Is no. 632 a religious or irreligious poem? Explain.

6. Death is sometimes represented as a lover coming in a dark cloak, sometimes as a skeleton with a scythe. How is he represented in no. 712, and what is the effect?

7. What is the meaning of no. 739?

8. Compare the attitudes toward death expressed in no. 712 and no. 1100.

9. Miss Dickinson is an economical writer. Having selected a poem, write a prose account of it, spelling out all the possible implications. What is lost?

Sidney Lanier (pages 131-135)
(See Sample Answers to Questions, p. 117)

1. Lanier was a Georgian, and might therefore be considered a "regional writer." Does the regional aspect appear very clearly? If it does, in what respects?

2. Make a list of the writers referred to in "The Crystal." What does each represent to Lanier?

John Banister Tabb (pages 135-136)
(See Sample Answers to Questions, p. 117)

1. Timrod (pages 124-126), Lanier (pages 131-135), and John Banister Tabb were all Southern poets. Do their poems appear to have anything in common?

2. What poet, if any, that you have read in *American Poetry* writes in a style somewhat similar to Tabb's style?

Edgar Lee Masters (pages 136-139)
(See Sample Answers to Questions, p. 117)

1. Masters' poems have a prose quality. Explain.

2. Characterize the irony Masters employs.

Edwin Arlington Robinson (pages 139-143)
(See Sample Answers to Questions, p. 118)

1. Is there anything notable about the rhythms of "Luke Havergal"?

2. Why does Cliff Klingenhagen drink wormwood?

3. "New England" is a regional poem. Explain.

Stephen Crane (pages 143-145)
(See Sample Answers to Questions, p. 118)

1. Crane is an ironic poet. Write an essay (350 to 400 words) on this subject.

2. Crane and Emily Dickinson, although they both lived and died in the nineteenth century, are held to be "modern poets." Why should this be so?

Robert Frost (pages 145-156)
(See Sample Answers to Questions, pp. 118, 119)

1. Which position—having a wall or not having one—does the poem "Mending Wall" recommend?

2. Is "The Wood-Pile" a bitter reflection on waste and decay? How would you characterize it? Is it an ironic poem?

3. Does Frost, in "After Apple-Picking," imply that one should enjoy work, do it to the best of one's ability, or simply do it to get it done? Read the poem carefully several times before answering.

4. Does the manner in which the story of murder is told, in "The Witch of Coös," add to or minimize the horror of it?

5. Is "Stopping by Woods on a Snowy Evening" a statement in favor of the poetic-minded man as opposed to the practical man? If not, how would you characterize it?

6. What is the point of "West-running Brook"?

7. Do "The Onset" (page 151) and "Acquainted With the Night" (page 152) have any themes in common?

8. Write a paraphrase of "The Gift Outright."

9. Are "Neither Out Far nor In Deep" and "The Bear" about the same subject?

Carl Sandburg (pages 156-157)
(See Sample Answers to Questions, p. 119)

1. Sandburg is often treated as a follower of Whitman. Write an essay (300 words) comparing the poetry of Whitman and that of Sandburg.

2. Sandburg, like Masters, employs for the most part a prose-like idiom. Compare the styles of the two men.

Wallace Stevens (pages 158-162)
(See Sample Answers to Questions, p. 119)

1. Write a paraphrase of "Sunday Morning."

2. Why does Stevens want bright night-gowns? What do they symbolize?

3. In "The Emperor of Ice-Cream" there is a mixture of the commonplace world, everyday experiences, and reverence for the dead woman. How might Stevens justify this?

4. In what sense (see "The Idea of Order in Key West") does or can an individual impose order on the outside world?

5. "Mozart, 1935" is a commentary on art in a period of economic depression. What is Stevens' view of the matter?

6. Read "Of Modern Poetry" very carefully. How, according to Stevens, does our age differ from earlier ages?

7. Compare "No Possum, No Sop, No Taters" with Frost's "Acquainted with the Night" (pages 152-153).

8. What is Stevens, in "The Poems of our Climate," saying about flaws and imperfections in relation to the beautiful?

Vachel Lindsay (pages 163-167)
(See Sample Answers to Questions, p. 120)

1. Read "The Congo" aloud.

2. What point does Lindsay make in "The Eagle That Is Forgotten"?

William Carlos Williams (pages 167-169)
(See Sample Answers to Questions, p. 120)

1. Shapiro places Williams in the Whitman line of poets. How would you justify this?

2. Is "The Dance," printed as prose, truly a poem? Explain.

3. Is "Classic Scene" an Imagist poem?

4. Does the poetry of Williams have any readily perceived similarity to his "The Great American Novel"? (See *American Short Novels*, pages 307-343.)

Elinor Wylie (pages 169-170)
(See Sample Answers to Questions, p.120)

1. What is the rhyme scheme of "Wild Peaches"?

2. Do you see any similarities, in style or in subject matter, between "Wild Peaches" and "Venetian Glass Nephew"? (See *American Short Novels*, pages 344-396.)

Ezra Pound   (pages 170-173)
(See Sample Answers to Questions, p. 120)

1. "The River-Merchant's Wife: A Letter" seems timeless. How does Pound achieve this effect?

2. Study "The Seafarer" for its alliteration and compound words. What effects, uncommon in modern poetry, are achieved by them?

3. Explicate "In a Station of the Metro."

4. William Carlos Williams and Pound were college friends and wrote letters, in their later years, to each other about poetry. Can you see any similarities in their work?

John Gould Fletcher   (pages 173-175)
(See Sample Answers to Questions, p. 120)

1. Fletcher wrote Imagist poetry. Is "Elegy on an Empty Skyscraper" an Imagist poem?

2. What is the theme of the poem?

Robinson Jeffers   (pages 175-178)
(See Sample Answers to Questions, p. 121)

1. What is the point of "To the Stone-Cutters"?

2. What is the theme of "Shine, Perishing Republic"?

3. Why does Jeffers admire hawks?

Marianne Moore (pages 178-179)
(See Sample Answers to Questions, p. 121)

1. Write a paraphrase of "Poetry." Compare it with Stevens' "Of Modern Poetry" (pages 161-162) and "The Poems of Our Climate" (page 162).

2. "What Are Years?" is about a paradoxical situation. Explain.

John Crowe Ransom (pages 179-182)
(See Sample Answers to Questions, p. 121)

1. Is the irony in "Bells for John Whiteside's Daughter" harsh or bitter? How would you characterize it?

2. Compare "Philomela" to Miss Moore's "Poetry."

3. What is the meaning of the word "equilibrists"? Is the diction of "The Equilibrists" archaic, or how would you describe it? What is the poet's attitude toward honor?

4. The irony in "Janet Waking" is similar to that in "Bells for John Whiteside's Daughter." Why?

T. S. Eliot (pages 182-185)
(See Sample Answers to Questions, pp. 121, 122)

1. Waste-land images, seen in "Preludes" and elsewhere in Eliot's poetry, have dominated modern literature. Can you provide alternative images, of the city, country, universe, etc., to which readers might respond strongly? Have other poets (Whitman, Jeffers, Stevens, *et al.*) supplied them?

2. Many of the images in "Preludes" are ugly. Does this mean that they are unpoetic?

3. Make a list of the images Eliot employs in "Rhapsody on a Windy Night."

4. Read the "Journey of the Magi" aloud. Is it difficult, or easy, to comprehend?

5. What are some of the symbols in "Journey of the Magi"?

6. Is there a conversational prose manner to "Journey of the Magi"? Explain.

Conrad Aiken (pages 185-186)
(See Sample Answers to Questions, p. 122)

1. Does "Morning Song of Senlin" seem at all suggestive of Eliot's poetry?

2. What sort of irony does Aiken employ?

Edna St. Vincent Millay (pages 186-187)
(See Sample Answers to Questions, p. 122)

1. Why, do you think, Miss Millay called her verses "First Fig" and "Second Fig"?

2. What sonnet form is employed in "Epitaph for the Race of Man"?

Archibald MacLeish (pages 187-190)
(See Sample Answers to Questions, p. 122)

1. There are several paradoxical statements in "Ars Poetica." What are they?

2. What are the allusions in "The Too-Late Born"?

3. Characterize the tone of "Empire Builders," and of "Brave New World." What is the allusion to in the phrase "brave new world"?

4. "You, Andrew Marvell" is about civilization moving westward. Explain the image.

Stephen Vincent Benét (pages 194-195)
(See Sample Answers to Questions, p. 123)

1. Make a list of American place names similar to those used by Benét. Are they Indian, French, Latin, English, or what, in origin?

2. Is there any justification for saying "The Song of the Breath" has a Whitman quality?

Hart Crane (pages 195-205)
(See Sample Answers to Questions, p. 123)

1. Write a paraphrase of "Praise for an Urn."

2. Does "Proem: To Brooklyn Bridge" catch a sense of New York City?

3. Does "The Harbor Dawn" catch a sense of the sea and the harbor at daybreak?

4. In "Van Winkle" and "The River" there are many historical allusions as well as twentieth century descriptions. Do the historical allusions create any sense of a fixed, orderly tradition?

5. "National Winter Garden," so named for a theater, develops a symbol of lust. What function does this seem to have in the whole poem?

6. In "The Tunnel" Crane sees an image of Poe. What function does this seem to have in the poem?

7. In *The Twenties,* Frederick Hoffman says this about Crane's "The Bridge":

> He has at last returned to his beginnings—the Bridge itself, and the full measure of its symbolic and mystical figuration. The cables radiating from the towers (the "harp"), the shape of the surface (the "altar"), and the curve of the span are all drawn in, to describe the "myth" which is America. They are also symbolic, in their unity and their geometric design, of the patterns of the turning world, as the previous sections of the poem have led us to anticipate. The Bridge is "synoptic" of "all tides below"; it incorporates all parts, not only America's but those of Tyre and Troy. . . .

It is the ultimate knowledge, "steeled Cognizance," whose "curveship" unites all patterns of curve, mundane and celestial:

O Thou steeled Cognizance whose leap commits
The agile precincts of the lark's return;
Within whose lariat sweep encinctured sing
In single chrysalis the many twain,—

It presents the one absolute "intrinsic Myth," in its "Swift peal of secular light." It is therefore the culmination of Crane's search for a secular myth, not dependent upon past dogmas but "intrinsic," containing certainties and its symbology within itself. As a product of the "fury fused" of science, it is constantly renewed and strengthened as science adds fresh chemistry to its song. To it Crane addresses his final prayer—the Bridge now stands where the "hand of God" once was. The prayer is not unqualifiedly rapturous; it is burdened with a final expression of doubt and humility. . . . "The serpent with the eagle in the leaves. . . ." *The Bridge* thus concludes on the note of unease and uncertainty with which it began.

Viking, 1955, p. 238.

Using this comment as a guide, write an essay (400 to 450 words) on "The Bridge."

Allen Tate (pages 205-207)
(See Sample Answers to Questions, p. 123)

1. Allen Tate once said that he recognized as a primary subject in his own poems "man suffering from unbelief." What evidence do these poems provide in illustration of this comment?

2. What sonnet form is employed in "Sonnets at Christmas"?

Kenneth Fearing (pages 207-208)
(See Sample Answers to Questions, p. 123)

1. What poet that you have read thus far seems closest in spirit to Fearing?

2. Fearing is concerned about the way the statistical average, the human being as represented in advertisements, etc., intrudes into our private lives. Why is it a danger?

Richard Eberhart (pages 208-210)
(See Sample Answers to Questions, p. 124)

1. Eberhart employs traditional poetic themes. What are they? Does he work any variations on them?

2. Scan the first eight lines of "The Groundhog." Does the metrical pattern seem appropriate to the subject?

Robert Penn Warren (pages 210-212)
(See Sample Answers to Questions, p. 124)

1. What are some of the symbols of original sin that Warren employs? Make a similar list of your own.

2. The imagery in "Bearded Oaks" is mostly from the sea. Show how the imagery is interrelated. The line "Twin atolls on a shelf of shade" is ambiguous, or multi-meaningful. Explicate the line.

3. Is the theme of "Crime" similar to the theme of "Original Sin"?

Theodore Roethke (pages 212-215)
(See Sample Answers to Questions, p. 125)

1. What does Roethke mean, in "Dolor," by the desolation of "public places"?

2. Roethke is preoccupied with the life we live below the level of rationality, of consciousness. Make a list of the images he employs to catch this lower or purely physical level of life.

Elizabeth Bishop (pages 216-217)
(See Sample Answers to Questions, p. 124)

1. What is the point of "A Miracle for Breakfast"?

2. What are some of the observations made by Miss Bishop in "Florida"? Select another state, where you live or one that interests you, and make a list of observations about it you might work into a poem.

Karl Shapiro (pages 217-221)
(See Sample Answers to Questions, p. 125)

1. Write a paraphrase of "Adam and Eve."

2. In what ways does Shapiro's story of Adam and Eve differ from the Biblical story?

Delmore Schwartz (pages 221-223)
(See Sample Answers to Questions, p. 125)

1. What is the significance of the dog named Ego in "The Repetitive Heart"?

2. "Starlight like Intuition Pierced the Twelve" explores some of the paradoxes of Christianity. Explain.

Randall Jarrell (pages 223-225)
(See Sample Answers to Questions, p. 125)

1. Jarrell says that dying in a war, as a member of a bombing crew, is a different, more irrational way of dying. Why?

2. What is the theme of "The Orient Express"?

John Berryman (pages 225-228)
(See Sample Answers to Questions, p. 125)

1. Write a biographical sketch of Anne Bradstreet as she emerges from a reading of Berryman's verses.

2. Does Berryman employ Anne Bradstreet's own rhythms? (Refer to her poems, pages 9-12)

John Ciardi (pages 228-229)
(See Sample Answers to Questions, p. 125)

1. What are some of the meanings Ciardi finds in the symbolism of the river?

Peter Viereck (pages 229-230)
(See Sample Answers to Questions, p. 126)

1. What is the theme of "The Day's No Rounder Than Its Angles Are"?

Robert Lowell (pages 230-231)
(See Sample Answers to Questions, p. 126)

1. Certain critics have said that Robert Lowell resembles the seventeenth century metaphysical poets. Can you see any resemblances between Edward Taylor (pages 12-14) and Lowell?

2. What is the symbolism of "The Drunken Fisherman"?

Richard Wilbur (pages 231-232)
(See Sample Answers to Questions, p. 126)

1. The subject of "The Death of a Toad" might seem insignificant. How has Wilbur managed to charge it with significance?

2. "Juggler" has to do with the delight we feel at watching the juggler temporarily overcome gravity. Can you think of any similar topics about which poems might be written?

On Poetry and Poets (pages 233-236)
(See Sample Answers to Questions, pp. 126-127)

Write essays (400 to 450 words) on two of the following topics, referring to any of the comments in "On Poetry and Poets," or to one or more of the poets in *American Poetry*:

1. The Meaning of Modernism

2. Poets in the Whitman Tradition

3. Poets in the Poe Tradition

4. What Is Peculiarly *American* About American Poetry?

5. Regional Poets

6. Is Frost Truly a Simple Poet?

7. Poems that Define Poetry

8. A topic of your own choosing

SAMPLE ANSWERS TO QUESTIONS —

Introduction

1. His chief points are that American poets have tried to break with English literary conventions, and that Americans, except for a few intellectuals and exiles, have historical amnesia.

2. Anne Bradstreet in the seventeenth century, and Philip Freneau in the eighteenth.

3. Shapiro sees Poe as sloughing off the European consciousness but not replacing it with a new consciousness; he sees him as a disintegrating force. Whitman, on the other hand, celebrates a new world and a new consciousness.

4. In the Poe line, generally speaking, he places Eliot, Pound, Cummings, and the "exiles" of the 1920's. He sees few in the Whitman line. He doesn't place Frost in the Whitman line, seeing him as more English and Victorian than American and contemporary. He does place Sandburg, Fletcher, Lindsay, and especially Hart Crane and William Carlos Williams.

Anne Bradstreet

1. Shakespeare, Raleigh, James I, Captain John Smith, Governor Winthrop.

2. Some of her settings. The verses are not different in convention from the English practices.

3. No.

4. A mixture of playfulness and piety.

Edward Taylor

1. My own being turn into a spinning wheel, etc.

2. He stays pretty close to it. One can be pious and witty at the same time. Yes there are internal rhymes.

3. More complicated.

4-5. Yes, he compares unlikely objects and things. The comparison of the relationship of two souls to "gold to airy thinness beat" is both unexpected and beautiful. Donne has greater verbal facility and subtlety.

Philip Freneau

1. Stresses words restraint, decorum, brilliance, wit, clarity, logic.

2. Yes, but instinctively he seems to belong to the romantic movement.

William Cullen Bryant

1. Freneau's God seems the God of the Deists, who stressed mechanism. Bryant's God seems somehow less concerned with the ordering of the universe in a mechanistic way.

2. Cooper employs it. Faulkner in "The Bear." Emerson.

3. Yes, see the ending.

4. Mystery, health, the future.

5. Man of justice, mercy, and melancholy in his own person.

Ralph Waldo Emerson

1. Healing powers of nature. Individualism.

2. Yes, a kind of cosmic irony. Things of this world in comparison with things of eternity.

3. This is a theme found in Emerson's essays also. Refer to Leary.

Henry Wadsworth Longfellow

1. A number of biblical allusions.

2. The images are generally suggestive of peace and comfort.

3. Possibly in "The Children's Hour," but generally not.

John Greenleaf Whittier

1. Whittier employs a firm, stiff beat in his lines, unlike the others.

2. Yes.

3. Longfellow, Lowell, Holmes.

Edgar Allan Poe

1. Poe is preoccupied with death, melancholy beauty, not preaching.

2. Is concerned with laws, abstractions, not with beauty.

3. Images suggest a never-never land of romantic beauty.

4. "The weary, way-worn wanderer bore" and "How statue-like I see thee stand."

5. See "The Haunted Palace" and "Dream-Land."

6. "Lenore," "Ulalume," and "Annabel Lee."

Oliver Wendell Holmes

1. A little quieter, a little more subtle than Whittier's.

2. The wonders of the one horse shay are known. As well the logic of its structure is. This verse form lacks the bounce of Holmes' verse.

Jones Very

1. He has a metaphysical cast of mind, but he obviously belongs to the nineteenth century.

2. The lines in "The Latter Rain" have a quiet inevitability, the lines of "The Created" strive for more dramatic force and perhaps achieve it.

Henry David Thoreau

1. Yes, his poems are similar to his prose essays.

2. Not quite lusty, but they work at being cheerful.

Walt Whitman

1. The temperament of the reader is likely to play a part in the way this question is answered. There is no doubt that Whitman was a great self-dramatizer, but perhaps this is true of most writers, including a quiet recluse such as Emily Dickinson.

2. Of all three, but perhaps especially "process and change."

3. "Undrape! you are not guilty to me..." There is a crudity in this diction that most poets would not be guilty of.

4. Section 14.

5. Various forms of love.

6. Human beings cleaving to each other in affection.

7. Lilac, star, and bird.

8. "Bivouac on a Mountain Side" seems the most skillful. It catches a scene with a certain firmness of outline, and suggests a meaning that enlarges one's sense of the image.

9. Very important because it is a part of his rejection of established conventions, and a part of his organic theory.

Herman Melville

1. Melville's are much darker and horror-struck.

2. Yes, of leaders and sycophants.

3. It can be read literally and also as a symbol of forces that destroy hopes, aspirations and plans.

4. The mood is similar in all of them.

Bayard Taylor

1. See definition of "genteel tradition" in glossary, page 40.

2. "Bedouin Song" is a conventionally romantic poem. The rhythms seem almost predefined, not the poet's own, because the feeling is not his, it is borrowed feeling.

Henry Timrod

1. The poem presents images suggesting heat, fetidness, and droopiness, all implying the fact of death. The final line makes explicit what was implied in the preceding lines.

2. Timrod's health was ruined in the Civil War, and he died prematurely. He also witnessed the slaughter of many young men. Understandably his imagination was dominated by dreary landscapes, desolate scenes, cemeteries, and death.

Emily Dickinson

1. The person who has succeeded no longer knows the taste of victory with the sharpness it is imagined by one who has not succeeded.

2. Tends to be a homely, domestic diction.

3. All the imagery adds to the sense of solemnity and inevitability that the theme develops.

4. The poem has to do with discovering what we are and what we might have been.

5. Neither. Simply says we can conceive of God only insofar as our imaginations can create Him.

6. As a gentleman.

7. There are no final harbors of peace.

8. Not very different. The awe is less insisted on in no. 712.

9. Any poem of hers elaborated in prose sentences will lose its sharp, elliptical, witty flavor.

Sidney Lanier

1. Slightly, mostly in terms of place names.

2. Shakespeare, Socrates, Dante, Milton, Aeschylus, Langley, Caedmon, Keats.

John Banister Tabb

1. Tend to be melancholy, to be conscious of the South's defeat in the War.

2. Somewhat like Emily Dickinson.

Edgar Lee Masters

1. Avoids rhyme, and his verse forms are irregular.

2. The heat of living, arguing, fighting, loving, is cooled by death.

Edwin Arlington Robinson

1. Admonitory and exclamatory. The trochaic foot of many of the opening lines is unlike the easiness of the usual iambic foot.

2. He drinks it as a kind of antidote.

3. Robinson refers to regional characteristics.

Stephen Crane

1. Primarily Crane's poems deal in cosmic irony.

2. There is no expectation of softness or collaboration with the universe.

Robert Frost

1. Depends on the circumstances.

2. It is ironic, but not bitterly. It accepts the world as it is.

3. That one should work professionally, enjoying the physical effort and the skill and the rewards. It is the only kind of enjoyment we can know, Frost implies. It is a mistake to try to build up happiness at some distant point in the dim future.

4. Adds to it.

5. Neither. It has a word to say for both. The poetic minded man has also to be practical.

6. Advancement comes by moving against the current, not with it.

7. An image of a terrifying universe.

8. One has to experience the land before one belongs to it, etc.

9. Man strives to know, but he is limited in what he can know.

Carl Sandburg

1. Language is somewhat similar. Is there point of view? Subjects?

2. Sandburg's lines are looser, more wave-like, less restrained.

Wallace Stevens

1. Woman sitting in her dressing gown, enjoying Sunday breakfast, thinks about Christianity, and compares it with a religion of the sun and nature.

2. The bright night-gowns symbolize active imaginations and excitement.

3. In the presence of death we are awe-struck, and we express our reverence or respect for the dead. But life also goes on. Change is the principle we must recognize.

4. The universe itself is disorderly. It takes on shape and meaning and order only in the human mind.

5. Economic depression — the poem was from the 1930's — distracts from a concern with the beautiful, but the beautiful remains.

6. Ours is an age of search, of trying to find the right statements, the right symbols, the right meanings. In the past the meaning of civilized actions seemed to be less under question.

7. They are similar. Both see a harsh universe.

8. Flaws and imperfections make us aware of the more perfect.

Vachel Lindsay

1. Read it with a flourish and a certain abandon.

2. Altgeld in his own person may be forgotten, but his achievements live on in later generations.

William Carlos Williams

1. Williams searches for the novel, for the American quality.

2. Sidney said that verse form wasn't essential to poetry. Williams' lines have a rhythmical development, a vigorous, dancelike movement.

3. Yes. He is preoccupied with objects in isolation, with enjoyment, and not with culture spelled Culture.

Elinor Wylie

1. Rhyme scheme is abbaabbacdceed.

2. The poem undertakes to glorify the homespun. The story stresses the artifact. However, in a real sense Mrs. Wylie has turned homely things into brilliant artifacts. For example, the lines "every little creek is shot with silver from the Chesapeake," and "Bronze partridge, speckled quail."

Ezra Pound

1. It has the timeless quality of a picture that appeals to nothing in its immediate present.

2. There are an indefinite number of syllables in the lines, and the emphasis is on the stresses, which tend to be consonantal and harsh.

3. An isolated element that is beautiful against a nondescript background.

4. Preoccupation with experiment. Imagistic quality.

John Gould Fletcher

1-2. Contrast between what man can build and the dark, outer night. Partakes to some extent of their Imagist doctrines. But makes an explicit statement of the sort the Imagists were unlikely to make.

Robinson Jeffers

1. That no artifact can outlast the ravages of time.

2. Advice is not to get too involved in the vulgarities of democracy.

3. Their strength and courage.

Marianne Moore

1. Poetry can be written about any subject, score sheets or match books. To be poetry it must illuminate. Stevens was concerned with poetry in the twentieth century, with finding the right beliefs for it, and also with the place of the flawed in poetry.

2. This is a paradox because Miss Moore says that freedom as freedom is meaningless. There is only freedom in relation to restriction.

John Crowe Ransom

1. It is an avoiding of a sentimental response. The poet is sad, but he knows the world goes on.

2. In "Philomela" he says that the poet in the twentieth century cannot write like the poet in the sixteenth or nineteenth.

3. Quite similar.

T. S. Eliot

1. Nice farms, beautiful suburbs, etc. Stevens presented the hill with deer and quail on it, and Frost the small farm and the mountains. But Eliot's images of the city and of a waste land seem to have caught the imagination of the twentieth century.

2. An image can be ugly without being unpoetic.

3. Lamps, geraniums, pins, rancid butter, moon, etc.

4. If read without any expectation of difficulty it is easy to comprehend.

5. The three crosses, and the silver of Judas.

6. Yes, but there is a metrical pattern controlling it.

Conrad Aiken

1. He is a little like some of Eliot's "heroes," notably Prufrock.

2. Cosmic irony.

Edna St. Vincent Millay

1. Irony. Not worth a fig? Succulent as a fig?

2. Irregular.

Archibald MacLeish

1. MacLeish doesn't mean poems make no sense. He means they employ images and metaphors in making their statements.

2. To the "Song of Roland," the old French romance or epic.

3. MacLeish contrasts capitalistic conservatism with the original vigor and outward-going qualities of the founders of the country.

4. Civilization has moved westward since the beginning of Western history.

Stephen Vincent Benét

1. Des Moines, French, Prairie du Chien, French, Onondaga, Indian, etc.

2. There is an awareness of the living, palpitating human being.

Hart Crane

1. Creates a sense of awe in the presence of death, in thinking of one he has known.

2. It catches the relationship of the sea and the harbor of the city.

3. The world of Rip Van Winkle seems very distant from the world Crane described.

4. It is a part of the seamier side of the city's life.

5. Poe's image seems to question the great hopes with which the poem opened. It is the side of the city that means defeat, sweat, suffering.

6. Use the points Hoffman makes in his comment in your paper.

Allen Tate

1. All of the poems are about the absence of belief, or the search for belief and the ordering of human values.

2. Irregular.

Kenneth Fearing

1. Perhaps Cummings.

2. One can forget about one's individuality, trying to conform to all the images of a good citizen that are presented to us in ads, patriotic appeals, etc.

Richard Eberhart

1. The passage of time, and the soul's yearnings. His themes are not notably different from those of many other poets.

2. The metrical pattern of the first four lines seems very appropriate. The first two lines are poetic, rhetorical, the third draws the reader up short, and the fourth presents a response to what he has seen.

Robert Penn Warren

1. The wen, the old horse, the hound, etc.

2. Throughout the poem the sea imagery is made to function. In the line quoted, the lovers can be seen as the twin atolls, rising from the dark, dim sea of history and pre-history. Alive, they are on a "shelf of shade," living on mystery.

3. Yes, each of us looks for the secret that will give us happiness, a mind at ease and at peace.

Theodore Roethke

1. There is frequently a dankness and great desolation in public places.

2. Fish, roots, flowers, quartz, crabs, etc.

Elizabeth Bishop

1. She seems to be saying that the usual notion of miracles is too extravagant and that we should not fail to observe daily miracles, the way the sun plays on water, the movement of birds, etc.

2. Any state will have its own unique characteristics.

Karl Shapiro

1. Retell the story as Shapiro envisions it.

2. Look up the account in Genesis.

Delmore Schwartz

1. The dog appears to represent responsibility, the harsh side of obligation and duty.

2. The upshot of the poem is that although Christianity in a sense makes life easier and more peaceful it also makes it much harder and more difficult.

Randall Jarrell

1. A soldier dies not like an individual, but like a number, and a bombardier kills people he does not know and therefore presumably can not hate.

2. Jarrell is observing the pathos and sadness of individual lives and of human life everywhere ("a willing sadness, a forced joy").

John Berryman

1. She was a patient, loving woman who had experienced great hardships, as much of the spirit as the flesh.

2. No.

John Ciardi

1. He remembers the history that belongs to the river, the drownings, and the garbage, and the river as death.

Peter Viereck

1. It is a contrasting of the activities of the day and the deep stillness and peace of night; and night seems to suggest death.

Robert Lowell

1. There is the same preoccupation with theological or religious subjects, the same sense of a guilty world, and a desire for union with God.

2. The poet seems to see himself in a kind of waste land, where there is insufficient water, but still he must strive to catch Christ, the Fisherman.

Richard Wilbur

1. It is not merely the death of a toad he is describing, it is death as any of us might experience it.

2. Tightrope walking, or highjumping.

On Poetry and Poets

Be sure to read pages 233-236 very carefully.

1. The Meaning of Modernism
Stress language, problems of disbelief in twentieth century.

2. Poets in the Whitman Tradition
Lindsay, Fletcher maybe, Sandburg, Hart Crane, W. C. Williams.

3. Poets in the Poe Tradition
Symbolist movement (Poe in France), symbolism of the city (Eliot, Crane), Eliot, Conrad Aiken, *et al.* Stevens.

4. What Is Peculiarly *American* About American Poetry?
See Shapiro's introduction, and Auden's essay in the Leary volume.

5. Regional Poets
Frost and Robinson are the most obviously regional.

6. Is Frost Truly a Simple Poet?
In relation to Eliot probably yes. But there are a number of complicated themes at work in Frost and it is a great mistake to read his poems for the surface meaning only.

7. Poems That Define Poetry
MacLeish, "Ars Poetica," M. Moore, "Poetry," Stevens, "Poet of Our Climate."

8. Why I Prefer Short Fiction to Poetry (or the reverse).

Part V: AMERICAN DRAMA

EDITED BY ALAN DOWNER

Drama Glossary

Advance guard. Writers who explore their literary medium, who experiment and are in advance of the conventions and practices of their contemporaries.

Aside. In older drama, characters said things that were heard by the audience but not by other members of the cast. The device is almost never used in modern drama. See "The Contrast."

Chorus. A singing and dancing group in Greek drama. Used to comment on and interpret the action. T. S. Eliot has used a chorus in "Murder in the Cathedral" and in "Family Reunion."

Climax. The most intense moment of conflict, the turning point.

Closet drama. Drama not intended for production; to be read. Shelley, Tennyson, Browning, and others wrote closet dramas. Thomas Hardy's "The Dynasts" is a good example.

Coincidence. Simultaneous occurrence of two events, such as the unexpected coming together of "hero" and "villain" looking for the same object, say, a letter. Used to intensify excitement.

Comedy. Tragedy relates man to the universe, and deals primarily with moral questions. Comedy is more concerned with man's relation to society and his conduct in relation to society. Not all comedy—Chekov's "The Cherry Orchard" for example—is hilarious; it can be muted, even sad; or savage, and incisive in its thrust.

Conventions. See page 37.

Denouement. The untying of the plot, following or growing out of the climax.

Deus ex machina. "God out of the machine." In Greek drama a god, lowered to the stage by a mechanical device, intervenes in the action. In later drama the use of any agency that interferes with the logic of the action is often called a *deus ex machina*.

128

Drama. Tension of conflict. May involve a character struggling against himself, or against nature, society, or other persons; may involve the conflict of two ideas, or sets of values. Action reached a climax, then is resolved.

Expressionism. See page 40.

Farce. Low comedy, involving confused identities, slapstick, buffoonery, etc. Elemental comedy of situation. Used in pantomime.

Intrigue comedy. Comedy of situation involving strategems, conspiracy; sometimes employs amorous situations.

Melodrama. Melodrama is to tragedy what farce is to comedy. Melodrama grows out of dangerous situations of a dark or sinister nature, but involving no great issues. It has its effect in the titillation of the audience.

Peripety. Term from Aristotle's *Poetics.* An action that seems to be coming out well for the protagonist whips about and destroys. him. Factors that had seemed favorable to him turn out not to have been. A form of irony.

Poetic drama. Drama using the language of poetry. The language should not be imposed on the action; it should help project, explore, and deepen the action. Poetic drama was at its height in the Elizabethan era. William Butler Yeats and T. S. Eliot have written poetric dramas. Maxwell Anderson wrote "Winterset," a melodramatic story of gangsters, justice gone astray, and young love in the language of verse.

Tragedy. Much debated term. Generally accepted meaning: protagonist undergoes a morally significant struggle that can be regarded as man's attempt to fathom eschatological (the-ends-of-man) "laws." Involves suffering and usually death. Earlier tragic protagonists were "high born." Modern tragedy involves the ordinary man.

Unity, unities. See page 92.

QUESTIONS —

Introduction (pages 1-12)
(See Sample Answers to Questions, p. 136)

NOTE: Page references are to *American Drama,* except where in italic, as above, *"See Sample Answers to Questions, p. 136,"* which refer to pages in this volume.

1. What direction (pages 2-3) did William Dunlap, writing in 1821, believe American drama would take? How would it differ from European drama?

2. See the term "Enlightenment" (page 39 of A Literary Glossary). Did Royall Tyler see himself as a product of the Enlightenment?

3. In what ways, according to Downer, does Tyler's "The Contrast" differ from Sheridan's "The School for Scandal" (page 3)?

4. Downer relates the Enlightenment to Romanticism (page 4). Explain. How did they affect the subject matter of drama?

5. See the term "Myth" (page 42) of A Literary Glossary). Downer discusses the American myth (pages 4-6). What are some of the elements of this myth?

6. Downer says there are three stages in the development of realism (pages 6-8). What are they?

7. The gist of Downer's remarks on the modern American theater, 1900 to the present, is that it incorporates but is not limited by the older realism (pages 8-12). Write an essay (250 to 300 words) on this topic.

ROYALL TYLER *"The Contrast"* (pages 13-47)
(See Sample Answers to Questions, pp. 136, 137)

1. Is the prologue (pages 13-14) jingoistic? If not, how would you characterize it?

2. List the main characters and other persons referred to. Comment on the nature of the names.

3. Explain the virtues Tyler attributes to the Americans, the vices he attributes to the English.

4. Does Tyler seem to have been self-conscious about the English? Is he at all defensive about American culture?

5. Characterize Colonel Manly. Is he a stiff, incredible paragon of virtue, or something different? Was the audience intended to find him somewhat humorous?

6. Characterize the American quality of Jonathan. Is he a complement to Colonel Manly?

7. The servants provide a second plot for the action of the play. How does it affect or influence the principal action? (See the term *Double plot*, page 39.)

8. Does Tyler seem to have weighted the action in favor of the American cause and American way of life? Answer in some detail.

JAMES A. HERNE *"Shore Acres"* (pages 48-105)
(See Sample Answers to Questions, pp. 137, 138)

1. Characterize the pace or tempo of "Shore Acres." Does it move more quickly or more slowly than "The Contrast"? Does the tempo seem appropriate? Why?

2. Do all of the characters have a role in forwarding the movement of the play? Do any of them seem unnecessary?

3. Are the characters mere types or are some of them, at least, fairly complicated?

4. Does there seem to be any reason for Ann Berry's speech mannerisms?

5. Which is the most interesting character? Why?

6. How are the regional elements of "Shore Acres" revealed?

7. Is Uncle Nat's fear, Act II, scene 1 (page 89), that he won't be able to save the "Liddy Ann" and his subsequent discovery that he can essential to the action, or is it merely good theatrically?

8. Clearly there are highly melodramatic* elements and scenes in "Shore Acres." What are they?

---
* See Glossary, p. 129

9. Is Blake a melodramatic villain?

10. Does the "American myth" function in the play?

11. Why is the final pantomimic scene (page 105) more dramatically effective than a witty curtain line would be?

WILLIAM VAUGHN MOODY *"The Great Divide"*
(pages 106-139)
(See Sample Answers to Questions, pp. 138, 139)

1. See the definition of "Genteel Tradition" (page 40). Is "The Great Divide" a criticism of the genteel tradition? Consider Ruth's leaving her husband, Polly's speech (page 132), Ruth's being a "divided woman," etc.

2. Is the play in part a dramatization of the "American myth"? In this regard, is it similar to "The Contrast" and "Shore Acres"?

3. Does Polly play a role similar to Uncle Nat's role in "Shore Acres"? Explain.

4. Is the near rape of Ruth at all related to the rude exploitation of the American continent?

5. What is the symbolism of the "Great Divide" (page 138)? Relate this question to question number 1.

6. Is Ghent to be taken as a symbolic American?

7. What are the moments of theatrical suspense in "The Great Divide"?

8. Does Dr. Newbury function as a kind of chorus, commenting on the action? (See Glossary, page 128.)

9. Does "The Great Divide" strike you as belonging only to its own period, the very early years of the twentieth century? Could it be played successfully on the stage today?

EUGENE O'NEILL *"The Hairy Ape"* (pages 140-166)
(See Sample Answers to Questions, p. 139)

1. "See Expressionism" (A Literary Glossary, page 40). Relate the definition to O'Neill's directions for producing "The Hairy Ape" (page 141).

2. Is "The Hairy Ape" primarily a leftist play, that is, is it basically concerned with a social doctrine? With materialism? With technology?

3. Do Mildred and the Aunt seem to be stereotypes? What do they represent? Does Mildred, even as a stereotype, seem overdone?

4. What is the plight of Yank?

5. Is his plight represented sympathetically? Is he a villain or a victim?

6. Characterize the people coming from church in scene 5 (pages 156-158). What do they symbolize?

7. If O'Neill is concerned with the "American myth," how does his concern differ from Herne's in "Shore Acres" and Moody's in "The Great Divide"?

8. How many times does the "cage" image occur?

ROBERT EMMET SHERWOOD *"The Petrified Forest"*
(pages 167-209)
(See Sample Answers to Questions, pp. 139, 140)

1. Imagine that O'Neill had written the description of the scene on page 168. How might he have asked for a more stylized, expressionistic setting?

2. Sherwood is concerned with the "American myth." Is his position similar to O'Neill's, Moody's, or different from both?

3. Squier identifies himself (page 182) as one of the "Hollow Men." What is this allusion? Since the play is set in the 1930's, what significance does this have? Why does Squier want to be buried in the Petrified Forest (page 194)?

4. One critic has referred to "The Petrified Forest" as "philosophical melodrama." Explain.

5. What is the point of the allusion to "A Tale of Two Cities" (page 198)?

6. What virtues do Duke Mantee and Squier have in common?

7. Downer calls (page 12) "The Petrified Forest" "a controlled allegory." Explain.

8. Does "The Petrified Forest" seem to have developed and extended American stagecraft?

THORNTON WILDER *"The Long Christmas Dinner"*
(pages 210-221)
(See Sample Answers to Questions, p. 140)

1. Write an essay (350 to 400 words) on the dramaturgy employed in "The Long Christmas Dinner."

2. The play is a mixture of allegory and realism. Would it be improved if it were one or the other?

3. If the play were three or five acts rather than one would it be more or less effective? In other words, does the theme require telescoped action or an extended action?

4. Does the play involve the American experience in any clearly recognizable way? Explain.

5. Are the three generations shown to be very different in their customs and responses or very much alike because of the similarities of the human experience, regardless of the generation?

TENNESSEE WILLIAMS *"The Glass Menagerie"*
(pages 222-260)
(See Sample Answers to Questions, pp. 140, 141)

1. Which of the three characters — Amanda, Laura, or Tom — seems to have the firmest hold on reality?

2. Are any of the characters lacking in dignity?

3. Why is the grinning picture of Amanda's husband grotesque?

4. What is the symbolism of the glass menagerie? What is the significance of Tom's smashing it (page 224) during the quarrel with Amanda?

5. Are the movies Tom's glass menagerie?

6. Does Jim O'Connor make it possible for Laura to escape?

7. One critic has said that Tennessee Williams is America's most dedicated advance-guard dramatist. Explain.

LIST OF ADDITIONAL PLAYS:

AUGUSTINE DALY   *Under the Gaslight*

DAVID BELASCO   *The Girl of the Golden West*

ELMER RICE   *Street Scene*

EUGENE O'NEILL   *The Emperor Jones*

MARC CONNELLY   *The Green Pastures*

MAXWELL ANDERSON   *Winterset*

ROBERT SHERWOOD   *Abe Lincoln in Illinois*

THORNTON WILDER   *Our Town*

WILLIAM SAROYAN   *The Time of Your Life*

TENNESSEE WILLIAMS   *A Streetcar Named Desire*

T. S. ELIOT   *The Cocktail Party*

ARTHUR MILLER   *Death of a Salesman*

WILLIAM INGE   *Come Back, Little Sheba*

SAMPLE ANSWERS TO QUESTIONS —

Introduction

1. Dunlap said that American was a republic, with free institutions, and therefore American drama will project and interpret the republic, its doctrines and institutions.

2. Yes, he did. And he also wrote the play to instruct his fellow citizens in the matter.

3. Sheridan criticized those who deviated from the rules of society, but Tyler was critical of the conformist. He draws his principles from his own experiences, and also from his ideal, George Washington.

3. Romanticism, in one of its senses, stresses the nobility and the capacities of the individual. So of course does the Enlightenment insofar as it puts great faith in the power of man's reason.

4. The early American had many images of himself. Sometimes he was a revolutionary veteran, sometimes a Yankee peddler, or a frontiersman. He was unique in the world. The Indian also became a mythical hero. He was pictured as the unconquerable underdog.

5. Downer says the first stage of realism was a realism of surfaces, producing the appearance of actuality in settings. The second was realism of content. The third emphasized not merely a plot that reflected actuality but a theme that tried to tell the truth.

6. In your paper, include discussions of the Provincetown Players, O'Neill's experiments, Wilder's continued preoccupation with the "American dream," and the post World War II playwrights, William Inge, Arthur Miller, and Tennessee Williams.

ROYALL TYLER *"The Contrast"*

1. It is on the edge of being jingoistic. Perhaps it is also a bit defensive. Tyler, after all, knew he was breaking new ground in trying to write an American play.

2. Colonel Manly's name suggests his character. Dimple suggests the character's irresponsibility, etc. Mr. Van Rough is a hard-headed type. Mr. Transfer is a broker. Etc.

3. The English, Tyler says, are all manners and no genuine substance. They cultivate a tired smile in place of a hearty laugh, and they cultivate amoral conduct. The Americans are hearty, natural, moral.

4. A little defensive perhaps. But he seems genuinely committed to defending or justifying the American types, as he presents them.

5. Possibly Tyler intended Manly to be slightly humorous, but generally he is presented as a figure of virtue.

6. Jonathan is a country type, but he is virtuous, and has the democratic virtues. He works for Manly but they respect each other, and Jonathan does not fawn.

7. The servants are the counterparts of the principal characters.

8. Yes. He makes Dimple and his servant empty fops, cheats, and generally despicable.

JAMES A. HERNE *"Shore Acres"*

1. The movement of "The Contrast" is rather jerky. The movement of "Shore Acres" is slower but more rhythmical. The treatment of the subject is expansive, and the tempo therefore seems appropriate.

2. Milly, the child, Perley the servant, and the Mail Carrier do not help forward the action to any extent.

3. Most of them are flat; types.

4. No, except that it helps characterize her.

5. Uncle Nat, the sacrificing brother. He engineers good events in the lives of those close to him.

6. The settings (mountains in the distance, the sea), and the language.

7. It isn't necessary to the movement of the play, but it is very effective theatrically. One notes the shift from inside the lighthouse to the outside, so that one sees the lights almost as those aboard the *Liddy Ann* see it.

8. The scene involving the *Liddy Ann* is one. The return of the young couple in the storm, arriving in time to save the old homestead, is another.

9. He promises to be at first, but then is humanized.

10. Yes, the young man, Sam, goes west and makes his fortune there.

11. Creates sense of peacefulness that a line or two probably couldn't achieve.

WILLIAM VAUGHAN MOODY *"The Great Divide"*

1. Yes, it is a criticism of the "genteel tradition." Ruth represents that tradition. Love should have no animal vigor in it, the "genteel" side of Ruth says. But the other side of her responds to Ghent. Finally the "genteel" side breaks down.

2. It is much more explicitly dependent on the American myth than "Shore Acres."

3. Somewhat similar. She "explains" what the author, Moody, is getting at.

4. It might have been related, but Moody doesn't do anything much with the idea.

5. Ghent, as the Westerner, says he belongs beyond the Rockies, beyond the Great Divide, but Ruth, child of a Puritan heritage, belongs in genteel New England. Thus the separation of the two. But no, no, Ruth says, they belong together!

6. Yes. He is the man of action.

7. One, whether Ruth will be raped, and two, whether, near the end of the play, she will rejoin Ghent.

8. Yes.

9. It is rather dated. Probably it would be amusing if played as a period piece.

EUGENE O'NEILL *"The Hairy Ape"*

1. O'Neill says the settings and the action should suggest that the men have been dehumanized and brutalized by their surroundings. The setting, he says, should be stylized, not naturalistic.

2. No. It is symbolic of the perversion of human strength by technological developments.

Mildred is extravagantly spoiled, snobbish, and mean-spirited.

4-5. He has been accustomed to the brutalities of the stokers and their world. Sight of Mildred, slumming in their midst, arouses his anger. He tries to escape from the stokehole but is unable to. He is more victim than villain.

6. They are mechanical creatures.

7. O'Neill says that the progress in machinery has been at the cost of dehumanizing the people who live with machines.

8. Rather frequently.

ROBERT EMMET SHERWOOD *"The Petrified Forest"*

1. O'Neill might have a gray dust covering the walls, etc., symbolizing the deadness of most of the characters, etc.

2. He is closer to O'Neill. Something, he implies, has happened to the old dream. But there is still hope.

3. To T. S. Eliot's "The Hollow Men."

4. Because he himself belongs to the waste land. The action is melodramatic, with the cops and robbers situation. But the problem,

how to renew life, is a philosophical one. Squier gives his life to make a good life for Gabby possible.

5. In *A Tale of Two Cities* Sidney Carton lays down his life for a friend, saying, "Greater love than this no man hath, in laying down his life for his friend."

6. They act, trying not to be acted upon, trying not to be passive agents.

7. What the characters represent is clear. Each represents an idea. They also are seen against the background of the desert, a wasteland.

8. No.

THORNTON WILDER *"The Long Christmas Dinner"*

1. In writing your paper, you might describe the settings employed in some of the other plays you have read, then compare these with the setting and techniques Wilder employs.

2. No. The realism makes the allegory easier to take, and the allegory keeps the realism from being inert and insignificant.

3. The play might have been a bit longer, but if it were a long play the point might seem tiresomely drawn out.

4. One recognizes that Wilder is treating an American family, in several generations. The play might be taken as a mildly ironic comment of the great expectations of Americans. Death, Wilder says, is always there, a kind of silent partner, who finally dictates the terms to us.

5. The generations are pretty much alike.

TENNESSEE WILLIAMS *"The Glass Menagerie"*

1. Amanda.

2. No.

3. The smile seems a foolish one in that it continues despite the defeats the family suffers and the fact that the father had left them.

4. It is the little fragile world of her dreams, unreal like them.

5. Yes, except that he is not as involved with escape as Laura is.

6. He seems to offer her escape, but then says he is engaged to another girl. Laura is not capable of escaping on her own.

7. It is a play involving society, psychology, a region, and it employs all of the technical advances that O'Neill, Wilder and others discovered.

Part VI: SPECIAL AIDS FOR FURTHER UNDERSTANDING OF AMERICAN LITERATURE

QUESTIONS —

Recognition of a Writer's Style
(See Sample Answers to Questions, pp. 145, 146)

Buffon, the French critic, is often quoted as having said, "Style is the man." And it is true that a writer expresses himself in a style that is peculiarly his own. Certain writers — Henry James or Whitman, for example — are almost immediately recognizable. Others are less distinctive, but, even so, with close attention on the part of the reader are frequentably recognizable.

There tends also to be a period style, seventeenth, eighteenth, nineteenth, or twentieth century. Anne Bradstreet or Edgar Allan Poe are clearly not twentieth century writers, and Ernest Hemingway is clearly not a nineteenth century writer.

The following are excerpts from writers represented in *Reader's Bookshelf of American Literature*, but the passages are from works not reprinted in it.

　　1. Indicate the period in which you believe that passage was written.

　　2. Indicate, if possible, the author.

　　3. Give the reasons that led you to select the period and the author.

The passages and authors are identified on pages 145-146.

　　1. Journals, memoirs, elaborate essays shall not fail hereafter to commemorate the heroes who have made their appearance on this new American stage, to the end that Europe may either lavishly praise or severely censure their virtues and their faults. It requires the inquisitive eye of an unnoticed individual mixing in crowds to find out and select for private amusement more obscure, though not less pathetic scenes. Scenes of sorrow and affliction are equally moving to the bowels of humanity. Find them where you will, there is a strange but peculiar sort of pleasure in contemplating them; it is a mournful feast for some particular souls. A pile of ruins is always striking, but when the object of contemplation is too extensive, our divided and wearied faculties receive impressions proportionally feeble; we possess but a certain quantity of tears and compassion. But when the scale is diminished, when we descend from the destruction of an extensive government of a nation to that of several individuals, to that

of a once opulent, happy and virtuous family, there we pause, for it is more analogous to our own situation. . . .

    2. I had eight birds hatcht in one nest,
        Four Cocks there were, and Hens the rest,
        I nurst them up with pain and care,
        Nor cost nor labour did I spare.
        Till at the last they felt their wing.
        Mounted the Trees and learned to sing;
        Chief of the Brood then took his flight,
        To Regions far, and left me quite:
        My mournful chirps I after send,
        Till he return, or I do end,
        Leave not the nest, thy Dam and Sire,
        Fly back and sing amidst this Quire. . . .

    3. Thine eyes shall see the light of distant skies;
        Yet, Cole! thy heart shall bear to Europe's strand
        A living image of our own bright land,
        Such as upon thy glorious canvas lies;
        Lone lakes — savannas where the bison roves —
        Rocks rich with summer garlands — solemn streams —
        Skies, where the desert eagle wheels and screams —
        Spring bloom and autumn blaze of boundless groves.
        Fair scenes shall greet thee where thou goest — fair,
        But different — everywhere the trace of men,
        Paths, homes, graves, ruins, from the lowest glen
        To where life shrinks from the fierce Alpine air —
        Gaze on them, till their tears shall dim thy sight,
        But keep that earlier, wilder image bright.

    4. The "Red Death" had long devastated the country. No pestilence had ever been so fatal, or so hideous. Blood was its Avatar and its seal — the redness and the horror of blood. There were sharp pains and sudden dizziness, and then profuse bleeding at the pores, with dissolution. The scarlet stains upon the body, and especially upon the face of the victim, were the pest ban which shut him out from the aid and from the sympathy of his fellow men. And the whole seizure, progress, and termination of the disease were the incidents of half an hour.

    5. Lull me to sleep, ye winds, whose fitful sound
        Seems from some faint Aeolian harp-string caught;
        Seal up the hundred wakeful eyes of thought
        As Hermes with his lyre in sleep profound
        The hundred wakeful eyes of Argus bound;
        For I am weary, and am overwrought
        With too much toil, with too much care distraught,
        And with the iron crown of anguish crowned.

Lay thy soft hand upon my brow and cheek,
O peaceful Sleep! until from pain released
I breathe again uninterrupted breath!
Ah, with what subtle meaning did the Greek
Call thee the lesser mystery at the feast
Whereof the greater mystery is death!

6. Very happy she looked. There was no sign of her being older; she was gravely, decently, demurely pretty as before. If she had seemed before a thin-stemmed, mild-hued flower of Puritanism, it may be imagined whether in her present situation this delicate bloom was less apparent. Beside her an old gentleman was drinking absinthe; behind her the *dame de comptoir* in the pink ribbons was calling *"Alcibiade! Alcibiade!"* to the long-aproned waiter. I explained to Miss Spencer that my companion had lately been her shipmate, and my brother-in-law came up and was introduced to her. But she looked at him as if she had never seen him before, and I remembered that he had told me that her eyes were always fixed upon the eastward horizon. She had evidently not noticed him, and, still timidly smiling, she made no attempt to pretend that she had. I staid with her at the café door, and he went back to the hotel and to his wife. I said to Miss Spencer that this meeting of ours in the first hour of her landing was really very strange; but that I was delighted to be there and receive her first impressions.

7. "The marvellous thing is that it's painless," he said. "That's how you know when it starts."
"Is it really?"
"Absolutely. I'm awfully sorry about the odor, though. That must bother you."
"Don't! Please don't."
"Look at them," he said. "Now is it sight or is it scent that brings them like that?"
The cot the man lay on was in the wide shade of a mimosa tree and as he looked out past the shade into the glare of the plain there were three of the big birds squatting obscenely, while in the sky a dozen more sailed, making quiet moving shadows as they passed.

8. I heard a fly buzz when I died;
The stillness round my form
Was like the stillness in the air
Between the heaves of storm.

The eyes beside had wrung them dry,
And breaths were gathering sure
For that last onset, when the king
Be witnessed in his power.

I willed my keepsakes, signed away
   What portion of me I
Could make assignable — and then
   There interposed a fly,

With blue, uncertain, stumbling buzz,
   Between the light and me;
And then the windows failed, and then
   I could not see to see.

9. The man in the street is fed
      with lies in peace, gas in war,
      and he may live now
      just around the corner from you
      trying to sell
      the only thing he has left to sell,
      the power of his hand and brain
      to labor for wages, for pay,
      for cash of the realm.
   And there are no takers, he can't connect.

10. The great Pullman was whirling onward with such dignity of motion that a glance from the window seemed simply to prove that the plains of Texas were pouring eastward. Vast flats of green grass, dull-hued spaces of mesquit and cactus, little groups of frame houses, woods of light and tender trees, all were sweeping into the east, sweeping over the horizon, a precipice.

SAMPLE ANSWERS TO QUESTIONS —

Recognition of a Writer's Style

Identifications:

1. Crèvecoeur, from "The American Belisarius," *Sketches of Eighteenth Century America,* probably written before the end of the Revolution.

2. Anne Bradstreet, from "In Reference to Her Children," 1656.

3. William Cullen Bryant, "To Cole, the Painter, Departing for Europe," 1820's.

4. Edgar Allan Poe, from "The Masque of the Red Death," 1845.

5. Henry Wadsworth Longfellow, "Sleep," 1875.

6. Henry James, from "Four Meetings," 1877.

7. Ernest Hemingway, from "The Snows of Kilimanjaro," 1936.

8. Emily Dickinson, "I Heard a Fly Buzz When I Died," before 1886.

9. Carl Sandburg, from "The People, Yes," 1936.

10. Stephen Crane, from "The Bride Comes to Yellow Sky," 1898.

QUESTIONS —

Terms from the New Criticism
(See Sample Answers to Questions, pp. 150, 151)

In the late 1930's and early 1940's, a series of textbooks were published, most notably *Understanding Poetry* and *Understanding Fiction,* by Cleanth Brooks and Robert Penn Warren, which asked technical questions about poems and short stories and ignored or almost ignored the biography of the writer and the period in which the poem or short story was written.

These textbooks were indebted to various volumes of literary criticism that collectively have been called the New Criticism. There is some difference of opinion about who is and who is not a New Critic. But probably most scholars would say that R. P. Blackmur, Cleanth Brooks, Kenneth Burke, T. S. Eliot, William Empson, John Crowe Ransom, I. A. Richards, Allen Tate and Yvor Winters are New Critics. There are many other, frequently younger critics, who are indebted to them. And perhaps one can say that almost all the criticism being written today is indebted to the movement called the New Criticism. This criticism tends to be analytical and aesthetic, to be less concerned with sociological or historical matters than with formal and literary matters.

The reason for introducing the New Criticism here is that there are a number of terms or concepts, developed by one or another of the New Critics, that are useful in analyzing or discussing literature. The following are a few of the terms one is likely to find in the writing of one or more of the New Critics:

aesthetic distance.   In drama, for example, the stage itself, the lighting, the costuming, and the heightened language and sometimes the posturing of the actors help to differentiate the action from real life. Devices for similar distancing and heightening are used in poetry and fiction. The language, especially poetic language, is different from everyday language. Characters are exaggerated or simplified for dramatic purposes.

    1. Discuss Henry James' "The Real Thing" (*American Short Stories,* pages 87-103) in relation to "aesthetic distance."

    2. Discuss Wallace Stevens' "Sunday Morning" (*American Poetry,* pages 158-159) in relation to "aesthetic distance."

affective.   The appeal that literature makes to our sensibilities, our emotions rather than directly or explicitly to the more clearly rational side of our minds.

1. Does the use of color in "The Blue Hotel" (*American Short Stories*, pages 143-163) contribute subtly and indirectly to the meaning?

2. Does the imagery in Eliot's "Preludes" (*American Poetry*, pages 182-183) move you even though you might be hard put to say precisely what each of the verses means?

intention. The term means the theme or meaning of a poem or story as this can be discovered from a close and careful examination of the literary work itself. *The intentional fallacy:* Critics hold that one should not depend on what the author may have said his meaning was, that in the evidence of the work itself one must find the poem or short story or novel's meaning. Authors, they say, are not always reliable or accurate reporters or commentators on their own work.

1. What is the *intention,* or meaning of Wallace Stevens' "The Emperor of Ice Cream" (*American Poetry*, page 160)?

2. What is the intention, or meaning, of Melville's "Bartleby the Scrivener" (*American Short Stories*, pages 64-87)?

objective A set of objects, a situation or chain of events which are
correlative. the aesthetic equivalent for the idea or emotion, or both, which gave rise to them; the dramatic or objective representation, the literary projection of an idea (theme) or emotion. Thus *Hamlet, Prince of Denmark* is the dramatization, or "objective correlative" of the suspicion that "there's something rotten in Denmark!"

1. Discuss Marianne Moore's "Poetry" (*American Poetry*, page 178) in relation to the objective correlative.

2. Twain apparently believed that most people are hypocritical and would cheat or steal if in no danger of being caught or exposed. This was his "germ" or idea for "The Man That Corrupted Hadleyburg" (*American Short Novels*, pages 68-96). Explain the nature

and appropriateness of his "objective correlative," his "situation" or "chain of events" for projective his germ in literary form.

3. Discuss O'Neill's "The Hairy Ape" (*American Drama,* pages 140-166) in relation to the "objective correlative."

tension.   In poetry the connotations should not contradict the denotations; they should complement and mutually enrich each other. In poetry and in fiction, it means that the theme—as in *Romeo and Juliet,* two lovers go willingly and inevitably into death because of their great love for one another—is not merely asserted, the author undertakes to justify or to "prove" it. Thus, in *Romeo and Juliet* the sanctity of romantic love, as the main characters see it, is challenged by the mere bawdiness of Mercutio and the low-minded expediency of the Nurse. In other words, the worth of romantic love is set against the opposing views of Mercutio and the Nurse.

1. Comment on the connotations and denotation in Warren's "Bearded Oaks" (*American Poetry,* page 211).

2. What is the tension in Melville's "Billy Budd" (*American Short Novels,* page 18-67)?

3. What is the tension in Marianne Moore's "What Are Years?" (*American Poetry,* page 179)?

4. What is the tension in Robert Frost's "Mending Wall" (*American Poetry,* pages 145-146)?

SAMPLE ANSWERS TO QUESTIONS —

Terms from the New Criticism

aesthetic distance

1. In James' story one is aware of a kind of allegory. The servants represent real life, and the older couple true gentility. In art, it is necessary to posture, and the servants posture before the artist. The story ends, with the neatness of a joke, when the genteel couple (the "real thing") take up the job of being servants, and the servants the job of pretending to be the "real thing." In other words, a theme or point is being dramatized, a theme that James wants artists and their audiences to understand.

2. The opening scene in "Sunday Morning" is realistically described, but the imaginings in the woman's head, her juxtaposing the sepuchre and the mountain with the deer and quail, serve to dramatize the theme. They enable the reader to understand what Stevens is saying, but they do not seem immediately real or actual.

affective

1. The colors in "The Blue Hotel" are like the colors used in stage lighting. They help make the story as eerie as it is.

2. All of the images suggest dankness, dustiness, tiredness, dreariness.

intention

1. Stevens does not make a precise or explicit statement about what "The Emperor of Ice Cream Means." There are certain objects described and the reader is asked to decide what they represent. "Concupiscent curds," "yesterday's newspapers," "horny feet," etc.

2. Melville describes Bartleby's actions, he does not tell you what to decide about it. Is he a hero, a fool, a quitter? One must decide on the basis of information inside the story. Two readers might well come to different conclusions about Bartleby.

objective correlative

1. Miss Moore makes an explicit statement about what a poem is and what a poem is not. She then provides a list of objects and situations about which poems might be written. They are the objective equivalents for the explicit statement.

2. Twain devised the situation of the man gulling the whole town of Hadleyburg. He plays on the town's avarice like an expert fisherman, giving them enough line to let them believe they are escaping, playing with them, then finally drawing them in. If one accepts Twain's thesis about human kind, one would have to acknowledge that his story exhibits human avarice and hypocrisy.

3. O'Neill wants to show us man dehumanized by mechanization, and he does this in every scene, using both settings and the actions of his characters to demonstrate it.

tension

1. See answer No. 2 (Warren) on page 149.

2. One is never wholly certain which view or interpretation of the story is right. The various possibilities pull against one another.

3. The paradox that only in restraint is there freedom.

4. Neither walls nor the absence of walls is advocated. There usefulness or their foolishness depends on the situation.

A SELECTED BIBLIOGRAPHY OF THE NEW CRITICISM:

R. P. Blackmur, *The Double Agent.* New York: Arrow Editions, 1935.

Cleanth Brooks, *Modern Poetry and the Tradition.* Chapel Hill: University of North Carolina Press, 1939.

_____ *The Well Wrought Urn.* New York: Reynal and Hitchcock, 1947.

———————— and Robert Penn Warren, *Understanding Fiction*. New York: Crofts, 1943.

———————— and Robert Penn Warren, *Understanding Poetry*, New York: Holt, 1938.

Kenneth Burke, *Counterstatement*. New York: Harcourt, Brace, 1931.

T. S. Eliot, *Selected Essays, 1917-1922*. New York: Harcourt, Brace, 1932.

William Empson, *Seven Types of Ambiguity*. New York: Norton, 1938.

William Van O'Connor, editor, *Forms of Modern Fiction*. Bloomington, Indiana: Indiana University Midland Books, 1957.

William Van O'Connor, *Sense and Sensibility in Modern Poetry*. Chicago: University of Chicago Press, 1948.

———————— and Leonard Unger, *Poems for Study*. New York: Rinehart, 1953.

Ezra Pound, *Literary Essays of Ezra Pound*. London: Faber and Faber, 1954.

John Crowe Ransom, *The World's Body*. New York: Scribner's, 1938.

R. W. Stallman, *The Critic's Notebook*. Minneapolis: University of Minnesota Press, 1950.

Allen Tate, *The Man of Letters in the Modern World*. New York: Meridian, 1955.

Lionel Trilling, *The Liberal Imagination*. New York: Viking, 1950.

Leonard Unger, *The Man in the Name*. Minneapolis: University of Minnesota Press, 1956.

Yvor Winters, *In Defense of Reason*. New York: Swallow Press and William Morrow, 1947.

SPECIAL THEMES IN AMERICAN LITERATURE:

Malcolm Cowley. *Exiles' Return.* New York: Viking, 1931. Revised 1951. Deals with 1920's and expatriate writers.

Bernard Duffey. *The Chicago Renaissance in American Letters.* East Lansing, Michigan: Michigan State University Press, 1954.

Frederick Hoffman. *Freudianism and the Literary Mind.* Baton Rouge, Louisiana: Louisiana State University Press, 2nd edition, 1957.

Perry Miller. *The New England Mind.* Cambridge, Massachusetts: Harvard University Press, 1954.

Constance Rourke. *American Humor: a Study of the National Character.* New York: Harcourt, Brace, 1931.

Louis Rubin and Robert Jacobs. *Southern Renascence: the Literature of the Modern South.* Baltimore: Johns Hopkins University Press, 1953.

Henry Smith. *Virgin Land: The West as Symbol and Myth.* Cambridge, Massachusetts: Harvard University Press, 1950.

Benjamin Spencer. *The Quest for Nationality.* Syracuse, New York: Syracuse University Press, 1957.

Randall Stewart. *American Literature and Christian Doctrine.* Baton Rouge, Louisiana: Louisiana State University Press, 1945.

Louis Wright. *The Cultural Life of the American Colonies, 1607-1763.* New York: Harper & Brothers, 1957.

Suggestions Regarding the Exercises Based on Special Themes in American Literature

1. List of topics: (1) The *American* quality in American Fiction (2) Regional Elements in American literature (3) The American Dream in American Drama (4) The Grotesque in American Literature (5) The Younger American Poets (6) Poe's Influence (7) Whitman's Influence.

2. Think about your topic carefully, and reread anything you can remember that might give you ideas to consider.

Exercises:

1. You have read extensively in American literature in these five volumes, *Reader's Bookshelf of American Literature*. Make a list of seven or eight topics about which articles or books might be written.

2. Having selected one of the topics from your list, write an essay (350-400 words) on it.

Literary Periodicals

To see what is currently being written about American literature, and, indeed, what contributions by new as well as by established writers are being made, it is necessary to follow the literary journals. Not all libraries will have each of the magazines listed below, but they will have some of them.

American Literature

Published four times a year. It is the professional journal for scholars and teachers of American literature.

Atlantic Monthly

A long-established journal, publishing articles on politics, eminent figures, concepts, etc. Features book reviews and literary questions.

College English

A professional journal for college English teachers. Many articles on American writers. Book reviews.

English Journal

A professional journal for high school English teachers. Similar to *College English.*

Harper's Magazine

Long-established journal. Similar in character to *Atlantic Monthly.*

Kenyon Review

A literary quarterly featuring criticism, short stories, poetry, and book reviews. Formerly edited by John Crowe Ransom, poet and critic, and currently by Robie Macaulay, novelist and short story writer.

Paris Review

Began after World War II. Features work of the post-war generation. Excellent interviews with writers.

Partisan Review

A literary quarterly that emphasizes European literature and speculation; also has political cast.

Poetry Magazine

The oldest and probably the best of the poetry magazines. Published Eliot, Pound, Frost, Stevens, and many others. Also does book reviews.

Sewanee Review

The oldest literary quarterly in the United States. Formerly edited by Allen Tate, poet and critic. Features literary criticism and literary history. Publishes poems, short stories, and omnibus reviews.

South Atlantic Quarterly

Features academic articles on American history and literature. Good book reviews.

Story Magazine

First published in 1930's, it discovered many good short story writers. Now being published again. Editors: Whit Burnett and William Peden.

Twentieth Century Literature

Critical studies of modern literature. Gives frequent extended criticism and attention to American writers.

University of Kansas City Review

Gives most of its space to articles on American literature.

Virginia Quarterly Review

A long-established review. Emphasizes Southern history and literature. Published writers such as Robert Penn Warren and Allen Tate.

The Yale Review

Political articles, sociological, but also many articles on literary criticism, and long book reviews.

Exercises:

Visit the library most convenient to you.

1. Which of these library periodicals do they carry?

2. Do they display (1) *New York Times Book Review*, (2) *Herald Tribune Books*, (3) *The Saturday Review?*

3. Write an essay (300 words) on the two or three magazines you would find most helpful to you as a student of American literature.

Suggestions Regarding the Exercises Based on Literary Periodicals

1-2. Most libraries will have *Atlantic, Harper's, N.Y. Times,* etc. Small libraries may not have some of the ones listed. If you are interested in seeing them a librarian can tell you where to order copies.

3. Any of the magazines listed would be helpful. Some of the professional magazines might be hard going for young, beginning students.

Suggestions Regarding the Exercises Based on Histories of American Literature

1-2. Most libraries will have one or more of these volumes. In examining a volume, ask yourself whether it is historical, critical, biographical, light or serious in treatment. At what audience is it aimed, etc.?

Histories of American Literature

1. Marcus Cunliffe. *The Literature of the United States.* Baltimore: Penguin, 1954.

2. James D. Hart. *The Oxford Companion to American Literature.* New York: Oxford University Press, 1956.

3. F. O. Matthiessen. *American Renaissance.* New York: Oxford University Press, 1941.

4. Robert Spiller, *et al. Literary History of the United States.* 3 vols. New York: Macmillan, 1948. Two volumes of literary history, one of bibliography.

5. Robert Spiller, *et al. Literary History of the United States.* Revised in 1953 in one volume, with a new chapter, "Postscript at Mid-Century," and a 23-page bibliography.

6. *University of Minnesota Pamphlets on American Writers.* Edited by W. V. O'Connor, Allen Tate, and R. P. Warren. In 1959, pamphlets on Twain, James, Hemingway, Faulkner, Frost, Wolfe, and others.

7. Arthur Quinn, *et al. The Literature of the American People.* New York: 1951.

8. Edmund Wilson, ed. *The Shock of Recognition: the Development of American Literature Recorded by the Men Who Made It.* New York: Oxford University Press, 1955.

9. Frederick J. Hoffman and William Van O'Connor, editors, *20th Century Literature in America,* Chicago: H. Regnery Co., 1951-2.
Fifty Years of American Drama, 1900-1950, by Alan Downer
The Modern Novel in America, 1900-1950, by Frederick J. Hoffman
Achievement in American Poetry, 1900-1950, by Louise Bogan
The Rise of Short Fiction in America, 1900-1950, by Ray West
Men, Ideas and Judgments, by James Gray, May Brodbeck and Walter Metzger
An Age of Criticism, by William Van O'Connor

Exercises:

1. Which of these volumes are available to you?

2. Write an essay (350 to 400 words) characterizing the volumes you have been able to examine.

Biographical
Encyclopedia

of

American Authors

from

The Reader's
Encyclopedia

BY

WILLIAM ROSE BENÉT

PUBLISHED BY

Thomas Y. Crowell Company

NEW YORK

ADAMS, HENRY

Few American families were as distinguished as that into which Henry Brooks Adams was born on February 16, 1838. His great-grandfather was America's second President; his grandfather its sixth. His father, Charles Francis Adams, was soon to become a Congressman and famous diplomat, and on both sides of his family there was a century-old tradition of leadership in Boston society and American public life. Despite this heritage, the shy, introverted youth who graduated from Harvard in 1858 sought no public eminence. He was destined to become a thoughtful, scholarly historian and influential philosopher; but it is characteristic that when, late in life, he wrote his most important books, he disdained publication and had them privately printed for friends.

Following his graduation, Adams voyaged to Europe to study, returning in 1860. He went to work as his father's secretary in Congress, and in 1861, when his father was named ambassador to England, he accompanied him as private secretary, remaining seven years. Upon his return he began a career in journalism; but, under family pressure, he accepted a professorship in history at Harvard in 1870, where he taught for seven years. In 1872 he married Marian Hooper, who died by her own hand (poison) in 1885.

While he taught at Harvard, Adams pursued a second career as editor of the *North American Review*, but in 1877 he resigned both positions, moved to the less demanding society of Washington, and devoted himself to his writing. In 1885, following the tragedy of his wife's death, Adams traveled to Japan, returning the following year to complete his monumental history of the United States during the Jefferson and Madison administrations. He left the United States again, this time for travel in Europe, and when he returned, steeped himself in the study of 12th century Europe, which resulted in his famous book, *Mont-Saint-Michel and Chartres* (privately printed 1904; published 1913).

For a lesser historian, the subject would have been merely a dry and esoteric study. But Adams brought to his work his now fully-matured theory of history, and this book represented one side of his famous image of the Virgin and the Dynamo. To most historians of his day, history was merely a record of human events with no especial connection; to an enlightened few, influenced by Darwinian theory, it was the drama of man's progress. Adams, however, had a new and shocking concept. He viewed history as the outward operation of powerful, underlying forces in dynamic interplay. He contrasted the closed, secure world of the Middle Ages (represented by its devotion to the image of the Virgin) with the turbulent, often chaotic world of modern industrial society (and its reverence for the energy of the Dynamo). Thus, the world he depicted in *Mont-Saint-Michel and Chartres* became a mirror against which he held the image of his contemporary world, and found it lacking.

As counterfoil to *Mont-Saint-Michel*, Adams wrote *The Education of Henry Adams* (privately printed 1907; published 1918), an intellectual autobiography in which he sought to reveal the shortcomings of American culture. The two books, with their searching analysis of the place of the modern American in world culture and reverent concern for the preservation of meaningful traditions, became an invaluable contribution to the very culture he thought to undermine, and have profoundly influenced the flowering of American thought. His death on March 27, 1918, was virtually unnoticed by an America which, engaged in a world war, seemed to be unconsciously fulfilling his direst predictions of its future.

AIKEN, CONRAD

Possibly because it could not be viewed as a whole, or even a progressing continuum, the work of Conrad Potter Aiken has only recently received the serious critical attention and acclaim it deserves.

Aiken was born in Savannah, Georgia, on August 5, 1889. His father was a doctor, and the deep impression he made on the boy can be found in Aiken's recurring medical themes. In 1900 Aiken went to live with an aunt; for reasons unknown, his father had killed Aiken's mother and then committed suicide. At Harvard, he was editor of the *Advocate* and class poet. A small inheritance left him independent of means, and a fierce, unbending will made him independent of spirit. Following his graduation he devoted himself entirely to writing; his first book of poems, *Earth Triumphant,* appeared in 1914. After that, a steady stream of publications revealed a gradual growth from imitative work to a highly individual style. During World War I he was exempted from military service on his claim that production of poetry is an "essential industry."

Selected Poems (1929) indicated the wide range of feeling and lyrical expression he had already developed, and won for him the Pulitzer Prize. Occasionally, Aiken wrote in prose, producing both novels and stories basically poetic in both theme and language. His novels in particular showed him a master of the complex psychology of motive and rationalization, as in *Blue Voyage* (1927), and *The Great Circle* (1933). The essentially impressionistic manner of his prose did not "take" in the era of hard-boiled realism and social consciousness, but *Ushant,* his fictional autobiography, written in the same style, found an enthusiastic readership when it appeared in 1952. With this work and *Collected Poems* (1953), which gathered the work of forty years into one volume, critics were better able to give his work proper appraisal. *Ushant, Collected Poems,* and the *Short Stories of Conrad Aiken* (1950) presented a formidable body of literary production. The development from the imitative and largely imagist early poems to the sen-

sitive, integral maturity of the later work mirrored the growth, not only of one intelligent sensibility, but of American poetry in the century. In 1956, after the publication of *Letter From Li Po,* Aiken was awarded the Bollingen Prize for Poetry. An earlier play, *Mr. Arcularis,* much-revised, received a TV production in 1957. In the same year *Sheepfold Hill,* his most recent work, was published, followed in 1958 by a collection of his critical essays, *A Reviewer's ABC*.

ANDERSON, SHERWOOD

Sherwood Anderson was born on September 13, 1876 in Camden, Ohio. His family was so rootless that each of the seven children was born in a different Ohio town. At fourteen, Anderson quit school and took a series of odd jobs in a vagrant pattern not unlike that of his father. When war broke out with Spain, he enlisted in the Army and served in Cuba. On his return he went to Chicago to work for a while as an advertising copy-writer, but nostalgia prompted a return to the scenes of his youth in Ohio. He successfully managed a paint factory in Elyria until one day, while dictating a letter, he stopped abruptly in the middle and walked out, never to return. He went to New York where he worked in advertising while beginning his serious writing. Anderson's first novel, *Windy McPherson's Son,* a buoyant, irreverent portrait of his father, was published in 1916. *Winesburg, Ohio* (1919) was a short-story sequence that movingly portrayed the frustrations of small-town life. His best novel, *Poor White,* appeared the following year, and in 1921 he published more stories in the *Winesburg* vein, *The Triumph of the Egg.* Anderson owed much of his success to his frankness on sexual themes and his forthright depiction of the secret passions that motivate men. Often misunderstood, his work was thought of as shocking, or even obscene. This reputation attracted a large readership, and it is not surprising that some of his worst writing sold best, like *Dark Laughter* (1925). In 1924 Anderson settled in Marion, Va., where character-

PHOTO BY GEORGE CSERNA

W. H. AUDEN

istically, he edited both newspapers, one Republican, the other Democrat, for many years. In a typical gesture, he announced in 1941 a trip to South America as an unofficial good-will ambassador, but he became ill en route. He was removed from the ship at Colon, Panama; on March 8, 1941, he died there of peritonitis.

AUDEN, W. H.

The English-born poet Wystan Hugh Auden has lived in the United States since 1939, and is a naturalized citizen. He was born in York on February 21, 1907, and received his education at Oxford University. His first book, *Poems*, appeared in 1930, and until his emigration to America he was considered a leader of the young, new, rebellious school of English poets. With Christopher Isherwood, he wrote two experimental plays that denounced the bourgeois mentality, *The Ascent of F6* and *The Dog Beneath The Skin*. In his poems he drew sharp contrasts between sayers and doers, and showed a gift for the satirical bite. Auden and the poets with whom he was associated were given to manifesto-like defenses of Marxism, attacks on bourgeois philistinism, and a sharp appreciation of the glories and foibles of the machine age. The poetry, in consequence, tended toward talkiness, raciness, and glib facility; but in English poetry, liberation

from a stuffy moralism and pretentious preciosity was sorely needed, and Auden's poems tore down fences eloquently and effectively.

His first important work in America was *For The Time Being* (1944), a Christmas oratorio. A collection of his earlier poems followed (1945), and in 1947 he published *The Age of Anxiety*, an excellent, if somewhat overextended urban morality play (Auden called it an "eclogue") in brilliant alliterative verse. It won him a Pulitzer Prize. His more recent works have shown the same versatility of his early poems, but far richer in maturity of tone, technical control, and perhaps more deeply-felt emotion: *Nones* (1951), and *The Shield of Achilles* (1955). With Chester Kallmann he collaborated on the libretto of Igor Stravinsky's opera, *The Rake's Progress*, adapted from the drawings of Hogarth. They have since translated several opera libretti, notably *The Magic Flute*.

BARRETT, WILLIAM

A New Yorker by birth, William Barrett has studied and taught in that city most of his life. Born on December 30, 1913, he was educated during the '30s at the City College of New York and Columbia University. His principal interest is philosophy, of which he is a professor at New York University, but Barrett has contributed frequent, and usually perceptive, literary reviews and criticisms to a number of newspapers and magazines. He has also published a variety of articles on philosophy to scholarly academic journals, and has written a study of existentialism, *Irrational Man* (1958). He is the editor of *Zen Buddhism*, a selection from the writings of D. T. Suzuki.

BERRYMAN, JOHN

John Berryman was born in McAlester, Oklahoma, on October 25, 1914. Educated at Columbia University, he has taught variously at Wayne University, Harvard, Princeton, and the University of Washington. His first poems appeared in several "little magazines," twenty of them being published in *Five*

Young American Poets: 1940. Poems
(1942) was his own first book, followed
by *The Dispossessed* (1948), confirm-
ing the promise of his earlier work. A
long silence followed, broken in 1956
when Berryman published his long, exquisite poem, *Homage to Mistress Bradstreet*, which brought him new recognition and stature.

BENÉT, STEPHEN VINCENT

Despite the long military tradition of
the family (three successive generations
of West Pointers), both Stephen Vincent
Benét and his brother William Rose
Benét pursued exclusively literary careers. Born in Bethlehem, Pennsylvania,
on July 22, 1898, Stephen was raised
on a variety of Army posts, mainly in
California. Even before he went to Yale,
the young poet had published his first
book, *Five Men and Pompey* (1915), a
collection of six dramatic monologues.
In 1920, after receiving his M.A. at
Yale, he studied at the Sorbonne. He
married Rosemary Carr in Chicago in
1921. In 1926 Benét received a Guggenheim Fellowship which enabled him
to work in France (where living was
cheaper), on the long poem he had
planned in his youth, incorporating the
dramatic events in American history
which were so closely tied to his family's. The book-length poem, published
in 1928, was *John Brown's Body*, for
which Benét was awarded the Pulitzer
Prize. In 1929 Benét returned to New
York, to become a free-lance writer. His
The Devil and Daniel Webster, a short
story that has become a minor classic,
was published in the *Saturday Evening
Post* in 1937. Benét wrote the libretto
for the opera based on this story (col-
laborating with the composer Douglas
Moore), and during the early years of
the war produced books and pamphlets
on America and American ideals for the
Office of War Information. At the time
of his death, on March 13, 1943, he was
engaged in writing a long poem dealing
with the history and traditions of the
American West. The unfinished work
was published in 1943, entitled *Western
Star*. His poetry found a wide audience

more than ten years after his death
when Paul Gregory staged a concert
reading of *John Brown's Body* that was
a hit on Broadway and successfully
toured the country.

BISHOP, ELIZABETH

Although her production has been
slender, Elizabeth Bishop is recognized
as one of America's finest poets. Born in
Worcester, Massachusetts, on February
8, 1911, she was educated at Vassar
College, graduating in 1934. Her first
book, *North and South* (1946), was an
immediate success; it had won the
Houghton Mifflin Poetry Fellowship
award of $1,000 the previous year. She
has received other prizes and honors as
well. In 1949 she was Consultant in
Poetry to the Library of Congress, and
in 1958 she was named honorary consultant in American letters. Her most
recent work was *Poems*, published in
1955.

UPI PHOTO

ELIZABETH BISHOP

BLACKMUR, R. P.

One of the soundest American critics of the 20th century is Richard Palmer
Blackmur. He was born in Springfield,
Massachusetts, on January 21, 1904.
Despite a lack of formal higher education, he developed a considerable reputation as a free-lance poet and critic,
mostly during the 30s. His first book,
The Double Agent, appeared in 1935,

but his best work has emerged since his fruitful association with Princeton University in 1940. Following a succession of fellowships, he joined the faculty permanently as a professor of literature. His critical essays are remarkable not only for their insights and originality, but also for their deft, provocative style. His best-known books include *Language As Gesture* (1952); *The Lion and the Honeycomb* (1955); and the sagacious study, *Form and Value in Modern Poetry* (1957) (a paperback). He is the editor of *American Short Novels* in this present series.

BRADSTREET, ANNE

Anne Bradstreet was born in England around 1612, daughter of Thomas Dudley, steward to the Earl of Lincoln. Although little is known of her early life, she seems to have acquired an excellent education in the Earl's household, including study of the arts and of languages. Her father was a Puritan, but Anne's liberal education imbued her with liberal views, and it was not until she married Simon Bradstreet in 1628 that she joined the dissenters. In 1630, both the Bradstreets and the Dudleys came to America, settling in the stern rigors of Puritan Salem. Anne, used to the comfortable ways of the English estates, was slow in adjusting to the hard life in the Bay Colony, and bitter complaints against its discomforts appear occasionally in her poems. As time wore on, however, both her husband and father became prominent in colonial affairs (they were both governors), and Mistress Bradstreet accommodated herself to their way of life, as she had to their religion. Intellectually gifted, she exercised great influence in their affairs and probably enjoyed her important role. In 1649, a brother of hers returning to England took along the manuscripts of her poems and published them there under the title, *The Tenth Muse*. The following year the book was published in Boston.

No one claims for Anne Bradstreet greatness as a poet. Most of her verses are commonplace imitations of popular styles of the day, although such acquaintance with literature was rare in a woman at that time. Her best poems, however, have the freshness and vitality that only a new society can impart, and many are valuable because they deal with the problems and mores of Colonial New England. She died on Sept. 16, 1672, surrounded by children and grandchildren. Many notable Americans are descended from her, including such writers as Wendell Phillips, Oliver Wendell Holmes, and Richard Henry Dana.

BROOKS, VAN WYCK

Van Wyck Brooks, distinguished critic, biographer, and literary historian, was born in Plainfield, New Jersey, on February 16, 1886. Educated at Harvard, he taught briefly at Stanford University, worked with a New York publishing company, and was literary editor of *The Freeman*. In his early books, Brooks displayed an interest in and profound understanding of contemporary (turn-of-the-century) French and English literature, but his attention turned gradually to his own national tradition, exploding in the trail-blazing *America's Coming-of-Age* (1915). In that volume he strongly averred the claim of American literature to serious attention and study. Brooks' critical method is basically biographical, an attempt to explain an author's work through his own life. The method depends heavily on the impressions and imagination of the critic, and Brooks has been frequently criticized for carrying his conclusions too far or for being inadequate to the materials under discussion. *The Ordeal of Mark Twain* (1920) spurred a long debate with Bernard De Voto on the accuracy of his interpretation. With *The Flowering of New England* (1936), Brooks began a five-volume historical study of American literature, called "Makers and Finders," concluding in 1952 with the publication of *The Confident Years*. The following year, *The Writer in America* came as a valuable and incisive summing up. *Howells: His Life and World* (1959) retracted some opinions expressed in *The Ordeal of*

Mark Twain. He has written a three-part autobiography, *Scenes and Portraits* (1954), *Days of the Phoenix* (1957), and *From the Shadow of the Mountain* (1961).

BRYANT, WILLIAM CULLEN

During the nineteenth century, William Cullen Bryant was regarded not only as one of the great practitioners of American poetry, but as its virtual founder. The present century has been broader in its perspectives and far more severe in its appreciation, relegating Bryant to a minor position in the tapestry of American letters. His achievement was unquestionably less than the pretensions made for him by his contemporaries, but he nevertheless composed some of America's most memorable poems.

Bryant was born on November 3, 1794, in Cummington, Massachusetts, and received a sporadic education, including Latin and Greek under the tutelage of two divines, and classics and mathematics during a brief stay at Williams College. Lacking funds, he had to forego his planned career at Yale, and read law instead. At the age of twenty-one he was admitted to the bar, practicing for nine years at Great Barrington, Massachusetts. By that time he had already written and published some of his finest poems. *The Embargo,* his first book of poems, all topical satires, was published in 1808, when Bryant was only thirteen; at seventeen, he wrote and published his best-known poem, *Thanatopsis* (in its first version); *To a Water-Fowl* was printed when he was only twenty-one. In 1825, he moved to New York, where he became an editor, and eventually the only editor and chief owner, of the *Evening 'Post.* Bryant's poetic production, though widely acclaimed, declined steadily in quality; but his editorship, and his central position in New York literary circles, was influential in the development of American literature throughout most of the century. In his later years he produced a poor translation of Homer's epics, redeemed by the fact that it introduced

WILLIAM CULLEN BRYANT

those classics to many Americans for the first time. He died on June 12, 1878.

CASSILL, R. V.

Ronald Verlin Cassill was born in Cedar Falls, Iowa, on May 17, 1919. He was educated at the State University of Iowa and at the Sorbonne. His first serious novel (he has written a number of paperback potboilers) was *Eagle on the Coin,* published in 1950. By then, Cassill was already known as a first-rate short-story writer, and it is in that genre that he is still best known, although he has written numerous articles, reviews, and critical pieces. His stories were featured along with those of J. B. Hall and Herbert Gold in *Fifteen by Three* (1957), and he has since published another novel, *Clem Anderson* (1961).

CHAPMAN, JOHN JAY

John Jay Chapman was born in New York City on March 2, 1862. His father, president of the New York Stock Exchange, was ruined by the Panic of 1870, but young Chapman went to Harvard anyway, working his way through and graduating in 1884. He was admitted to the bar in 1888 and practiced law, which he hated, until the turn of the century. In that time he had earned a sufficient fortune to give up the law for life. He was active in New York reform politics, but his outspokenness, his unpredictable opinions, and his unstable, passionate nature precluded a political career. In contrast to his public self, Chapman's writings are thoughtful, reasoned, and imaginative. His first book, *Emerson* (1898), rescued that writer from the tyranny of misused labels and re-interpreted his significance for a skeptical generation. Chapman brought this same freshness of viewpoint to all his critical works, which he wrote in a vigorous, engaging style. Among his better-known books are *Causes and Consequences* (1898), *Learning* (1911), *The Greek Genius* (1915), and *Dante* (1927). He died, following an operation, on November 4, 1933. Long neglected, his work recently enjoyed a revival and the subsequent re-appraisal has restored Chapman to the front rank of American critics.

CHASE, RICHARD

Descended from a long line of New Englanders that stretches back to the 17th century, Richard Volney Chase was born in Lakeport, New Hampshire, on October 12, 1914. He graduated from Dartmouth College and received both his M. A. and Ph. D. at Columbia University, where he is now a professor of English. Writing mostly on American literature, he has contributed articles and essays to a number of magazines and critical journals. A rare blend of careful scholarship and incisive imagination has illuminated his work on classic Americans: *Herman Melville* (1949), *Emily Dickinson* (1951) and *Walt Whitman Reconsidered* (1955). Professor Chase's most recent book, *The American Novel and Its Tradition* (1957), is an original and provocative study that probes the characteristic forms of American fiction and has aroused new interest in several neglected masterpieces.

CIARDI, JOHN

The multiple career of John Ciardi since his birth in Boston on June 24, 1916, has included teaching, editing, and translating, all carried on simultaneously. His most significant and valuable work, however, is his poetry, for Ciardi

UPI PHOTO

JOHN CIARDI

is one of the finest poets of his generation. He was raised and educated in Medford, Massachusetts, and began writing poetry during his college years (Tufts College, B.A., 1938; University of Michigan, M. A., 1939). For these early poems, published in *Homeward to America*, he received the Hopwood Award in 1939. For three years he taught at the University of Kansas City. When the United States entered the war, Ciardi enlisted in the Army Air Corps, serving as a gunner on a B-29. After his discharge he taught at Harvard (1946-1949), the Salzburg Seminar of American Studies (1950-51), and since 1953 at Rutgers University, where he is now Professor of English. Every summer since 1947 he has been on the poetry faculty of the Bread Loaf Writers' Conference at Middlebury College, and since 1955 has served as chairman. In 1949 he formed his present association with Twayne Publishing Co., a New York book publishing house specializing in poetry and scholarly works. For several years he contributed regular poetry reviews to the *Nation*, and in 1953 he became poetry editor of the *Saturday Review*. Five volumes of his poems have appeared since the war, notably *As If* (1955) and *I Marry You* (1958).

Ciardi writes in a tough, almost hard-boiled style that gives his poetry a sense of solidity and architectural firmness. His language is direct, unevasive, consciously abhorring coyness and "prettifying." The refusal to be sentimental or foolishly nostalgic does not entirely eliminate romantic emotionalism, and a profound sensitivity underlying the deliberate understatement animates his best poems, making them spring to life. This same power emerges in his translation of Dante's *Inferno* (1954), which restores the vigor of Dante's language in a sanguine denial of the genteel literary tradition.

CLARK, WALTER VAN TILBURG

Walter Van Tilburg Clark was born in East Orland, Maine, on August 3, 1909. In 1917, the family moved to Reno, Nevada, where Clark's father became president of the University of Nevada. Clark studied there, receiving his M. A. in 1932, then journeyed east to the University of Vermont, where he received another master's degree in 1934. In the ensuing ten years, Clark taught in Cazenovia, New York; returning to Nevada in 1945, he settled in the Washoe Valley. For the past few years he has taught English and writing at San Francisco State College, living in Mill Valley, Calif.

Clark's first novel, *The Ox-Bow Incident*, was published in 1940. An ironic study of a lynching, this short book packs a powerful wallop. It became one of the most moving films ever to emerge from Hollywood. His publications since then include *The City of Trembling Leaves* (1945), *The Track of the Cat* (1949) (novels), and *The Watchful Gods, and Other Stories* (1950).

CRANE, HART

Harold Hart Crane was born in Garretsville, Ohio, July 12, 1899. During his childhood, Crane's parents moved to Cleveland where his father became a wealthy candy manufacturer and where, soon afterward, they were divorced. The interior conflict which was to lead in later years to alcoholism, violence, homosexuality and, ultimately, self-annihilation clearly had its beginnings during this period. A gifted youth, Crane began writing poetry at 13, despite his father's constant discouragement of "this

poetic nonsense." He went to Cuba at 17 and stayed for nearly a year with his mother at his grandfather's plantation on the Isle of Pines. Traveling from there to New York and on to Paris, he returned to Cleveland in 1917, when the U. S. entered the war. Reluctantly, Crane went to work for his father, abandoning his plans to attend college. In constant rebellion, he escaped to New York several times, where he worked as an advertising copywriter. Each time he returned home sheepishly to the domination of his father; but in 1920, his escape was final.

Advertising proved as much drudgery as the candy business, but Crane soon found a patron, Otto Kahn, who was willing to support him while he fashioned his poems. His first book, *White Buildings,* appeared in 1926 and heralded the emergence of an important poetic talent on the American scene. Crane's wild personal life, his violent temper, particularly during his frequent drunken episodes, and his flagrant homosexuality were overlooked or apologized for by his friends and others who admired his powerful, intense poems. Their patience was retarded in 1930 when Crane's modern symbolic epic, *The Bridge,* was published. An intensely personal, deeply realized vision of American culture, *The Bridge* was immediately recognized as one of the most important poems of the era. *Poetry: A Magazine of Verse* awarded Crane the Helen Haire Levinson prize, and soon thereafter he was named a Guggenheim Fellow. Voyaging to Mexico to absorb atmosphere for a long poem on Latin America, he found himself unable to create. For a writer who had sacrificed all conventional life for his art and who was seething with interior conflict, it must have been a desperate moment. On April 27, 1932, in transit between Mexico and New York, Hart Crane threw himself overboard into the Gulf of Mexico and disappeared forever.

CRANE, STEPHEN

The brief, luminous career of Stephen Crane began in Newark, New

Jersey, where, on November 1, 1871, he was born. His father was an itinerant minister who preached in and around Port Jervis, and it was there that Crane spent his childhood. When his father died, in 1880, the family moved to Columbia County, New York. Young Stephen received a sporadic education there, interrupted by periods of work to help support the family. He managed to get to Lafayette College and later to Syracuse University, working his way through as a correspondent for the New York *Tribune;* in 1890, after his mother's death, he gave up his schooling and went to New York to try his hand at journalism. Work was unsteady, and Crane found himself at the bottom of New York society, living in run-down rooming houses in the slums, frequently bordering on starvation. It was in this atmosphere that he wrote *Maggie: A Girl of the Streets,* a true-to-life portrait of urban life which proved too starkly real to find a publisher. Crane borrowed some money and published it himself in 1892, but the book found few readers and most of the copies were used to stoke the stove in his Bowery room.

Among the few readers of *Maggie,* however, were Hamlin Garland and William Dean Howells, who immediately recognized Crane's talent and encouraged him to continue writing. Through their efforts, *The Red Badge of Courage* was published in 1895. Despite its financial failure, this novel earned overnight fame for its author, and he was inundated with offers of newspaper work. In 1895 he traveled to Texas and Mexico as a correspondent; the following year he was in Greece covering the war with Turkey; and in 1897 he was sent to Cuba to report the ferment that was soon to explode into war. While en route home from Cuba, Crane was shipwrecked and cast adrift in an open boat, an experience powerfully described in his novelette, *The Open Boat.*

The experience also permanently impaired his health, and in 1898 he traveled to England to recover. There he met again Cora Taylor, who had helped to nurse him back to health in Florida, and married her. To evade malicious gossip in America (Cora Taylor had once been madam in a bordello), the Cranes settled in a house in England where Joseph Conrad was a frequent visitor. That year Crane returned to Cuba as war carrespondent for the New York *World,* but his health failed quickly and he returned, dying of consumption. A hasty trip to Germany was arranged, but it was too late—soon after his arrival, on June 5, 1900, he died.

Although he lived entirely in the 19th century, Crane was more modern than any of his contemporaries and his writing is more of our century than theirs. *Maggie,* it is true, was in the naturalistic style of the turn of the century; indeed, its sordid truthfulness and sympathy for any human experience is a model for that type of fiction. *The Red Badge of Courage* displays a further dimension of his understanding—a profound psychological insight. Few of the book's readers, even today, can believe that this tale of fear and courage in the Civil War was written by a man born six years after it was over, who never saw war until after it was published. Crane's lucid style and uncanny sense for the telling detail inform some of the best stories written in America, such as *The Open Boat* and *The Blue Hotel.*

His poems, which found no audience during his lifetime, are at the vanguard of modern American poetry. These unrhymed verses in a variety of experimental meters betray an intellect of almost feminine sensitivity ruthlessly determined that poetry should be not merely a pretty way of uttering commonplaces, but a vehicle for expressing inmost convictions and deepest impressions.

CRÈVECOEUR, MICHAEL GUILLAUME ST. JEAN DE (J. HECTOR ST. JOHN, PSEUD.)

Nothing is known about the life of Michael Guillaume St. Jean de Crèvecoeur before 1764, except that he was born in France on January 31, 1735. It is likely that he was the Crèvecoeur who is recorded as having served under

Montcalm in Canada and explored the western regions as surveyor and map-maker for the French. If he were, it is understandable why he would want to hide the facts when, in 1764, he became a British subject in the American colonies, and anglicized his name. In that year he bought a farm in Orange County, New York, and in 1769 he married Mehetable Tippet, daughter of a Yonkers merchant. It was here that he wrote the *Letters of an American Farmer,* the work for which he is remembered. These lively sketches of American life disclose a profound love of the American landscape, a frank view of colonial society, and a fondness for the homely details of pastoral existence. Perhaps more important, they are an early recognition of the important differences between America and its European heritage, and of the possibility of a unique American culture.

A Tory during the Revolution, Crèvecoeur decided to return to France, setting out in 1780, but unable to cross until after his arrest and release as a spy. He returned in 1783 as French consul, and discovered that his home and farm were destroyed. Meanwhile his book had been translated into French, prompting a disastrous migration of Frenchmen, who, moved by Crève-coeur's description of the beauties of America, settled in the Ohio valley and were massacred by Indians. In 1790, he returned to France, resigning his consul-ship and retiring to Rouen. There he wrote several books in French, and there, on November 12, 1813, he died. None of his French works ever captured the flavor and style of the famous *Letters* and they are not remembered to-day. But in 1922, several more manuscripts in English were discovered, and they had all the charm and honesty of his famous book. They were published in 1925 as *Sketches of 18th Century America.*

DICKINSON, EMILY

The events in the life of Emily Elizabeth Dickinson were few; she never married, she traveled little, and, although now recognized as one of the

From The Life and Letters of Emily Dickinson
by Martha Dickinson Bianchi
(Houghton Mifflin Company)
EMILY DICKINSON

greatest of American poets, she published almost nothing during her lifetime. Most of her life was spent in Amherst, Massachusetts, where she was born on December 10, 1830. Her father, Edward Dickinson, was a prominent lawyer, active in public affairs, who served in the state legislature, in Congress, and as treasurer of Amherst College. He helped young Emily to get more education than women then normally received, first at Amherst Academy, then for one year (1847-48) at Mount Holyoke College for women in nearby South Hadley. There she became friendly with Helen Hunt, a classmate, later Helen Hunt Jackson, author of the well-known romance, *Ramona.* In 1854, while her father was in Congress, Emily traveled to Washington and, during her return, stayed briefly in Philadelphia. Except for occasional trips to Boston and excursions in the area around Amherst, that was the extent of her travels. In the early 60s, she sent off some of her poems to Thomas Wentworth Higginson, a noted literary figure, soliciting his aid in learning the craft of poetry. How serious she was in her request we shall never know, but her careful choice of her best work for this initial letter, and the uncommon shrewdness revealed in her poetry, lead to the conclusion that she more probably sought more confirmation of her obvious talents. Whatever her motive, Higginson was properly bowled over, and began a lifelong correspondence with the young poet. Despite his encouragement, she would not allow any publication of her poems. One was published by the Springfield *Republican* in 1866, where it was sent without Emily's knowledge by her sister; another appeared in *A Masque of Poets,* Helen Hunt Jackson's 1878 anthology, and that was all.

The period of her most prolific, and most significant, writing was 1858 to 1865, but she wrote continuously, if not as much or as well, until her death, arranging her poems in neatly tied packets, like so many dearly remembered love letters or souvenirs. When her father died in 1874 she managed the household, seldom venturing from Amherst. In this quiet way she lived out her days, which came to an end on May 15, 1886.

If her life was uneventful and secluded, her interior consciousness was turbulent and supremely active; it is richly documented in her poems. Despite the popular image of the New England spinster, Emily Dickinson was neither wispy nor waspish. She combined a brilliantly perceptive sensitivity with a fine speculative mentality to achieve a profound metaphysical understanding. Her poetic intuition was faultless, and she was able to communicate deep feelings and thoughts in brief, bold strokes. The invented forms and peculiar rhymes were experimental in their day, but their wholesale adoption into modern prosody testifies to their aptness and permanent validity, which have placed their creator not only in the top ranks of American poets, but in the vanguard of modern poetic expression.

The world would never have had these wonderful poems but for the decision of Emily's sister, Lavinia. Confronted with the legacy of these odd packets of verse, Lavinia decided, in 1890, to essay publication. *Poems* was so unexpectedly successful that it was followed almost immediately by another volume (1891). Further volumes appeared in 1896 and 1914, all collected in *The Complete Poems of Emily Dick-*

inson (1924). Even then, there was more to come; a new volume appeared in 1929.

At first, Lavinia was uncertain of the reception these strange poems might receive, and in the early volumes the poems were "corrected," to conform more with popular notions of versification. Some of the forms were simplified, words changed, rhythms "smoothed." Later poems were subjected to less manipulation—but they were not restored to their original forms until 1955, in the variorum edition of T. H. Johnson, who also arranged them as closely as possible into chronological order and removed the insipid titles that had been attached to some of the untitled verses. From this scholarly restoration, Emily Dickinson's reputation emerged more than ever, one of unassailable greatness.

DREISER, THEODORE

The supreme irony of Theodore Dreiser's life was that recognition of his literary merit was slow in coming among America's readers and critics, but once granted, was heaped on him far in excess of his actual achievement. Early in his career it required considerable daring to defend him against attack; in the later years, unfavorable reviews were written apologetically.

Dreiser was born in Terre Haute, Indiana, on August 27, 1871, and raised in nearby Warsaw. He attended Indiana University briefly, then embarked on a twenty-year journalistic career. He worked as a reporter for newspapers in Chicago and St. Louis, and went to New York in 1894. By 1907 he was editor-in-chief of the Butterick Publications (magazines). His first book, and in some ways his best, was *Sister Carrie* (1900), which was suppressed at the instigation of the publisher's wife before a single copy was sold. For the next few years Dreiser wrote short stories (later collected in *Free, and Other Stories*), but published no novels until his retirement from the magazines in 1910. *Jennie Gerhardt* appeared in 1911; followed by *The Financier* (1912); its sequel, *The Titan* (1914); and a detailed account of the artistic temperament, *The "Genius"*

(1915). Through these books, Dreiser became a leader in the naturalist movement, carrying a penchant for minute detail to often absurd extremes; but the new generation of novelists looked to him for guidance in throwing off the shackles of conventional optimism and sentimentality which bound even the realist Howells. There ensued a stream of dull novels and plays until 1925, when Dreiser finally captured the imagination of America with *An American Tragedy,* a woeful tale of crime induced by poverty and ambition, and peculiarly abetted by the topsy-turvy American social order. Despite Dreiser's characteristically crude style, the book's obvious sincerity, rugged power, and, partially, its supposed luridness, insured its popularity. It was also dramatized and filmed. Dreiser published little in his later years, but his reputation insured the posthumous publication of two late novels, *The Bulwark* (1946) and *The Stoic* (1947). He had never graduated from the tediousness of his style, however, and neither book, despite some excellent characterization and psychological insight, fared well. He died December 28, 1945.

RICHARD EBERHART

EBERHART, RICHARD

Born in Austin, Minnesota, on April 5, 1904, Richard Eberhart was educated at Dartmouth, Cambridge University (St. John's College), and Harvard. In 1930, while working as a tutor to Prajadhipok, King of Siam, he published his first book, *A Bravery of Earth,* a brilliant performance for so young a poet. When the book, *New Signatures,* appeared in London in 1932, Eberhart was the only American poet represented among the new English voices of Spender, Auden, and C. Day Lewis. His early poems, written while he was a teacher at St. Mark's School in Southborough, Massachusetts, were published in *Reading The Spirit* (1936) and *Song and Idea* (1940), and *Poems, New & Selected* (1944). During World War II he served in the Navy, and in the years since has taught at several schools (at Dartmouth since 1956), worked as a business executive and board chairman (continuously since 1946), and has produced several volumes of poems that represent little progress in his characteristic style and motifs. *Undercliff* (1953) collected all his post-war poems to that date. In 1950, he was one of the founders of the Poet's Theater in Cambridge, Massachusetts, and has been a guiding luminary in its activity. His own play, *The Visionary Farms* (1952) has received several experimental productions.

ELIOT, T. S.

For nearly half a century the poems, plays and essays of Thomas Stearns Eliot have exerted an enormous influence on Western literature. He is, in the words of *Life* magazine, "the world's most distinguished poet" and, in 1948, was awarded the Nobel Prize for literature. Born in St. Louis, Missouri, on September 26, 1888, Eliot followed his ancestors (including one, Rev. Andrew Eliot, who had been President there) to Harvard, entering in 1906. Despite his Midwestern rearing, Eliot fitted easily into the Boston of his forebears, and he is remembered by classmates as a brilliant though reticent student, precise in his bearing and seri-

T. S. ELIOT UPI PHOTO

ous in his attitude. While at Harvard he edited the *Advocate* and was a member of both literary clubs, the Stylus and the Signet. He received his B. A. in only three years and one year later, his M. A. Returning to Harvard after a year at the Sorbonne, Eliot worked for his Ph.D. but, although his dissertation was accepted, he never took the degree. A traveling scholarship took him to Germany just before the war, and later that year he was at Oxford. In 1915, Eliot settled permanently in England. During the last years of the war he served as assistant editor of the *Egoist,* and began publishing both poetry and criticism: *Prufrock and Other Observations* (1917) and *Ezra Pound, His Metric and Poetry.* His *Poems* (1919) betrayed his interest in the French symbolists and his criticism (*The Sacred Wood,* 1922, and *Andrew Marvell,* 1922) revealed his preoccupation with the English metaphysical poets. These were synthesized with a profound, almost esoteric involvement with folklore and myth in the influential poem, *The Waste Land* (1922). Voicing the disillusionment of the "lost generation," *The Waste Land,* in a brilliant juxtaposition of evocative quotation and stunningly eloquent snatches of original verse, depicted the deterioration and sterility of the post-war world. Its theme was echoed again and again in contemporary writing, but perhaps farther reaching was the influence of its style and form. The insistence on the cadence

of everyday speech continues to affect the writing of poetry today, while the emphasis on allusion and contrast by juxtaposition have become normal modes not only in writing, but in all the arts. He died January 4, 1965 in his London home.

EMERSON, RALPH WALDO

Born in Boston on May 25, 1803, Ralph Waldo Emerson relied on his aunt, Mary Moody Emerson, for help and guidance in his boyhood struggle for education. His mother, widowed in 1811 with six children under ten, was hardly able to provide for them, but with the help of "Aunt Mary" young Emerson was able to glean from an assortment of tutors and schools enough preparation to enter Harvard when he was fourteen, working his way through as messenger boy to the President. Graduating as class poet in 1817, he was filled with literary ambitions; but necessity drove him to teaching, which he pursued successfully for the next seven years. In 1825 he forsook teaching, determined to make a career of the ministry, despite inner misgivings. He entered Harvard's divinity school that year, but ill health soon forced him to leave, and in the next few years he alternated occasional preaching with convalescence. The Second Church of Boston offered him a post in 1829, and soon thereafter he was in full charge. That same year Emerson married Ellen Tucker, a delicate consumptive who died less than two years later.

RALPH WALDO EMERSON

His ministerial career was quite successful, but Emerson was continually plagued by doubts; in the summer of 1832 he broke finally, not only with his congregation, but with the church. Departing that winter for Europe on a kind of literary pilgrimage, Emerson came in contact with Walter Savage Landor in Italy, met John Stuart Mill and Coleridge in London, visited Wordsworth in the lake country, and, at Craigenputtock in Scotland, began a life-long friendship with Thomas Carlyle.

Upon his return, Emerson went to live with his mother in Concord, Massachusetts, and in 1835, following his marriage to Lydia (later Lidian) Jackson, bought a house of his own, which was his residence until his death. He gave lectures and occasional sermons to earn a living, and began to meet with a circle of friends who were soon to become known as "the Transcendentalists"; Margaret Fuller, H. D. Thoreau, Nathaniel Hawthorne, A. Bronson Alcott, Jones Very. In 1836 he published his first book, *Nature,* which found only a small, but very select audience. As Emerson's reputation grew, interest in his lectures increased. Harvard invited him to deliver the Phi Beta Kappa oration in the summer of 1837, and Emerson responded with *The American Scholar,* an eloquent appeal for courage and action among American thinkers, for final freedom from the tyranny of European ideas, for the beginning of a new era. This revolutionary address was followed the next year by an address to the graduating class of Divinity College, Cambridge, which shocked polite Boston society and set New England on its ear. Calling the church dead and hopeless, he informed the young divines that they would have to undergo considerable awakening before they could touch the living world. He urged the graduating class to find a new revelation, appropriate to a new era, declaring that the institutions of the church were helpless to achieve salvation, and that only through the individual soul was regeneration possible.

This idea was the core of his philosophy, which he developed in essays, poems, and lectures over the next two decades. Basically, Emerson believed that through his own soul each man was able to participate in an experience of God (or the Over-Soul), of which nature is the material embodiment. Thus, natural law and moral law are parallel expressions of the operation of the Over-Soul, and intuitive insight can attune men's minds to divine will, thus achieving perfection. Emerson never systematized this complex philosophy, but the above simplification does more damage to its tone than to its content. For the force of Emerson's writing and his influence lies not in a system of ideas, but in a *way* of thinking, and in the almost telegraphic style in which it is expressed. Emerson was the master of the pithy sentence, the comprehending paragraph. But frequently his essays seem merely a hodge-podge of brilliant paragraphs strung together without apparent scheme.

His poems, despite frequent lapses of diction and a tendency to didacticism, are easily as great a monument to his achievement as his prose writings. Uncommitted to European conventions and willing to use homely images and colloquial language, Emerson in his best poems sounds strangely modern, even today.

As a continuing influence, he is notable not only for his central position in the best writing of his time—his friendship, for example, with Hawthorne and Thoreau, or his encouragement of Whitman—but also for his vision of an indigenous American literature devoted to the dynamic energy of the American experience which he regarded as a force that could free American letters from its European bondage.

In the two decades preceding the Civil War, his fame burgeoned, his influence spread, and his lecture circuits widened in scope, extending into the West. Emerson managed to evade the more far-fetched schemes that sprang up under his influence, such as Brook Farm and Fruitlands, but he was vocal in his objections to slavery. He began to collect his essays and lectures into published volumes, notably *Essays—Second Series* (1844), *Representative Men* (1850), and *English Traits* (1856). Following 1860, Emerson declined slowly into the senility which marked his old age, and on April 27, 1882, he died.

FARRELL, JAMES T.

The poverty-ridden Irish Catholic neighborhoods in which he was reared are the dismal settings of Chicago-born James Thomas Farrell's best fiction. He seems in his writing to be seeking a wider perspective than the stultifying confines of this oppressive environment permit. Born on February 27, 1904, Farrell was educated in parochial schools, followed by three years at the University of Chicago, until 1929. To support himself when he began writing he held a variety of jobs, including filling station attendant and Railway Express clerk. In 1932 *Young Lonigan* was published. This unflinching naturalistic account of boyhood on city streets was followed by *The Young Manhood of Studs Lonigan* (1934) and *Judgment Day* (1935), forming the *Studs Lonigan* trilogy that appeared in a single volume in 1935. The entire work, tracing the failure of its hero's growth and his development into a malformed maturity forms a sensitive, subtle indictment of the failure of the American dream in the depression years. The later tetralogy on Danny O'Neill, using some of the same settings and characters as the Lonigan books, was neither artistically nor commercially so successful. *A World I Never Made* (1936), *No Star Is Lost* (1938), *Father and Son* (1940), and *My Days Of Anger* (1943) although important as documents in the history of American naturalistic novel, fail to maintain the interest and feeling evoked in the Lonigan books, partially because they verbosely repeat materials more succinctly stated earlier, partly because they tend toward an optimism unwarranted by the facts of the situation and compromise the forthright honesty of the earlier work.

With the completion of the O'Neill tetralogy, Farrell seemed to have written himself out as a novelist. The continued excellence of his many short stories was unmatched in the longer work, and neither *Bernard Clare* (1946) nor its sequel, *The Road Between* (1949), met with success. Always a cogent spokesman for the kind of social realism which his own works best represent, Farrell has in recent years emerged as a notable critic. He early denied that Marxism could determine adequate literary standards, thus bewildering many of his left-wing admirers, who had seen his work as documents of Marxist realism. Farrell's criticism has been collected in *The League of Frightened Philistines* (1945), *Literature and Morality* (1947), and *Reflections at Fifty and Other Essays* (1954).

WILLIAM FAULKNER

FAULKNER, WILLIAM

Through a series of novels marked by violence, guilt, terror, and sexuality, William Faulkner has constructed an elaborate, involved modern epic that has earned him a reputation as one of this century's greatest writers.

Born in New Albany, Mississippi, on September 25, 1897, Faulkner has resided most of his life in Oxford, the hub of Lafayette County and location of the University of Mississippi. Following a stint with the Royal Air Force during World War I, Faulkner attended the University, then traveled in various parts of the South. His first book, a volume of poems, appeared in 1924 and two years later, prompted by Sherwood Anderson, whom he met in New Orleans, Faulkner published *Soldier's Pay*. His novels and short stories since then have won him increasing respect, despite occasional lapses into mediocrity. In *Sartoris* (1929), he began his great saga of the decline of the Southern ideal, and the rise of the evil Snopes family in mythical Yoknapatawpha County (closely resembling Lafayette County). Many of his novels are experimental in form, the most interesting being *The Sound and The Fury*, in which a family's history is related through the consciousness of several of its members, one section representing the weirdly disjointed mentality of an idiot. Other new techniques often create exciting, bizarre effects in his novels: stories move backward chronologically, from the present into the past; sometimes two disconnected stories are carried on simultaneously; and occasionally he drops hints in different parts of the narrative, relative to an event which is never explicitly described. This results in a frequently baffling, but always absorbing style, although Faulkner's habit of stretching a single sentence to a length of several pages has met with criticism. Opinion differs as to which of Faulkner's books are most successful. *Sanctuary* (1931), for example, was written, in Faulkner's frank admission, as a deliberate "shocker." Some critics have condemned its obvious sensationalism, but others have seen in it an allegory of contemporary moral decay. Its sequel, *Requiem For A Nun* (1951) helped integrate it into the totality of Faulkner's work. There is little disagreement that *Light in August* (1932), a tale of miscegenation and guilt, is a masterpiece; *The Hamlet* (1940), first of a three-part study of the Snopes ascendancy (*The Mansion*, 1959, and *The Town*, 1960, complete the cycle), is praised by some critics; and the allegorical novel, *A Fable* (Pulitzer Prize, 1954), has been called his greatest work. Other books include *As I Lay Dying* (1930), the twin novel, *The Wild Palms* (interwoven with *The Old Man*, 1939), and *Intruder In The Dust* (1948).

In 1949, Faulkner was awarded the Nobel Prize. In his Stockholm acceptance speech he defined the literary artist's subject matter as "the human heart in conflict with itself." The total effect of Faulkner's work is the extension of that conflict into the fiber of society. His characteristic violence and eruption of chaos reflect the socially corrosive effect of individual conflict. Haunted by the power of evil, he has cast its dark shadow across the hearts of his characters, showing how it lurks there, ready to spring into general corruption, and warns of ultimate decay. He died July 6, 1962 in Oxford, Miss.

FEARING, KENNETH

Poet-novelist Kenneth Flexner Fearing was born on July 28, 1902, in Oak Park, Illinois, where he was raised and received his early education. Following his graduation from the University of Wisconsin in 1924, he went to New York to work as a free-lance editor and press agent. Beginning with *Angel Arms* (1929), Fearing has published a steady stream of poems remarkable for their concision and their attention to the more bizarre and lugubrious aspects of modern life. They form a sort of cumulative satiric threnody. *Angel Arms* was followed by *Poems* (1935), *Dead Reckoning* (1938), *Collected Poems* (1940), *Afternoon of a Pawnbroker* (1943), and *Stranger At Coney Island* (1949). A collection of the best of these, *Selected Poems*, was published in 1956.

As a novelist, Fearing has specialized in the psychological mystery story, elevating that form to genuine significance. At his best, as in *Dagger in the Mind* (1941) and *The Big Clock* (1946), a startling tale in which the victim of the hero's pursuit is himself, Fearing has transformed the genre into an exciting vehicle for acid comment on the condition of man in contemporary society. His most recent novels are *The Loneliest Girl in the World* (1951) and *The Generous Heart* (1954). He died June 26, 1961 in New York City.

FLETCHER, JOHN GOULD

As a leading figure of the Imagist movement, John Gould Fletcher was a highly-rated poet when the movement was in vogue. He was born in Little Rock, Arkansas, on January 3, 1886, gifted with a tragically delicate sensibility. His early years were marked by restlessness when away from the Southern scene in which he was reared. In the years following World War I, his most successful Imagist experiments were published in *Goblins and Pagodas* (1916), *Japanese Prints* (1918), and *Preludes and Symphonies* (1922). As these titles indicate, he was greatly influenced by Oriental art, and by musical forms. His poems also revealed a preoccupation with the phenomenon of color. His best work was collected in *Selected Poems* (1938). *Burning Mountain* (1946) indicated, finally, a breaking-away from the confining vision and form that animated his earlier poems, and gave promise of a new and vigorous maturity. The promise was never fulfilled: on May 10, 1950, he was found drowned in a pool near his home, an apparent suicide.

FRANKLIN, BENJAMIN

The remarkable versatility of Benjamin Franklin is a commonplace of history. Taken with his other formidable achievements, his literary accomplishments seem almost incidental; yet they remain an important aspect of this eighteenth-century genius.

Franklin was born in Boston on January 17, 1706, a chandler's son, but was himself a printer by trade, having been apprenticed at the age of 11. Following an unsuccessful move to New York, he went to Philadelphia; he arrived penniless, but soon became a leading citizen. His publication, *Poor Richard's Almanack*, gave currency to his wise and witty aphorisms, which were published in book form in *The Way of Wealth* (1758). Franklin's non-literary accomplishments are world famous: he proved the identity of lightning and electricity; he invented bifocals; he founded Philadelphia's first fire company; he originated a number of institutions, including the circulating library, the University of Pennsylvania, and the *Saturday Evening Post;* he was a leading statesman, active in the framing of the Pennsylvania Constitution and the Declaration of Independence; and was a highly respected and successful ambassador to France during the Revolution.

In his writings, Franklin was a sympathetic defender of the American Indian (*Remarks Concerning the Savages of North America*, 1784); a prophetic opponent of colonialist tyranny (*Rules By Which A Great Empire May Be Reduced To A Small One*, 1773); and a witty enemy of slavery (*On The Slave Trade*, 1790).

His best-known book, the *Autobiography*, was begun in 1771, and covered only the first fifty years of his long life. Written with characteristic vitality and warm humor, and emphasizing the pragmatic "get ahead" philosophy that was his guide, the book still makes for fascinating reading. Franklin died on April 17, 1790.

PHILIP FRENEAU

FRENEAU, PHILIP

Philip Morin Freneau was born on January 2, 1752, into a New York family of established wealth and position. Well-tutored in youth, he entered the College of New Jersey (later Princeton) as a sophomore when he was only fifteen. Upon his graduation, unsettled as to a career, Freneau turned to writing, an activity which increased in intensity as the Revolution got underway. A dedicated democrat, he devoted most of his skills to anti-Tory and anti-British satire; as a journalist in the early days of the United States he spoke out against Federalism, which he believed would lead to monarchy. Beginning in the 1770s with a voyage to the West Indies, Freneau developed a passion for the sea that was to stay with him most of his life. He alternated journalism with seagoing until very late in his long life.

Meanwhile, he was continually engaged in the writing of poetry. Despite the lack of an audience in those hectic early days, Freneau produced volumes of verse, much of it notably on indigenous themes, like "The Indian Burying-Ground" and "To the Memory of the Brave Americans." He was an American poet in the age before "American literature" began, although he lived to witness those beginnings in the early careers of Irving, Cooper, and Bryant. Freneau died at the age of 80 on December 19, 1832, when he lost his way in a blizzard on his way home from a country store.

ROBERT FROST

FROST, ROBERT

Among modern American poets, Robert Lee Frost is indeed a rare, anomalous figure. In an age of excited, often drastic, experimentation, he has clung to traditional forms and meters, giving them new vitality. In an era when poets have lost their audience, he has developed a widespread, often worshipful, popularity. In a century whose poetry is peppered with scholarly allusions and obscure metaphors, his is clear, colloquial, almost extravagantly simple.

Although easily identified as a New England poet, with roots deep in its soil, Frost was born on March 25, 1874, in San Francisco, and his work was first published in England. Dissatisfied with the education he was receiving at Dartmouth, he left abruptly, never to return. The ensuing years were filled with toil. For a while he taught in a country school, then edited a country weekly. He found work as a cobbler, a millhand, and for eleven years worked a farm in New Hampshire. Then one day, at his wife's prompting, he left for England, settling in Beaconsfield. There, in 1913, his first book, *A Boy's Will*, was published. *North of Boston* (1914) followed, and in 1915 he returned to the United States in triumph. He settled again in New England, gradually acquiring several farms, and continued writing. Frost has been the object of an ever-growing chorus of praise, and the recipient of innumerable honors and prizes. (He has been awarded the Pulitzer Prize four times.) His books include *Mountain Interval* (1916), *New Hampshire* (1923), *West-Running Brook* (1928), *A Further Range* (1936), *The Witness Tree* (1942), *Collected Poems* (1949), and *Aforesaid* (1954).

Several of Frost's poems have become so popular, and are so often quoted, that they have begun to seem cliché. *Mending Wall, The Road Not Taken, Stopping By Woods On a Snowy Evening, Birches,* because they strike a responsive chord in such a mass of readers, are often taken to be simple-minded, sentimental verses. But the poems are far more complex than they seem on the surface, and they often elude explication by ablest critics. His ability to communicate so immediately, directly, and concretely, while his meaning remains puzzlingly intricate, giving each poem a perpetual freshness, is a token of a mastery that borders on wizardry.

If critics find his work totally Yankee, it is because the poems communicate toughness and pessimism laced with dry humor and an unlabored naturalness, the characteristic Yankee mode. Frost has worked wonders with the dialogue poem, notably in *Death of the Hired Man*, and with folklore, as in *The Witch of Coos*. His more expansive mood was tapped by John F. Kennedy at the presidential inauguration in 1961, when Frost recited *The Gift Outright*, with one line changed in tribute to the "New Frontier." He died on January 29, 1963 in Boston, Mass.

GARLAND, HAMLIN

Hannibal Hamlin Garland was born on September 14, 1860, in the midst of a presidential campaign, and was named for Lincoln's running mate. When he was young, his family moved from his birthplace near West Salem, Wisconsin, to Iowa, where Garland was raised. The chinch bug drove them from adversity in Iowa to adversity in the Dakota Territory, culminating in Garland's resolution to reverse the direction of movement in an effort to reverse the family fortunes. To some extent, he was successful. When he went east, Garland became a friend and admirer of William Dean Howells, who urged the young adventurer to write. The first fruits were a series of sketches, in fictional form, based on his experiences in the Midwest, collected in 1891 in *Main-Travelled Roads*, his first and best book. Thereafter, Garland became an ardent social reformer, casting his ideas in a sequence of novels, stories, and essays that have little literary merit, despite their historical interest. In 1913, looking back on two decades of ineffectual literary effort, Garland considered himself a failure, but triumph awaited him. In that year he began his richly evocative and popular autobiography, *A Son of The Middle Border*. Its enthusiastic reception inspired him to write a series of sequels, produced over the next 12 years. A *Daughter of the Middle Border* (1921), which won a Pulitzer Prize; *Trailmakers of the Middle Border* (1926); and *Back-Trailers of the Middle Border* (1928). None of the sequels, however, matched the literary distinction of the original. In 1929 Garland moved to Los Angeles to live with his daughter; there he remained, writing—and nothing of note—until his death on March 4, 1940.

HALL, DONALD

The young poet and critic, Donald Hall, was born in 1928 in New Haven, Connecticut. He was educated at Harvard, where he exhibited an early talent for poetry, and won several prizes for his writing and translation. A Henry Fellow, he voyaged to Oxford, where his poem *Exile* also received an award. Upon his return to the United States, Hall spent three years at Harvard as a Junior Fellow, during which time his first book, *Exiles and Marriages* (1955), appeared. In 1957 he began his present tenure as a professor of English at the University of Michigan, and the following year published a new volume of poems, *Dark Houses*. A vigorous new voice in American poetry himself, Hall has been ready to promote new writing in America at every opportunity, and many of his critical essays are devoted to the younger poets. Together with Robert Pack and Louis Simpson, he edited *New Poets in England and America*. In 1961 he published a personal narrative, *String Too Short To Be Saved*.

HARTE, BRET

Francis Brett Harte was born at Albany, New York, August 25, 1836. His early childhood was interrupted by frequent changes of residence as his father vainly tried to support the family by various scholarly pursuits. At thirteen the boy had to end his own sketchy schooling in order to go to work. Yet he had already read avidly in his father's library—especially the works of Charles Dickens—and, at eleven, two years after his father's death, he had published a poem in the *New York Sunday Morning Atlas*.

In 1854 Harte went to California.

He worked at various jobs for seven years while contributing prose and verse to newspapers. During this time he obtained, often indirectly, the knowledge of life in California mining country that he later exploited so fruitfully in his stories. During the next seven years, now in San Francisco, he acquired considerable literary reputation, thanks in part to the patronage of Jessie Benton Frémont. It was only in 1868, however, with his regular contributions to the new *Overland Monthly,* that he discovered the literary medium that was to win him wide fame: the short story set in the Far West, filled with colorful characters, and treated with humor and pathos in the manner of his favorite author, Dickens.

The celebrity he achieved in the next three years with *The Luck of Roaring Camp, The Outcasts of Poker Flat,* the comic poem about the "Heathen Chinee," and other productions in the same vein lured him to the East. There the *Atlantic Monthly* offered him $10,000 for his literary output for the coming year. For a short time he was popular on the lecture platform and lionized in the salon—but from the day he abandoned the West, he never again wrote a truly successful work. Several collections of his short stories, an attempt at the novel *(Gabriel Conroy)* and two at the drama (including *Ah Sin,* written with Mark Twain about Harte's most famous character) received at best only moderate approval.

In serious financial straits, Harte accepted in 1878 a consulship at Crefeld, Prussia, and later one at Glasgow, which he kept until 1885. In England he found his fame still bright. He lived there until his death on May 5, 1902, but succeeded in producing nothing more than tired variations on his familiar California sketches.

Except in his final years, Harte was a painstaking writer; but his subject matter and his intellectual grasp of life were so limited that his original notion of applying a Dickensian technique to a new setting soon degenerated into a pat and monotonous formula.

NATHANIEL HAWTHORNE

HAWTHORNÈ, NATHANIEL

Nathaniel Hawthorne was born in Salem, Massachusetts, on July 4, 1804. His father died only four years later, leaving the family in financial peril that finally forced his mother to move to a lonely farm in Raymond, Maine. There the youth cultivated an early predilection for solitude. In 1825 he graduated from Bowdoin College, where he formed several friendships that were to prove important in later years. He returned to Salem and led a secluded life, devoting himself to the reading of Augustan writers, wild romances, and New England history, and to his own writing. *Fanshawe,* his first novel, a slight tale of college life, was published anonymously in 1828 and found few readers. In the years following, Hawthorne supported himself by contributing stories and sketches to several magazines, collected in *Twice-Told Tales* (1837), the first intimations of the literary genius that was yet to blossom fully.

In 1839, through a Bowdoin classmate, the historian George Bancroft, Hawthorne secured a post at the Boston Custom House, where he worked for two years. Following his return to Salem, he joined briefly the idealistic colony at Brook Farm, but in 1842 he married and moved to Concord, Massachusetts. A second volume of *Twice-Told Tales* appeared in 1845, and in 1850 he published more stories in *Mosses From An Old Manse*. By this time, Hawthorne's style had fully matured, and his incisive perception of the residence of good and evil in the human heart had already received eloquent expression in some of his shorter tales. He turned now to the full-length romance, and with a burst of creative energy produced in rapid succession *The Scarlet Letter* (1850), *The House of the Seven Gables* (1851), *The Blithedale Romance* (1852), and *The Snow-Image* (short stories, 1852).

In *The Scarlet Letter*, a familiar classic of American fiction, Hawthorne's preoccupation with New England history bore its richest fruit. Deeply aware that the Puritan tradition had deteriorated from its original profound spirituality into pseudo-moralistic materialism, and possibly haunted by the knowledge that a remote ancestor, Captain Hathorne, had participated in the Salem witch-burnings, Hawthorne sought in the archives and histories of 17th century New England the secret of the surrender of goodness to the forces of evil. The decay of the Puritan tradition served as a historical analogy to the everyday mystery of the confrontation of evil in the labyrinthine human heart.

The Bay Colony setting serves as background for many of Hawthorne's shorter tales, like *Young Goodman Brown*, *The Gentle Boy*, and *The Maypole of Merry Mount*. But the sustained atmosphere in *The Scarlet Letter* is a triumph of style and artistic imagination. Despite its complex symbolism and virtually cosmic allegory, its distant setting and ambiguous tone, this tale of sin and redemption strikes the reader immediately with the clarity of its psychological insight and its movement toward comprehensible truth.

The House of the Seven Gables has a more contemporary setting, but one visited with a curse from that earlier era. It is a simple tale of love and death with sombre, symbolic overtones. Again, structure and style triumph, and *The House* vies with *The Scarlet Letter* for the rank of Hawthorne's finest work. In *The Blithedale Romance* he turned to his experiences at Brook Farm for story and setting; but the theme remained the same — the hidden recesses of evil in the human heart — and the book is best understood in the context of his other work.

In 1852, Hawthorne wrote a campaign biography of his friend and Bowdoin classmate, Franklin Pierce. With the election of Pierce to the presidency, Hawthorne was rewarded with an appointment as consul at Liverpool, where he lived until 1857. The following year he traveled in Italy for his health, and there gathered material for his last novel, *The Marble Faun* (1860). Upon his return to the United States he wrote a series of sketches on life in England, collected in *Our Old Home* (1863). When he died on May 18, 1864, he left unfinished two novels that were later published in their incompleted form: *Dr. Grimshawe's Secret* and *Septimius Felton*. If these works demonstrated a decline in his powers, the publication of his notebooks by his widow revealed a more practiced eye and skilled pen than even his impressive published works disclosed, and gave final testimony to the greatness of his legacy.

HEMINGWAY, ERNEST

Nick Adams, Jake Barnes, Lieutenant Henry, Robert Jordan: to many Americans these ambiguous heroes are as familiar as next-door neighbors. They are fictional creations of Ernest Hemingway, one of the most popular, influential, and significant writers of this century.

Hemingway was born in Oak Park, Illinois, on July 21, 1899. Educated in the Oak Park public schools, he went to work for papers in the Midwest and Canada; drifted to Europe, where he worked as a war correspondent; and then settled in Paris. Here he began his serious writing, largely under the tutelage of Gertrude Stein. His first published work, *Three Stories and Ten Poems*, appeared in 1923. *In Our Time*

A. E. HOTCHNER

ERNEST HEMINGWAY

(1924), a loosely connected cycle of short stories was the first of his books published in America. In 1926, two books appeared: *The Torrents of Spring,* a satire parodying Sherwood Anderson; and *The Sun Also Rises,* which gave currency to Gertrude Stein's epithet, "lost generation," and provided a vivid and permanent portrait of its *mores.* The book also made Hemingway's widely imitated style the language of fiction for a generation and more. *Men Without Women,* more short stories, appeared in 1927, and two years later his most famous novel, *A Farewell To Arms.* By this time, Hemingway was recognized as a leading writer of his generation, from whose works a pattern of themes and ideas emerged. His style carried most of it: a tough, hard-boiled, mannered simplicity and directness that evaded moral judgment, conveyed physical rather than intellectual activity, and penetrated to the core of reality in swift, sure strokes. His heroes serve as unflinching mirrors in a world of brutal facts. Hemingway's preoccupation with unreflective physical courage has received more discussion than its appearance in his work would warrant, largely because the author and the legend surrounding him are inevitably linked with his writing. His passion for bullfighting (discussed in *Death In The Afternoon,* 1932,) and for big-game hunting (*The Green Hills of Africa,* 1935) have done much to exaggerate the importance of this aspect of his writings; but it figures importantly in *The Sun Also Rises,* and is the basic theme of *The Snows of Kilimanjaro, The Short Happy Life of Francis Macomber* (short stories), and, in the last analysis, of *For Whom The Bell Tolls* (1940).

During the Second World War, Hemingway was again a war correspondent, and was rumored to have taken a more active part in the fighting than correspondents are allowed by law. A government investigation cleared him of any breach of the Geneva Convention, but the award of a Bronze Star reopened suspicions. Like his heroes, Hemingway maintained a shrewd silence.

Aften ten years without publication, the long-awaited *Across The River and Into The Trees* (1950) appeared, but was received with universal disappointment. The book reads like a parody of Hemingway, and its faulty style and structure led many critics to conclude that the master had lost his touch. *The Old Man and The Sea* (1952) dispelled that premature judgment and was acclaimed everywhere. The book won Hemingway a long overdue Pulitzer Prize and, in 1954, the Nobel Prize for Literature.

After the publication of *The Old Man and the Sea* Hemingway lived for a time in Cuba, deep-sea fishing and battling the nemesis of all worshipers of physicality, age. He made occasional safaris, and in 1954, when he was believed dead following an air crash in Africa, he emerged from the jungle, bruised but visibly unshaken, out-Hemingwaying Hemingway. After 1958 he made his home in Ketchum, Idaho, where he died on July 2, 1961, of a self-inflicted shotgun wound. He had been undergoing treatment for hypertension and was reportedly concerned about his health.

HERNE, JAMES A.

James Ahern was born in Cohoes, New York, on the first of February, 1839, and changed his name when he embarked on his stage career twenty years later. Securing his first acting job by buying into a barnstorming company with his life savings of $165, Herne soon displayed the natural acting ability which was to develop into one of the best-known talents of his day. The first twenty years of his career were spent in travel, as was normal for theatrical folk, but despite his increasing competence and fame, Herne was dissatisfied with his achievements. In the mid-70's, while managing the Grand Opera House in New York, he decided to try his hand in San Francisco, and became stage director at the Baldwin Theatre. In 1878 he met and married Katherine Corcoran, who prompted him to write, and also became friends with the young stage manager David Belasco, with whom he collaborated on his first effort, *Hearts of Oak*. The play was a departure from the usual mode of its time, playing down melodrama and accenting realism. With Herne and his wife in the lead roles, *Hearts of Oak* was a success in its Baldwin Theatre opening, and subsequently across America. In ensuing years Herne wrote and produced plays of varying success, but his insistence on realism on the stage was influential in the theatrical revolution of the 90s. Herne achieved success again with his best play, *Shore Acres*, which opened in Chicago in 1892, again starring the author and his wife. *Shore Acres* introduced realism to the American stage, even though much of it seems stilted and contrived today. The idea of silence at the end, a scene in which the kitchen is hero, was one of the boldest strokes of Herne's imagination. Herne's other plays, like *The Reverend Griffith Davenport* (1899), a drama of a family torn by conflicting loyalties during the Civil War, or *Sag Harbor* (1899), which returned to the quiet New England of *Shore Acres*, also helped to break new ground. When he died on June 2, 1901,

Herne left a legacy of stage pioneering which made possible the modern American drama.

OLIVER WENDELL HOLMES

HOLMES, OLIVER WENDELL

The distinguished physician, poet, and essayist, Oliver Wendell Holmes, father of the famous jurist, was born in Cambridge, Massachusetts, on August 29, 1809. He was educated at Harvard, where he began by studying law, and later switched to medicine. His earliest poems were written during his Harvard years, and appeared in *The Collegian*, an undergraduate magazine. In 1830, a year following his graduation, Holmes composed the well-known poem *Old Ironsides,* in a successful appeal to prevent the scrapping of the famous frigate, *Constitution.*

He began his medical practice in Boston in 1836, following some years abroad to extend his studies. As a physician his career was easily as distinguished as his literary achievement, coupled with a long tenure (1847-1882) of the chair of anatomy and physiology at Harvard Medical School.

As a writer he could be serious or whimsical, as the mood stirred him. His witty, fanciful poem, *The Deacon's Masterpiece,* is as famous as the serious

Old Ironsides or *The Last Leaf*. His "medicated" novel, *Elsie Venner*, despite its recent revival, is hardly of great distinction; even less so is the dispirited tale, *The Guardian Angel*. But his essays, which began to appear in the *Atlantic Monthly* in 1857, when the magazine was founded, have earned him enduring fame. The most memorable are those connected by the "plot" of the Autocrat speaking to his fellow boarders at breakfast in a Boston boarding house: *The Autocrat of The Breakfast-Table*. Through these essays, Holmes himself became known in social Boston as "the Autocrat," despite the appearance of subsequent volumes in the same vein: *The Professor at The Breakfast-Table*, *The Poet at The Breakfast-Table*, and *Over The Teacups*. Noted not only for their irrepressible charm (in which they rival Lamb's "Elia"), but also for their canny observation of American modes and manners, these essays are marked by a versatile and peculiarly American sensibility. Holmes lived well into his eighties, spanning most of the century, and died on October 7, 1894.

HOWELLS, WILLIAM DEAN

The appellation "the dean of American letters" that attached to William Dean Howells for the last 30 years of his life was not only a pun on his name, but an accurate description of the position in American literary life to which he had risen. Born on March 1, 1837, at Martin's Ferry, Ohio, this son of a migratory journalist had little formal education, never completing more than the grammar school rudiments. Work in his father's printing office from the age of nine, and his father's fondness for writing fostered the boy's interest in books, however; on his own he studied Latin, German and Spanish. His boyhood was spent in a succession of Ohio towns, ending in Columbus, where he worked as reporter and editor on the *Ohio State Journal* from 1856 to 1861. During these years he wrote poems, some of which he published with a friend, John J. Piatt, in *Poems of Two Friends* (1860). Though the volume

was a total failure, five poems were published in the *Atlantic Monthly* and brought him to the attention of the American literary world. For Lincoln's 1860 Presidential campaign Howells wrote a biography which may have favorably influenced the Western states, and for which he was rewarded with an appointment as U. S. consul in Venice, where he stayed until 1865. Upon his return he undertook the journalistic literary career he was to pursue for the rest of his life. He worked at first for the newly founded *Nation*, but a few months later accepted a sub-editorship on the *Atlantic Monthly*. Five years later he was editor-in-chief, a position he held until 1885. From 1886 to 1891 he wrote a regular column for *Harper's Monthly*, "The Editor's Study," and the following year he edited the *Cosmopolitan Magazine*. He returned in 1900 to *Harper's*, where his "Easy Chair" column appeared until his death on May 11, 1920.

His high and respected position on America's leading literary magazines gave Howells a sounding board for his Tolstoy-influenced theory of realism in fiction. Briefly, Howells believed in the literary value of "real life," a dictum which helped to change the direction of American fiction from the romantic to the almost photographic reproduction of everyday life. Although he ultimately disapproved of the pessimistic turn this new fiction took, he was instrumental in bringing recognition to such writers as Henry James, Stephen Crane, and even Frank Norris.

Howells' own fiction was never entirely free, however, from romantic tendencies; in his best novels the blend of romanticism and realism accounts, to some extent, for their excellence. The recurring theme of Howells' work is the social confrontation of sophistication and innocence. In his early work, the theme appears in a series of comedies of manners, beginning with *Their Wedding Journey* (1872), more a travel sketch than a novel. With the appearance of *A Modern Instance* (1882) Howells showed himself a knowing and masterly delineator of the "real" American with this portrait of a disintegrating marriage, achieved with a wealth of realistic detail. His best-known novels quickly followed: *The Rise of Silas Lapham* (1885), which remains the classic depiction of the entry of the *nouveau riche* into cultured society; and a mellow romance of middle age, *Indian Summer* (1886). At about this time, Howells became a convinced Socialist, and the class struggle, a variation on his main theme, became the focus of his next ten novels. A *Hazard of New Fortunes* (1890) is probably the best of them, with its description of wealth and poverty, the literary life, and street-car strikes in New York; the Utopian *A Traveler from Altruria* (1894) is the most uncharacteristic, but perhaps the most curious and interesting. His final novel, *The Vacation of the Kelwyns* (1920) returns to a pastoral New England, and to the basic theme of innocence contrasted with sophistication.

At the end of his life, Howells found himself attacked by the new generation of American writers. He had written more than 50 volumes, including novels, short stories, unproduced plays, criticism, travel notes and autobiography. He lived to see his social ideas and literary ideals belittled by a generation that did not understand that it was Howells himself who created the receptive public and literary climate that made their writing possible. His narrow and orthodox taste and morality have been supplanted, but his finest writing continues to serve as a voice for his times and a model for new generations. Howells' place in American literature is secure.

IRVING, WASHINGTON

Washington Irving was born in New York on April 3, 1783. An indifferent student, his early education was at best fragmentary, and until 1798, when he entered a law office, it took no serious direction. Under the influence of his brothers he began writing early. In 1802 his brother Peter published the first installment of "The Letters of Jona-

WASHINGTON IRVING

than Oldstyle, Gent." His satires on New York society were beginning to receive favorable attention, but he departed for Europe in 1804, under his brothers' auspices, to mend his failing health. Returning two years later with bulging notebooks and a passion for writing, Irving all but forsook his law practice and embarked on a literary career. For a year the vehicle of his satire was a fortnightly paper called *Salmagundi: or, the Whim-Whams and Opinions of Lancelot Langstaff, Esq.* By this time he was well known in New York as a writer and wit, a reputation confirmed by *A History of New York* (1809) by "Diedrich Knickerbocker," the first great work of American comic literature. For the next six years Irving was engaged in a variety of inconsequential hackwork. In 1815 he set sail for England to work in the family business in Liverpool. The business failed in 1817, and Irving, driven more by necessity than desire, turned again to writing. Meeting Scott that year at Abbotsford, he received much-needed encouragement from one of his literary heroes, and began work on "Rip Van Winkle." For the next two years Irving produced a steady stream of essays, stories, and sketches, published in groups of four and five in New York. In 1820 he collected them in the English edition of *The Sketch Book* under the pseudonym

"Geoffrey Crayon." The book established him immediately in England—the first real recognition from Europe of a possible American culture. In 1822 he published *Bracebridge Hall,* a well-received collection of miscellaneous writing, and later that year departed for the continent. Travel for two years in France and Germany again filled his notebooks, and he returned to England briefly to publish *Tales of a Traveller* (1824). This was not so well received, and Irving departed again for the continent, understandably discouraged. For two years in France he studied Spanish, and in 1826 was invited to the U. S. Embassy in Madrid to undertake a translation of the *Life and Voyages of Columbus.* The next three years in Spain, spent in serious study and careful observation, produced not only the translation (in 1828) but *A Chronicle of the Conquest of Grenada* (1829), and, upon his return to America, *Alhambra* (1832). The remaining years of his life, some of it spent traveling to the American frontier, some in Europe, but most of it at his estate in Tarrytown, New York, were devoted to hackwork. During his final eleven years he worked intermittently on a childhood ambition, a biography of George Washington. He completed the fifth and final volume in 1859, just a few months before his death on November 28.

Washington Irving is best remembered as a pioneer—perhaps the first indigenous American author to achieve international fame—but he is little read today. Possibly the greatest tribute to his accomplishment is the fact that the story of Rip Van Winkle and the legend of Sleepy Hollow are well-known to many Americans who have never read Irving. His art has passed quietly into the American consciousness, firmly embedded in the American heritage.

JAMES, HENRY

Before Henry James, there were a number of great novelists—but to James we owe the first consciousness of the novel as an art form, and the first attempts to codify a theory of the novel. If this critical awareness were all he contributed, James would be always remembered. How much greater is our debt then, for James practiced what he preached, being a consummate novelist, short-story writer, and the virtual creator of the novella in English.

Henry James was born in New York City on April 15, 1843, son of a well-known theologian of the same name, and brother of William James, the famous psychologist and philosopher. He was educated both in New York and abroad and in 1862 entered Harvard Law School. Legal studies, however, interested him little, and he soon began contributing sketches and articles to several magazines, gradually developing the determination to live by his pen. His early stories, dealing mostly with the American scene, drew unreserved praise from a number of critics, but it was not until after he had traveled abroad again, for the first time as an adult, that he felt sufficiently secure to publish his first novel, *Roderick Hudson* (1875), in which his recurring theme of American innocence confronted by European cultivation received its first exposition. Feeling somehow uncomfortable and stifled in his native America, James left for Europe in 1875; in 1876 he settled in England, where he was to live out most of his life.

The American appeared in 1877, and two years later *Daisy Miller* was published. By this time he had earned a considerable international reputation, confirmed with the publication of his early masterpiece, *The Portrait of A Lady.* With this complex, superbly imagined and realized tale of the corruption of American innocence by an evil European influence, sharply depicted through the indestructible character of Isabel Archer, James' first period may be said to have come to an end.

In the latter half of the 80s, James wrote several social novels, notably *The Bostonians, The Princess Casamassima* (1886), and *The Tragic Muse,* which he felt permanently alienated his readers, and he turned to the theater in an effort to regain his audience. Actually, these novels, though limited in popularity during James' day, have endured as some of his finest works, while as a playwright he was a total failure. From 1890 to 1895 he published no long fiction, devoting most of his time to his writing for the stage; but it was during this period that he produced some of his best short stories, many of them covertly autobiographical, dealing with artists misunderstood by their public. James terminated his theatrical career following the fiasco of *Guy Domville* (1895), which was hooted from the stage in its first performance. In 1896, he moved to a house in Rye, where he began producing some of his more memorable novellas, foreshadowing the subtle psychological explorations of his later novels, and their tight, unified form. *The Spoils of Poynton* appeared in 1897; that year also saw *What Maisie Knew;* and in 1898, he published *The Turn of The Screw.* James expanded his form in *The Awkward Age* (1899) and *The Sacred Fount* (1901), followed by his last three great novels: *The Wings of the Dove* (1902), *The Ambassadors* (1903), and *The Golden Bowl* (1904). In these last works he paid such close attention to the details of psychological motivation, that he has been attacked for "writing in a social vacuum." Objects and everyday events are closely explored in a cumulative revelation of character and insight into motive that is stunning in its impact.

James was no less skilled as a critic, and is highly regarded for his *French Poets and Novelists* (1878); a biography of Hawthorne, an early and valuable appreciation (1879); *Partial Portraits* (1888); and *Notes on Novelists* (1914). His most valuable criticism, perhaps, was the series of prefaces to his own works, prepared for the collected edition. They were gathered by R. P. Blackmur and printed as *The Art of The Novel* in 1949. His travel books include *A Little Tour In France* (1885) and *The American Scene* (1905).

James became a British subject in July, 1915, to show his sympathy with the English people in World War I. For some years he was engaged in writing several volumes of autobiography, publishing *A Small Boy and Others* and *Notes of a Son and Brother. The Middle Years* was left uncompleted at his death, on February 28, 1916.

JARRELL, RANDALL

Like many of the poets of his generation, Randall Jarrell has pursued an academic career. He was born in Nashville, Tennessee, on May 16, 1914, and was educated at Vanderbilt University. In the pre-war years he taught at Kenyon College (1937-39) and the University of Texas (1939-42), publishing poems in a number of literary magazines. These were collected in his first book, *Blood For A Stranger* (1942). Following the war, a Guggenheim Fellowship (1946) enabled him to concentrate on his writing, resulting in *Losses* (1948), a book which gave a taut, lyrical voice to the hopes and frustrations of the post-war generation. Since 1947 Jarrell has taught at the Woman's College of the University of North Carolina. In 1953, he published *Poetry and the Age,* a penetrating analysis of the structure and function of poetry which has become a valuable text for thoughtful critics and students. His novel, *Pictures From an Institution* (1954), is an incisive, satirical view of the literary pretensions of American women's colleges. On March 14, 1961, he received one of the 1960 National Book Awards for his collection of poems, *The Woman at the Washington Zoo.*

JEFFERS, ROBINSON

Although born in the east, in Pittsburgh, Pennsylvania, on January 10, 1887, the poet Robinson Jeffers is usually associated with the West Coast. He was educated there, taking his degree at Occidental College in 1905, subsequently studying medicine at the University of Southern California and forestry at the University of Washington. These vain attempts to find a more financially rewarding career than the writing of poetry, to which he was always devoted, ended in 1914, when a small

UPI PHOTO

ROBINSON JEFFERS

legacy provided independent means. On the rugged California coast near Carmel he constructed a house and tower with his own hands out of rock from the cliffside, and there he lived, a virtual hermit. His earliest books, such as *Flagons and Apples* (1912) and *Californians* (1916) found few readers; but, beginning with *Roan Stallion* and *Tamar and Other Poems*, Jeffers developed a larger following. His poems were written "in the grand manner," rhetorical, eloquent, with long lines and rolling rhythms suggestive of dramatic verse. He wrote several works for the stage, including *Dear Judas, The Tower Beyond Tragedy* and the eminently successful *Medea*. Despite Jeffers' taste for Greek tragic themes, critics have found that his work falls short in both scope and feeling of true tragedy. The appeal for him in classical literature seemed to be its intimations of desperate violence and tortured sexuality, which are recurring elements and themes in his work. *The Double Age* (1948) met with a dubious reception, and the suggestion that his skill was at an ebb; but *Hungerfield and Other Poems* (1954), his most recent book, contains some of his finest work, reflecting further growth and maturation of his fine sensibility.

He died January 20, 1962 at Tor House, his Carmel Home.

KOUWENHOVEN, JOHN A.

John A. Kouwenhoven, one of America's foremost students of American culture, was born in Yonkers, New York, on December 13, 1909. He was educated at Wesleyan, where he was graduated in 1931, and at Columbia, receiving his M. A. in 1933. He was a teacher at Columbia until 1939, then for two years taught at Bennington College. In 1941 he became an editor of *Harper's Magazine* for five years. He returned to teaching in 1946, accepting an appointment at Barnard College, but he continued as a contributing editor at *Harper's* until 1953. During the years 1950-54, Professor Kouwenhoven was Chairman of the English department at Barnard. He has written several books, including *Adventures of America* (1938) and *Made in America* (1948). In 1953, for Columbia University's bicentennial, he prepared *A Historical Portrait of New York*.

LANIER, SIDNEY

The life of the Southern poet, Sidney Lanier, was so replete with the trappings of romance, that he seems almost a fictional figure. Born in Macon, Georgia, on February 3, 1842, he showed an early gift and prodigious appreciation for music. As a child he taught himself to play several musical instruments, and so overwhelmed himself with the delights of music that he was frequently transported into a rapturous trance. He entered Oglethorpe College as a sophomore when only 14, and taught there immediately after his graduation. When the Civil War began, he enlisted with the Macon volunteers, and participated in some of the war's severest fighting, nevertheless managing to study French, German, and Spanish in his spare time, and to entertain the troops with his musical virtuosity. Later, he saw service as a blockade runner, was captured, and spent five months in Point Lookout prison. Released in February, 1865, Lanier walked to his home in Macon, arriving exhausted and ill. In his debilitated condition, he contracted tuberculosis, against which he

SIDNEY LANIER

waged a 17-year struggle, not succumbing until September 7, 1881. At first he tried traveling in search of a suitable climate, working at teaching, clerking, and, for a short while, reading and practicing law with his father. But when he realized the hopelessness of combatting poor health with over-exertion, he settled into a more quiet life devoted to music and literature. He published a novel, *Tiger-Lilies* (1867) and *Poems* (1877). An accomplished flutist, he played for many years as first flutist of Baltimore's Peabody Symphony. His lectureship in literature at Johns Hopkins during his last years testifies to his recognized scholarship. Lanier was no less skilled a poet, fashioning exquisite lyrics that reflect his extremely sensitive nature and keen, musical ear. His welcome preoccupation with Southern themes and locales served as an inspiration for succeeding generations of Southern writers.

LINCOLN, ABRAHAM

Abraham Lincoln—born in a log cabin on February 12, 1809, felled by an assassin's bullet, April 15, 1865—is a familiar hero to most Americans. His actual life, mingled with the legends which grew around him, is part of the history of his country. Born in Kentucky, raised in Illinois, "honest Abe" ascended from obscure poverty through self-edu-

cation to the Presidency of the United States. Remembered as "the Great Emancipator" who held the Union together, the "Captain" who navigated the U. S. through bloody civil strife, much storied and sung by great American writers, and many not-so-great, he is seldom thought of as an American literary figure, though many Americans could recite the "Gettysburg Address" from memory. Still, the vast body of his writings and speeches form a monument to his achievements as a prose stylist. A dazzling variety of eloquence, each form suited to the need, is to be found in his speeches and voluminous correspondence. Somber when necessary, funny when suitable, always clear and to the point, his writings reflect the man who captured the American imagination in its moment of crisis and has held it captive since his untimely death.

LINDSAY, VACHEL

Nicholas Vachel Lindsay was born in Springfield, Illinois, on November 10, 1879. Originally intending to enter the ministry, he attended Hiram College in Ohio for three years, but abandoned this to study art, first at the Chicago Art Institute (1900-03) and then at the New York School of Art (1904-05). In 1906, jobless and broke, he set off on his famous walking tour of the South, trading copies of an early poem for room and board. The next four years were spent in lecturing for the YMCA and stumping Illinois as an anti-Salooner. In 1912 he tried a repeat of the Southern trip in the West, aiming for the coast but never getting beyond New Mexico. His first two volumes of poetry, *General William Booth Enters into Heaven* (1913) and *The Congo* (1914) displayed a haunting incantatory power, bardic, almost prophetic, and Lindsay's frequent public appearances chanting them became a popular sensation. The colloquial quality of his poetry, infused with a highly imaginative sense of the dignity of the everyday, seemed to embody the American dream, while its jazzy rhythms captured America's dynamic energy. Lindsay's later years were

marked by a waning of his powers;
when he died by his own hand on December 5, 1931, he was already a legend
of the past. But many of his poems retain their power, and their influence is
evident in the colloquialism of much
modern American poetry and the willingness of present-day poets to explore
the energetic folkways of America.

LONGFELLOW, HENRY WADSWORTH

The popularity of Henry Wadsworth Longfellow in his own day was
unparalleled: in his later years his birthday was publicly celebrated. In contrast,
the twentieth century has been harsh in
its judgments. His easy, often monotonous cadences, his glib morality and
sentimental tone, his glossy treatment of
history, all have felt the unkind cut of
hostile criticism—yet his finest poems
endure, and there is hardly an American
alive who is not familiar with some of
them.

Longfellow was born in Portland,
Maine, on February 27, 1807, the son
of a wealthy and influential Portland
lawyer. He attended Bowdoin College,
where he was a classmate of Hawthorne's, and where he talked and
dreamed of an indigenous American literature, determined to be a contributor
to it himself. Upon his graduation in
1825, the trustees offered him a professorship in modern languages, provided
he travel to Europe to sharpen his linguistic skills. Longfellow was abroad
until 1829, taking up his post on his
return. He married in 1831, but his wife
died four years later, while the couple
were on a European tour. That year his
first book, *Outre-Mer*, a record of his
first trip abroad, was published. In 1836
he went to Harvard as professor of modern languages, a position he held until
his resignation in 1854. He moved into
the famous Craigie House, and when he
was remarried in 1843, to Frances Appleton, the house was bought by her
father as a wedding present.

Meanwhile, Longfellow had made
his reputation as a poet. His first book
of poems, *Voices of the Night* (1839),

**HENRY WADSWORTH
LONGFELLOW**

met with enthusiastic acclaim, preparing
the way for the great success of *Ballads*
in 1841. That book contained some of
his best-remembered short poems: *The
Wreck of the Hesperus, The Village
Blacksmith,* and *Excelsior!*

Poems on Slavery appeared in 1842,
and the following year he published *The
Spanish Student. Evangeline* (1847)
and *Hiawatha* (1855) were translated
into numerous languages and ran
through several editions in France and
Italy; *The Courtship of Miles Standish*
(1858) sold 10,000 copies on its first
day in London. Following the death by
fire of his wife in 1861 (Longfellow was
severely burned in a heroic but unsuccessful attempt to save her), he became
more serious and perhaps too pretentious in his poetry. His translation of the
Divine Comedy introduced Dante to a
large American audience; but his own
Golden Legend, Judas Maccabeus, and
Christus, A Mystery, have few, if any,
saving graces. *The Hanging of the
Crane* (1874) indicated the possibility
that, in later years, he might have wed
his unquestionable skills to his larger
ambitions, a possibility partially confirmed by the manuscript he left unfinished at his death, *Michael Angelo*
(published posthumously, 1883). The
last three years of Longfellow's life were
spent in bed following a nervous collapse, and it is unlikely, had he recov-

ered, that he could have invigorated his declining powers. He died on March 24, 1882, at Craigie House.

LOWELL, AMY

Amy Lowell was born in Brookline, Massachusetts, February 9, 1874, a member of an old and distinguished New England family. She was educated entirely in private schools and frequently traveled abroad, but did not early discover that poetry was her "natural mode of expression"; her first poem was published in the *Atlantic Monthly* in 1910. Her first collection, *A Dome of Many-Coloured Glass*, appeared in 1912. Meeting Ezra Pound in England the following year, she identified herself with the newly developing Imagist School: she became so vocal an adherent that Pound later said the movement should be called "Amygism." Her work was strongly affected by her study of French and Oriental poetry. In 1922 she anonymously published *A Critical Fable*, a series of sketches of contemporary poets patterned on *A Fable for Critics* by her cousin James Russell Lowell. She devoted her last years mainly to a biography in two volumes of *John Keats*, 1925. She died May 12, 1925.

In the words of William Rose Benét, "Amy Lowell tended to be celebrated more for her personality than for the artistic value of her work." Arrogant, cigar-smoking, brutally frank, she nevertheless won devoted friends. The best poems in her eleven volumes (mainly written in the free verse she called "unrhymed cadence") are by no means without merit. They have frequently been included in anthologies.

LOWELL, JAMES RUSSELL

"Elmwood," the family home in Cambridge, Massachusetts, was the birthplace and lifelong residence of James Russell Lowell. He was born there on February 22, 1819, the scion of a distinguished Boston family. His father was for 40 years minister of the West Church (Unitarian), but young Lowell showed an early predilection for literature. At Harvard he was elected

class poet (1838), but was barred from reading his poem when he rose and bowed his acknowledgment of the honor in chapel; such behavior was thought unseemly. In 1840, after graduating from Law School, Lowell was engaged to Maria White, and four years later they were married. It is apparent that she was a strong influence upon him, the inspiration for his work. Mrs. Lowell was an abolitionist, and so it is not surprising that his *Poems: First Series* (1844) should contain a number of antislavery verses. Before the marriage, Lowell's work had been largely literary. For a while he published his own magazine, *The Pioneer* (1843), in which his excellent taste is visible in the inclusion of such writers as Poe, Whittier, and Hawthorne; soon after marrying, however, Lowell turned his hand to abolitionist work, writing editorials for the *Pennsylvania Freeman* and editing the *National Anti-Slavery Standard*. The midyear of his marriage marked the peak of his creative career. In one year, 1848, he published *Poems: Second Series, A Fable for Critics*, the first series of *The Biglow Papers*, and *The Vision of Sir Launfal*. In 1853, Maria Lowell was dead. For more than ten years following, he published no books at all. He accepted a professorship in French and Spanish at Harvard in 1855, holding that position until 1886, but this did not mean a retirement from public life. From 1857 to 1861, he was the first editor of the *Atlantic Monthly*. His staunch Republicanism was rewarded in 1877 with a post as minister to Spain. Three years later he was named minister to England, remaining there until 1885. Returning to Cambridge, Lowell retired to "Elmwood," where he died on August 12, 1891. Although he continued writing until his death, he was never able to capture again the spirit his wife had inspired.

LOWELL, ROBERT

Robert Traill Spence Lowell is related to the two other well-known American poets who bear the name of Lowell, and trace in one family the history of

UPI PHOTO

ROBERT LOWELL

poetry in America. In the family tradition, Lowell began his education at Harvard but, at a friend's suggestion, switched to Kenyon College, where his fruitful study with John Crowe Ransom persuaded him to write poetry. Lowell graduated in 1940. During the war, he served a jail sentence as a conscientious objector, and published his first book, *Land of Unlikeness*, in 1944. Most of these same poems were printed, with a number of additional poems, in the Pulitzer Prize-winning volume, *Lord Weary's Castle* (1947). Lowell's style shows Ransom's influence, but his poems reveal an intensely personal vision, intricately bound with a deep religious conviction, that borders on pure mysticism. More recent books are *The Mills of the Kavanaughs* (1951), and *Life Studies* (1959). The more recent poems seem more relaxed and mellower in tone, suggesting greater control of the intellectual faculties over the emotional.

MacLEISH, ARCHIBALD

A unique ability to give voice to the slightly sentimental social consciousness and the expansive, optimistic nationalism of American intellectuals in the 1930s, in a delicate, elliptical style that bore all the earmarks of fine poetry, gave Archibald MacLeish a reputation and critical reception far in excess of his achievement. Ironically, his more re-

cent work, displaying a heightened sensitivity and more incisive intelligence, has met with a reaction among critics that tends to underrate its quality.

MacLeish was born in Glencoe, Illinois, on May 7, 1892, and was educated at Yale, graduating in 1915. An interval of service in France during World War I interrupted his studies at Harvard Law School and may well have disrupted his entire view of his own career; for in 1923, having taken his law degree and practiced for several years, he abruptly gave up his legal work and traveled to France for a five-year sojourn, during which he wrote profusely under the influence of French styles and the newly emerging modes of Eliot and Pound. Earlier poems, published during his law school days betray in their titles their intense, personal content: *Songs for a Summer's Day* (1915) and *Tower of Ivory* (1917). In contrast, his new work proclaimed a more public interest: *Einstein* (1929), *New Found Land* (1930), and *Frescoes For Mr. Rockefeller's City* (1933). *Conquistador* (1932), for which MacLeish was awarded the Pulitzer Prize, is a book-length poem dealing with the conquest of Mexico, inconsistent in style and tone, which tended to wax oratorical on a variety of matters not connected with its subject. The tendency to produce "social documents" in a mystified, precious style reminiscent of, but not necessarily containing, poetry can best be seen in his radio plays, *Fall of The City* (1935) and *Air Raid* (1938). Although failing as poetry, these two works are notable for their attempt to write in verse for mass media, and for their early understanding of the widespread terrors awaiting the world, lurking in the growth of totalitarianism in Europe and compounded by "Democracy's" refusal to recognize the danger. *America Was Promises* (1939) expressed the poet's growing apprehension, and possibly, bitterness, but was mainly in the expansive mood of his earlier work.

MacLeish's increasing pre-occupation with the danger to the American dream posed by contemporary events

ARCHIBALD MacLEISH

UPI PHOTO

impelled him into public service. In 1939, he was named Librarian of Congress; in 1941 he assumed additional duties as director of the U. S. Office of Facts and Figures; when war broke out, his work was tripled by his appointment as assistant director of the Office of War Information. MacLeish resigned all these posts in 1944 to become Secretary of State until the war's end, then served on a number of international commissions until his retirement, in 1948, from public life. During these years his writing was entirely composed of hortatory tracts devoted to his public purposes: *The American Cause* (1941), *A Time to Speak* (1941), *A Time to Act* (1942), and similar books bespoke his urgent dread for America's future and his hope for survival in informed, concerted action. MacLeish's post-war poems, *Act-five* (1948) reverted, however, to more private considerations, and revealed a mature poet in command of his language and with a trenchant view of man's condition. Certainly more pessimistic than his earlier work, these poems nevertheless communicated a more profound understanding, and pointed to human possibilities without resort to propaganda. *Collected Poems* (1952) again won him a Pulitzer Prize, largely on the strength of the new direction he had taken in his later work, and perhaps more deservedly. His most re-

cent work, *J. B.* (1958), a play rendering the story of Job in verse and in a modern setting, again demonstrated the new depths of his understanding and his recognition that man's problems are more than merely political. The play won MacLeish a third Pulitzer Prize and had a successful Broadway run.

MASTERS, EDGAR LEE

Born in Garnett, Kansas, on August 23, 1868, Edgar Lee Masters moved at an early age to Petersburg and later to Lewiston, Illinois, where he was raised. He attended Knox College briefly, but left school to read law in his father's office. In 1891, he was admitted to the bar and took up practice with his father, but the next year he left abruptly for Chicago, where he began his own practice, pursued successfully until 1920. In Chicago he started to write poetry, mostly hackneyed and imitative, but soon began to publish the remarkable poems collected in *Spoon River Anthology* (1915). Conceived as a sequence of epitaphs and death-speeches, *Spoon River* gave voice to a dead past, to the great and the humble of a bygone America. Overnight, Masters was famous, and a few years later resolved to devote himself entirely to writing. Surprisingly, he was never again able to write as well. In the ensuing years, Masters wrote prodigiously—poems once again hackneyed and imitative, bad novels, and several volumes of gossipy, bitter autobiography. His egotism, intransigence, and bad writing endeared him to no one, and despite the homage paid to *Spoon River* as a seminal influence on American poetry, its author was neglected. For many years he lived secluded with his wife in New York's Hotel Chelsea. In 1944 he entered Bellevue Hospital, suffering from pneumonia and malnutrition. Aid poured in from admirers of his early poems and in 1946 the Academy of American Poets paid him belated recognition with an award of $5000. He died on March 5, 1950, in a Philadelphia convalescent home.

MELVILLE, HERMAN

At the beginning of his literary career, Herman Melville was a brilliant success. His books were bought and widely discussed, and he was hailed as an important American author. But as his books became more serious in intent and profound in content, his reputation dwindled, until he entirely disappeared from the literary scene and was almost totally forgotten at the time of his death. Melville's loss of reputation is one of the most colossal failures of judgment in America's reading public, and it is ironic that an America clamoring for an indigenous literature should have thus maltreated one of its greatest practitioners.

Melville was born in New York City on August 1, 1819. Educated briefly at Albany Academy, he was forced to abandon his schooling when his father died in 1831, leaving his mother and her brood of eight destitute. He had no formal education at all after he was fifteen; instead, he attempted several different ways of helping to support the family and, lacking success, ended by signing on the *Highlander,* Liverpool-bound, as a seaman, in 1837. This initial sea voyage seems to have profoundly stirred his imagination, and the experience is recorded in his early novel *Redburn* (1847). After returning to the United States to work briefly as a teacher, Melville could not resist the call of the sea. In 1841 he embarked for the South Seas aboard the *Acushnet,* beginning a three-year adventure that provided the material for all his early writing. The *Acushnet* was a whaler, prototype of the *Pequod* in *Moby Dick* (1851). Melville jumped ship in the Marquesas in 1842, living among the natives in a tropical paradise (*Typee,* his first novel, 1846, and *Mardi,* 1849). When his life seemed endangered, he escaped aboard an Australian whaler, the *Lucy Ann,* and settled for a while in Papeete (*Omoo,* 1847). He returned to America on the frigate *United States* (*White Jacket,* 1850).

The overnight success of *Typee* in 1846 determined Melville on a literary career. Lionized and acclaimed, he little realized that his books were more popular for their exotic settings and romantic incidents than for their literary merit. When, in 1850, he moved to Pittsfield, Massachusetts, to settle on his uncle's farm, he was already well-known, the author of five successful novels. In Pittsfield he met and became close friends with Hawthorne, who had just published *The Scarlet Letter* and was at work on *The House of the Seven Gables.* Just how influential Hawthorne was in regard to Melville's work is conjectural, but it is certain that they discussed and shared views of the value of allegory in literature, the advantage in depth of the romance over the novel, and a profound conviction that evil is a universal element of existence. That year Melville wrote his great epic, *Moby Dick.* Its dark symbolism, intense moral vision, the scope of its allusions, and its infuriatingly meticulous description of whaling and whaling lore puzzled and alienated his public. The book, hailed by Hawthorne and a few other discerning critics, met with only limited success. *Pierre* (1852), denser in style and more obscure in meaning, appealed to an even smaller audience, and when a fire at Harper's in 1853 destroyed the plates of all Melville's published work, it seemed an emblem of the almost total obscurity awaiting him. After *Israel Potter* (1855) had proved both an artistic and commercial failure, he turned to shorter fiction, probably to tap the magazine market. But he could not escape his new-found predilection for symbolic tales of the problem of evil, and magazine readers had no patience for such work as *Bartleby* or *Benito Cereno,* which Melville collected in *Piazza Tales* (1856).

By the time *The Confidence Man* was published in 1857, Melville had lost his audience entirely, and that strange and difficult comic novel could hardly have been expected to restore it. It was the last fiction published during his lifetime. For a few years the author traveled, to San Francisco, to Europe, and to the Holy Land; but in 1863 he moved his family to New York, settling permanently, and, driven by financial necessity, finally accepted a job as Customs inspector (1866-1885). His pen was not altogether stilled. He wrote during these years some of America's finest poetry, which he published privately (*Battle-Pieces* (1866) and *Clarel*, a long philosophical poem based on his Holy Land pilgrimage, 1876). Presumably, he also continued writing fiction, but nothing survives except the manuscript of *Billy Budd*, a beautifully written and extremely moving short novel probably written in his last year. It was found among his papers when he died in New York on September 28, 1891, a virtually forgotten genius, and was published in England in 1924, when a complete edition of his works helped revive interest in his neglected writings. It has also been dramatized.

MENCKEN, H. L.

For half a century, the unpredictably irascible Henry Louis Mencken thumbed his nose at all he found wrong with America and, in his bullying, insulting, ever-popular way, helped educate America to the 20th century.

Mencken was born in Baltimore on September 12, 1880, and went to work in his youth as a reporter for the Baltimore *Herald*. Always an ace newspaperman, he worked his way up to the editorship, transferred to the *Sun* papers in 1906. In 1908 he became literary editor of *The Smart Set*, rising to co-editor in 1914. Ten years later, he left to found *The American Mercury*, with George Jean Nathan; after Nathan withdrew he remained as editor until his resignation in 1933. In his role as editor, he was influential in publishing and promoting new, talented writers, notably Dreiser and Sinclair Lewis, and for introducing such foreign influences as Nietzsche, Shaw, and Ibsen.

Like all good journalists, Mencken was glib, facile, prolific—and if his opinions were often refreshingly unconventional, they were also all too often exasperatingly superficial. Mencken was a master of invective, which he scattered so lavishly as to diminish its force. For example, he invented the happy pejorative term "Bible Belt," but he heaped such unlimited scorn on that region as to make such benightedness incredible. Almost everything he wrote was saved and published, and it is too much to ask the present-day reader to wade through six volumes of the too-topical *Prejudices*. At least one prejudice, however, bore rich fruit. Prompted by intense Anglophobia, Mencken set out to prove how much the American language differs from English. The resulting three volume study, *The American Language* (including two supplements), was an invaluable contribution to American linguistics and lexicography.

Mencken's own style is a peppery colloquialism which makes up in vigor what it too often lacks in depth. Especially interesting is his three-volume autobiography, *Happy Days* (1940), *Newspaper Days* (1941), and *Heathen Days* (1943). In his later years no longer the center of controversy on questions of prohibitionism, Darwinism, realism, and hard-headed Republicanism, and found dead wrong by his fellow-countrymen in his "prejudice" for Germany, Mencken's rankling dissent turned to outright rancor and bitterness. He died on January 29, 1956, and with him passed a raucous, belligerent, but unforgettably vivacious era.

MILLAY, EDNA ST. VINCENT

Edna St. Vincent Millay, probably America's best-known woman poet, was born in Rockland, Maine, on February 22, 1892. While she was still a student at Vassar *The Lyric Year* published her *Renascence*, a fine poem, all the more remarkable as coming from a 17-year-old girl. Her talent for poetry was easily matched by her talent for self-dramatization, and by the time *Renascence and Other Poems*, her first book, was published, she was already widely known as a leading Greenwich Village "character," a notoriety that inevitably helped sell her books. *A Few Figs From Thistles* (1920) revealed a tough, sexy impudence which appealed to the reading public; indeed, she and Dorothy Parker are credited with prompting sympathy and setting models for the modern hard-boiled career woman. As an apostle of bohemianism and as an articulate spokesman for honest expression, Miss Millay was regarded as peculiarly modern in outlook; but her verses betray a fondness for traditional forms (like the sonnet, of which she was one of the ablest practitioners), easy rhythms, and vaguely sentimental rhetoric. Even when she tried to sound colloquial, her verses seem formal and mannered, but they continued to prove popular. For *The Harp-Weaver and Other Poems* she received the Pulitzer Prize in 1923. In that year she married Eugen Boissevain and moved to Austerlitz, New York, where her poems became more pastoral and lyrical, as in *The Buck In The Snow* (1928) and *Wine From These Grapes* (1934). In her later years, as her attention focused on political matters, her verse became more talky and rhetorical, murky in tone and turgid in style. Among the books of this period were *Conversation At Midnight* (1937), *Make Bright The Arrows* (1940), and *The Murder of Lidice* (1942).

As a playwright, notably in the verse-plays *Aria Da Capo* (1921) and *The King's Henchman,* a libretto for an opera by Deems Taylor, Miss Millay achieved the same peaks and troughs as in her poems. She died on October 19, 1950, still one of America's best-loved literary figures. Her last poems were gathered in *Mine The Harvest* (1954), her earlier successes in *Collected Poems* (1956).

MOORE, MARIANNE

The growth of Marianne (Craig) Moore's reputation as a poet represents not the gradual development of her own work so much as a growing maturity in American literary taste and understanding. From the beginning, Miss Moore has written beautiful poems compounded of elegantly precise images and complex, elliptical metaphors, giving concise, explosive expression to a wonderfully cultivated sensibility.

She was born in Kirkwood, Missouri, on November 15, 1887, and edu-

GEORGE PLATT-LYNES
MARIANNE MOORE

cated in Pennsylvania, where her family moved during her childhood. In 1909, she graduated from Bryn Mawr College and six years later began publishing her poems in *The Egoist* and Harriet Monroe's *Poetry* magazines. A slim volume of Miss Moore's verses was published in England in 1921, appearing in revised and expanded form in America, entitled *Observations* (1925). For this book, she received the coveted Dial Award, and was offered the editorship of *The Dial* on the strength of it, serving until its demise in 1929. In that year she moved to Brooklyn, of which beleaguered borough she has since been a loyal and dedicated resident. Her subsequent books such as *Pangolin & Other Verses* (1936), *What Are Years?* (1941), and *Nevertheless* (1944), found few readers because of their difficulty, but their evocative, cogent brilliance did not escape the attention of sensitive critics, who voiced admiration, even awe, of her work. When her writing was assembled in a single volume, *Collected Poems* (1951), however, the effect was stunning. That year, Miss Moore was awarded the Pulitzer Prize and the Bollingen Prize for Poetry. Public accolades did not disturb the even flow of her work, and she has since produced several volumes of the same arch, enticing, brittle, fluid, silvery, beguiling, antisequacious poetry, notably: *Predilec-*

tions (1955), *Like A Bulwark* (1956), and *O To Be a Dragon* (1959). Her 1955 translation of *The Fables of La Fontaine* demonstrated to Americans the reasons why the French consider it a masterpiece.

NORRIS, FRANK

Although born in Chicago on March 5, 1870, and widely traveled during his lifetime, Benjamin Franklin Norris, Jr., is most closely associated with California, where his family moved when he was fourteen. Early indications of a talent for drawing persuaded his family to send him abroad, first to London, then to Paris, to prepare for an art career. Norris, however, spent most of his time writing, and when he returned to California he set out to become a professional writer. As a journalist, he went to Africa to cover the Boer War, contracting a debilitating tropical fever which weakened him permanently. His coverage later of the war in Cuba was curtailed by a recurrence of the fever. He worked as a reader for Doubleday, Page & Co. in New York until 1900, when he settled once again in California.

Norris' reading of Zola engendered his ambition to become the great American of the Naturalist novelist school. Although his actual production fell short of this goal, he did become one of the most influential figures in this American literary movement. As a reader for Doubleday, he achieved the publication of Dreiser's *Sister Carrie;* as a critic and essayist he set the tone and the goals for the Naturalists; and as a novelist he created some of the best-known models for their approach. *McTeague* (1899) brilliantly depicted, in close detail, the degeneration of a San Francisco dentist and his wife through miserliness. *The Octopus* (1901) was a novel about the growing of wheat in California and the struggles of the farmers against the railroad. The first of a "wheat" trilogy, *The Octopus* was followed by the story of wheat distribution, *The Pit* (1903). Norris had planned to visit India for background to the third novel, about the consumption of wheat; but he was felled by an attack of appendicitis, followed by peritonitis, and died in San Francisco on October 25, 1902.

O'CONNOR, FLANNERY

Much Southern fiction falls into a kind of American Gothic tradition, edged with violence and laced with horror, extending from Poe to Faulkner. The work of Flannery O'Connor is part of this tradition, but, like that of its great practitioners, is highly individual, marked by a grave, personal style and an intense moral conviction. Miss O'Connor was born in Savannah, Georgia, on March 25, 1925, and raised in Milledgeville, where she currently lives on a farm, and where she graduated in 1945 from Georgia State College for Women. For the next two years she studied creative writing at the University of Iowa under Paul Engle. It was while she was at Iowa that her first published story appeared in *Accent. Wise Blood,* a novel about an itinerant preacher martyred in the South for his unorthodox opinions, appeared in 1952. A number of her short stories were collected in *A Good Man Is Hard To Find* (1955), and a second novel, *The Violent Bear It Away,* was published in 1960. In 1957, she contributed an essay, "The Fiction Writer and His Country" to Granville Hicks' symposium, *The Living Novel,* an argument for the universality of "regional literature." Miss O'Connor's own work gives eloquent proof. She died August 3, 1964 in Milledgeville, Georgia.

O'CONNOR, WILLIAM VAN

As critic and editor, William Van O'Connor has been influential in focusing public attention on the meaning and value of contemporary American literature. He was born in Syracuse, New York, on January 10, 1915, and educated at Syracuse University, receiving his M. A. in 1937. Before World War II, he taught at Ohio State University, and served in New Guinea and the Philippines as a staff sergeant during the war. Since 1946 he has been on the English faculty of the University of Minnesota. He is now at the University of California, Davis, California.

His first important critical work,

Sense and Sensibility in Modern Poetry, appeared in 1948; that same year he edited *Forms of Modern Fiction;* and in 1952, his *An Age of Criticism, 1900-1950* tackled the modern American phenomenon, creative criticism. He has written searching studies of Wallace Stevens (*The Shaping Spirit,* 1950) and William Faulkner (*The Tangled Fire,* 1954), and has edited or co-edited numerous collections, including *Poems for Study* (with Leonard Unger) (1953), *Modern Prose; Form and Style* (1959), and *A Casebook on Ezra Pound* (with Edward Stone) (1959). He is the general editor of this present collection, *The Readers' Bookshelf of American Literature.*

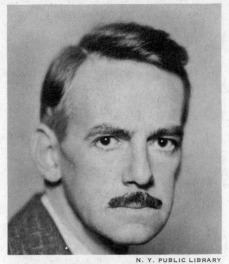

EUGENE O'NEILL

O'NEILL, EUGENE

Ella Quinlan, an actress, and wife of actor James O'Neill, gave birth to a boy on October 16, 1888, in New York, a son destined to outshine both his parents in the theater, destined, in fact, to become America's greatest playwright. Christened Eugene Gladstone O'Neill, he was educated in Catholic and private schools and in 1906 entered Princeton. His academic career was cut short in less than a year, when he was suspended for "general hell-raising." In the ensuing years his vagabond spirit found adventure and experience at sea, and on the waterfronts of the world's ports of call. In 1912 he worked for a while as a reporter on the New London *Telegraph,* contributing occasional poetry, but year's end found him in the hospital, a victim of tuberculosis. The year of recovery proved the turning point in O'Neill's life, for his interest turned to the drama. He read plays voraciously—both classical and modern—and began writing short plays of his own, some of which he published in *Thirst and Other One-Act Plays* (1914); but most of this early work never saw light, destroyed by the young playwright with ruthless self-criticism. Frustrated by the inability to set down his dramatic concepts, O'Neill enrolled in George Pierce Baker's famous "47 Workshop" at Harvard for technical training. But it was his asso-

ciation in 1916 with the Provincetown Players, and the enthusiasm of Susan Glaspell and George Cram Cook that finally brought the bottled-up experiences of his vagabond years to full flood on the stage. They produced *Bound East for Cardiff,* a one-act play, following its success with *The Long Voyage Home* and *Ile* in 1917 and *The Moon of The Caribbees* in 1918. This succession of stage triumphs paved the way for O'Neill's first Broadway production, *Beyond The Horizon* (1920), for which he received the Pulitzer Prize.

The next dozen years saw a sequence of innovations such as the American theater had not witnessed in its entire history, each uniquely successful and, more importantly, each contained in a striking drama that expressed the insight and vision of profoundly sensitive poetic intelligence. *The Emperor Jones* (1920) is almost entirely composed of a long monologue by a self-proclaimed dictator in flight, portraying in his own collapse from proud security to hysterical fear the sources in his own character of his destruction. Excitement is additionally generated by the repeated beating of a drum, beginning at a pace slightly slower than the average human pulse and gradually increasing in frequency, taking the heartbeat of the audience with it. More than a mechanical device to excite sensations, this feature of the play indicates O'Neill's deep understanding of the physical sources of emotional experience, an understanding dramatized in *The Hairy Ape* (1922). The confrontation between man and ape in this play's finale is a symbolic representation of the tragic disparity between psychological development and physical reality that plagues modern man, and that served as O'Neill's most recurrent theme. The tension between inner truth and the inner lie, and the conflict of both with external reality is the focus of most of his work.

In *Desire Under The Elms* (1924), O'Neill attempted to portray the corrosive effect of submerged emotions, and the destruction caused when they explode in violent passions. The idea was communicated more subtly and profoundly in *The Great God Brown* (1926), in which the characters alternately don and doff masks to portray their inner natures in juxtaposition with their external personalities. The result is a continuing, sometimes baffling, shift of character which accurately depicts the precarious minute-by-minute adjustments with which we confront experience.

Marco Millions (1928) showed O'Neill in an acidly satiric vein, underscoring his criticism of the materialistic attitude. A rich comic effect is achieved by supplanting Marco Polo with a modern high-pressure salesman and contrasting his America with the wise Orient. *Strange Interlude,* presented in 1928, is probably O'Neill's best-known play. Here, the idea of *The Great God Brown* achieves startling impact with the adoption of a different device: the interior monologue is spoken directly to the audience by stopping the action and having the characters step forward in soliloquy.

In 1931, the emotional complexity of domestic tragedy attempted in *Desire Under The Elms* was strikingly achieved in *Mourning Becomes Electra,* a reworking in American terms of Aeschylus' classic tragedies of the house of Atreus. Shifting the scene to post-Civil War New England, O'Neill was able to inform the rich texture of his own play

with the extra dimension of background supplied by the Greek original. *Ah Wilderness!* (1933) is a warm, wonderful comedy of a boy's growing-up. With the failure, in 1934, of *Days Without End,* O'Neill entered a long period of silence.

The Iceman Cometh (1946) marked his return to Broadway, and it was none too successful. Possibly because of its length (it had to be produced with an intermission for dinner), possibly because of its uncompromising presentation of the bottom of society, the play did not seem to "take." But a subsequent revival off-Broadway and a successful TV production proved its unquestionable appeal and the permanent validity of its searching comment—the need for dreams in the face of sordid reality.

To the sophisticated present-day reader, much of O'Neill seems verbose, self-conscious, tryingly naïf. When he died on November 27, 1953, he seemed already to be a dim figure of the past. However, the outstanding success of his posthumously produced plays, *A Long Day's Journey into Night* (1956) and *A Touch of the Poet* indicate the continued vitality of his work; and even a superficial view of the American theater, indeed of all theater, since his pioneering plays will clearly demonstrate the pervasiveness of his influence.

PAULDING, JAMES KIRKE

Because his father had pledged the entire family fortune to the Revolution, James Kirke Paulding was born into poverty on August 22, 1778, at Great Nine Partners, New York, and consequently had no formal education. His sister married William Irving, the poet brother of Washington Irving, and in 1797 Paulding went to New York, where he immediately became a close friend of the Irving family. He did some writing for Peter Irving's *Morning Chronicle,* and was a contributor to *Salmagundi,* the satirical Irving fortnightly. His sketches of U. S. naval commanders in the War of 1812, and the staunch patriotism of his *The U. S. and England* (1815) came to the attention of President Madison, who named him secretary of the Board of Navy Commissioners. In 1824, Monroe appointed him Navy agent for New York, a post he held until 1828, when he became Van Buren's Secretary of the Navy. All this time he was busy writing novels, satires, and his *Life of George Washington* (1835), the standard biography until Irving's. In 1849, he stopped writing altogether, retiring to Hyde Park, where he died on April 6, 1860. He is best remembered as a vocal defender of American civilization, and for his influence on the creation of an indigenous literature, best exemplified in the seminal friendship with Washington Irving.

EDGAR ALLAN POE

POE, EDGAR ALLAN

In Boston, on January 19, 1809, a son, Edgar, was born to David and Elizabeth Poe, itinerant actors. At the age of two, the frail infant was orphaned by the death of both parents, and adopted by a wealthy merchant of Richmond, John Allan, whose name he later added to his own. The young Poe was precocious, not only in intelligence and talent, but in dissipation. His career at the University of Virginia, begun in 1822, was peremptorily halted by his dismissal for dissolute habits. At the age of eighteen he left his home in Richmond and made his way to Boston, where he published his first book, *Tamerlane and Other Poems* (1827). Under the name of Edgar A. Perry, Poe then enlisted in the Army, rising to Sergeant-Major before his discharge two years later. In 1829, he published *Al Aaraaf:* the same year he wangled his way into West Point, where authorities soon discovered his unsuitability, and the following year he was dismissed. Soliciting subscriptions from Army and West Point friends, he published a collection, *Poems*, in 1831. Despite this multiple publication, his poetry attracted little notice, and he turned to the composition of prose works, for which he immediately displayed a genius. His short story, *MS. Found In a Bottle*, won a prize in 1833, and gave clear indication of the somber, macabre, intensely

imaginative tales to come. Virginia Clemm, a thirteen-year-old cousin, became his bride in 1836, and for the next 11 years she and her mother joined Poe in his restless pursuit of work and publication. Until 1837 Poe was literary editor of the *Southern Literary Messenger* in Richmond. The next year they were in New York, where he wrote and published his only novel, the *Narrative of A. Gordon Pym*. The following year they moved to Philadelphia for a five-year sojourn during which he contributed stories and essays to Burton's *Gentleman's Magazine*, becoming editor when it was reorganized as *Graham's Magazine*. Poe's book, *Tales of the Grotesque and Arabesque* appeared in 1840. In April, 1844, failing in his attempts to establish a magazine of his own, and unable to secure a desired government position, Poe moved his family to New York, where he worked on the *Evening News*. *The Raven,* his best known poem, appeared in that newspaper early in 1845, and after years of unrecognized struggle, Poe suddenly found himself famous. He was now able to publish *Tales* and *The Raven and Other Poems* with some hopes of profitable sales. For a while he was lionized in New York Society, but his unabated alcoholism again began closing doors. He managed to stay alive, despite the meagerness of his earnings, but his young, fragile wife, ravaged by consumption aggravated by malnutrition, succumbed in 1847. Two years later, following a trip to Richmond, Poe was found in the streets of Philadelphia in a delirium. What had happened in the five days preceding is still a total mystery. He was taken to a hospital, but never fully regained consciousness. On October 7, 1849, he died.

Critical estimates of Poe's work are at wide divergence. His best poems, although schoolroom familiars, lack the emotional power and vigor of language now expected of poetry. They seem, in most cases, to be merely word pictures or sound effects. The very vagueness of these poems, however, together with their sombre tone, has been a source of their appeal in France, where, through the translations and worshipful introductions of Charles Baudelaire, they have exerted a profound influence, and are credited with being the source of the symbolist movement.

By general agreement, it is in the tales that Poe's genius had its greatest flowering. He is at his best in those dark, impossible, terrifying nightmares, rich in symbolism and informed with basic psychological truth, like *The Fall of the House of Usher, William Wilson, Ligeia* and *The Tell-Tale Heart.* His tales of "ratiocination," particularly those featuring C. Auguste Dupin (*The Murders in the Rue Morgue, The Mystery of Marie Rogêt,* and *The Purloined Letter*), are considered the foundations of the modern detective story.

As a critic, Poe's reputation has fared better for the practical criticism than for his literary theories, which, for all their apparent resemblance to Coleridge, suffer from being either incompletely reasoned or impossibly unrealistic. Perhaps the greatest failing is their inconsistency with his own best literary practice.

PORTER, KATHERINE ANNE

Of her chosen form, the short novel, Katherine Anne Porter is an acknowledged mistress. She was born in Indian Creek, Texas, on May 15, 1894, and that region has served as the back-

UPI PHOTO

KATHERINE ANNE PORTER

ground for much of her fiction. She is a meticulous craftsman, revealing in her tales a thoughtful intelligence and a shrewd sense of character and motive. Her narratives are overlaid with a mysterious, symbolic tone that suggests, but does not explicitly divulge, fluencies of significance beneath the surface. Among her finest works are *Flowering Judas* (1930), *Noon Wine* (1937), and *Pale Horse, Pale Rider* (1939). Miss Porter has also done excellent translations from both Spanish and French. *The Days Before* (1952), a collection of her essays, reveals her as a knowing and able critic, deeply conscious of her own art.

POUND, EZRA

Since the beginning of his career, Ezra Loomis Pound, poet, critic, literary impresario, and manifestoist, alleged traitor and mental incompetent, has been a center of controversy. Estimates of his work have ranged from "genius" to "rantings," but no history of modern writing can neglect him as the focus of influences that have shaped its character and quality.

Born in Hailey, Idaho, on October 30, 1885, Pound was educated at Hamilton College and the University of Pennsylvania. Before completing his doctoral work, he departed for Europe, where he was to remain until 1945.

EZRA POUND

Living first in Italy, he settled in Rapallo in 1924 after more than a decade in France and England.

His first book of poems, *A Lume Spento,* was published in 1908. Subsequent volumes revealed his preoccupation with the revival of older forms and foreign literatures, which he felt would renew and invigorate poetry: such as *A Quinzaine for This Yule* (1908), *Provença* (1910), *Canzoni* (1911), *Cathay* (1915), and *Homage to Sextus Propertius* (1934). His search through world literature for models focused on the innovators those rare spirits who breathed new life into poetry in moments when decay had begun to set in —and it was Pound's interest that renamed the reputations of many neglected great writers: Cavalcanti, the Provençal troubadours, and Sextus Propertius. Referring to the influential translation of Li Po (*Cathay*), T. S. Eliot dubbed him "the inventor of Chinese poetry for our time."

The title *Make It New!* may be regarded as Pound's slogan during these early years. Endless theorizing on just what qualities give poetic language its power led to the development of Imagism, a movement Pound fathered, but later abandoned, owing to the excessive misunderstanding of his intentions by its practitioners. Imagism stressed the ne-

cessity for precise description in poetry and aimed at the concentration of emotion in objects and the hard physical facts of existence. Capturing a fleeting moment seemed to be the intent of most imagists, but Pound's own work in this genre, some of Amy Lowell's work, and most of William Carlos Williams' poems demonstrate how much deeper imagism could penetrate. Vorticism, the short-lived movement that followed, clearly showed that no amount of theoretical organization could inject quality into literature. Again, Ernest Fenollosa's speculations on the uses of the Chinese character in English poetry, widely broadcast by Pound, led to no significant work except that of Pound himself.

But if Pound's codified theories bore little fruit, his own profound understanding of the nature of poetry and an instinctive sense for what is right in language prompted his sponsorship, in an early day, of the work of T. S. Eliot, Wyndham Lewis, James Joyce, and William Carlos Williams. His friendship with W. B. Yeats unquestionably influenced that poet's later work, and through these seminal authors Pound has exerted a tremendous influence on our age.

Pound's insistence on clarity of imagery, liveliness of language and colloquiality of rhythm appears at its best in his early poems, collected in *Personae* (1926). These reveal a delicacy of feeling combined with an acid view of society that lends a bitter-sweet quality to almost all his work. In the early '20s, at a time when Pound was least optimistic for the future of the world and was beginning to develop his lifelong interest in the economic theory of social credit, he began the long series of poems he called *cantos,* intending to inscribe, through ellipsis, the entire history of civilization. Publication has already exceeded the originally announced 100 cantos and the end is not yet in sight. The first seventy-one, published over a number of years, were collected in *The Cantos* (1948); the next fourteen appear in *The Pisan Cantos* (1948); and the most recent additions to the series have been published in *Section: Rock-Drill, 85-95 de los Cantares* (1956) and *Thrones: 96-109 de los Cantares* (1959). Because they refer, by quotation and allusion, to countless works in a dozen literatures frequently reproduced in the original tongue, the *Cantos* are considered among the most difficult and obscure of all modern works; but highlighted moments of absolute clarity clearly indicate the continuance of Pound's poetic skill: critics who have mastered most or all of the poems are generally in agreement as to their permanent validity.

The poet's activities have not been quite so obscure as his writings. His interest in social credit led him to support Mussolini in pre-war Italy, a support which apparently continued right through the war, during which Pound made anti-American broadcasts on the Italian radio. For this offense, he was returned to the United States under a charge of treason, but was judged incompetent to prepare a defense and committed to St. Elizabeth's Hospital in Washington. The controversy surrounding this decision was revived in 1948 when Pound, despite his politics, was awarded the Bollingen Prize for Poetry. In 1958, the indictment having been withdrawn, he was released and returned to Italy.

His best critical writings, never organized into any cohesive system, espoused a variety of theories, but were always telling in their literary analysis and always lively in style. They were collected in *The Literary Essays* (1945), with an introduction by T. S. Eliot.

POWERS, J. F.

The award-winning short-story writer James Farl Powers was born in Jacksonville, Illinois, on July 8, 1917. Most of his youth was spent in Illinois, principally in Quincy and Chicago. His first stories appeared in *Accent*, and the young writer was so grateful for their publication that he dedicated his first collection of stories, *Prince of Darkness* (1947), to the editors of that magazine. Powers writes taut, cunning stories, many of them dealing with problems and characters of the Catholic Church, drawn from his own religious experiences and convictions. In recent years, most of his stories have appeared in the *New Yorker*. A second collection, *Presence of Grace* (1956), demonstrated further the range and striking effectiveness of this talented writer.

RAHV, PHILIP

The name of Philip Rahv has long been associated with *Partisan Review*, the influential literary magazine of which he was one of the founders and a longtime editor.

Rahv was born in the Ukraine on March 10, 1908. Rahv's family migrated to the United States in 1922, settling in Providence, Rhode Island. In the early '30s he began contributing critical articles to a variety of magazines and journals. Following the first appearance of *Partisan Review* in February, 1934, there was a struggle for control of the magazine among the members of the John Reed Club, who sponsored it, representing several shades of Marxist and communist opinion. When the purge trials began in the Soviet Union in 1936, *Partisan Review* suspended publication for several months of severe soul-searching debate among its editors and supporters. With the resumption of publication in 1937, Rahv and his co-editor William Philips had clearly won, for they retained control and completely re-organized the staff. The magazine became an outspoken anti-Stalinist organ, maintaining an independent leftist slant, which has considerably diminished over the years. It was also instrumental in establishing a large number of our present-day novelists, poets and critics, many of whom appeared for the first time in its pages.

A collection of Rahv's critical essays, *Image and Idea*, appeared in 1949. During the years 1944-45, his editorship of James' *The Bostonians* and *The Great Short Novels* helped initiate a James revival.

RANSOM, JOHN CROWE

As poet, critic, editor, and teacher, John Crowe Ransom has been one of the most influential literary figures of his generation. He was born in Pulaski, Tennessee, on April 30, 1888. Following his graduation from Vanderbilt University in 1909, he went to Oxford as a Rhodes scholar, remaining until 1914. Returning to the United States, he accepted a teaching position at Vanderbilt that he held, interrupted only by service as an artillery officer during the war, until 1937. There he founded and edited *The Fugitive,* through which he may be said to have initiated the "Southern renascence." Among the "Fugitives" who were his students at Vanderbilt were Allen Tate and Robert Penn Warren. Ransom's own poetry provided models for the young poets he tutored, and his editorial judgment and critical essays gave direction to what he himself called *The New Criticism* (1941). His poetry is marked by a precision of imagery and taut, controlled versification. The subject matter of his poems is frequently directly religious, and the other usually have religious overtones, as may be seen by some of his book titles: *Poems About God* (1919) and *Grace After Meat* (1924).

In 1937, Ransom went to Kenyon College, where he has taught ever since. The literary principles of *The Fugitive,* stripped of their regional character, found new promulgation in the pages of *Kenyon Review,* which he edited, and before long found general currency. The most recent collection of his poetry, *Selected Poems,* appeared in 1945.

ROBINSON, EDWIN ARLINGTON

The single-minded determination to be a poet which characterized his youth and early manhood finally brought Edwin Arlington Robinson fame and permanent literary stature, and rewarded America with a profound and influential body of poetry. Robinson was born in Head Tide, Maine, on December 22, 1869, and spent his early years in New England. He entered Harvard in 1891, but had to leave after two years to devote his time to writing. Struggling on the meager income from a small inherit-ance, Robinson lived with his family in Gardiner, Maine, and in 1896 published his first book, *Children of the Night,* at his own expense.

In 1896 he moved to New York, where he was to live for the rest of his life. In 1905, while Robinson labored as an inspector in the New York subway construction, his book *Captain Craig* (1902) came to the attention of Theodore Roosevelt, who greatly admired it and secured a clerkship for the poet in the New York Custom House. The publication of *The Town Down the River* (1910) won a small circle of admirers, and he felt secure enough to leave the Custom House; but it was not until 1916, when *The Man Against The Sky* appeared, that he really made his mark on the American literary scene. His poems, which retain their freshness and vigor today, must have seemed especially vital and vibrant when they were first published.

Robinson had the knack of infusing traditional forms with new life, chiefly through a spare style which had the force of daily speech and charged simple events with profound meaning. Although he was deeply involved with figures of heroic stature, particularly in a series of long Arthurian poems *(Merlin* (1917), *Lancelot* (1920), *and Tristram),* his most memorable poems deal with smaller figures from the American scene: *Richard Cory, Cliff Klingenhagen, Miniver Cheevy.*

When all his early work was published in 1921 as *Collected Poems,* Robinson was awarded the Pulitzer Prize. His next book, a long Browningesque study called *The Man Who Died Twice* (1924) won him the Pulitzer Prize again. By 1927, when *Tristram* appeared, he was America's best known contemporary poet. Not only did the book receive the Pulitzer Prize, but it proved a best-seller, the first volume of poetry to turn that trick since Whitman's *Leaves of Grass.*

Each summer, beginning in 1911, Robinson resided at the MacDowell Colony in Peterborough, New Hampshire, where, despite his habitual introversion, he was a personal inspiration as well as influence upon the work of aspiring artists.

Although he continued writing until his death in New York on April 6, 1935, his later work showed a decline in his power and control, tending toward didacticism. He was never able to recapture that quality he had set as a standard, not only for himself, but for all future American poets, so forcefully in the '20s.

ROETHKE, THEODORE

In marked contrast to his hefty physical appearance, Theodore Roethke's poems are characteristically delicate, almost fragile, and hauntingly evocative. He was born in Saginaw, Michigan, on May 25, 1908, the son of a flower-grower, and his early experiences in his father's greenhouse emerge full-blossomed in the frequent flower imagery of his work. Roethke was educated at the University of Michigan, receiving his B. A. in 1929. Following a year at the Law School and a year at Harvard, he returned to Michigan for graduate study, taking his M. A. in 1936. He has since taught at a variety of colleges, including Lafayette, Pennsylvania State, Bennington, and the University of Washington, where, since 1947, he has been on the English faculty.

Open House, Roethke's first book of poems, largely a collection of work that had appeared for several years in a number of periodicals, was published in 1941. His writing since has been slender in volume, but effective and powerful: *The Lost Son* (1948), *Praise To The End!* (1951), and *The Waking* (1953), for which he received the Pulitzer Prize in 1954. In 1958, when *Words For The Wind* appeared, he was awarded the Bollingen Prize for Poetry. He died August 1, 1963 in Seattle, Washington.

ROURKE, CONSTANCE

Born on November 14, 1885, in Cleveland, Ohio, Constance Mayfield Rourke devoted most of her life to the study of popular American culture and folklore, and its meaning to contemporary American society. Educated at Vassar (B. A. 1907) and at the Sorbonne,

Miss Rourke began her career as a teacher of English at Vassar College, 1910-1915. Perhaps her best-known work is *American Humor: A Study of the American Character*, which appeared in 1931, outlining the history and significance of several folk-hero and literary prototypes. However, she had already made a reputation among American scholars with *Trumpets of Jubilee* (1927), about the Beecher family and others, and *Troupers of the Gold Coast* (1928), which dealt with minstrels and itinerant theatre-folk of the 19th century. *Davy Crockett* (1934) extended the work she had done in *American Humor*, while in *Audubon* (1936) and *Charles Sheeler* (1938) she attempted to define an American art which integrated traditional American materials toward a view of the present. Miss Rourke died suddenly, following an accident, on March 23, 1941. The posthumous *Roots of American Culture* (1942) revealed an alert and informed critic at work on a meaningful definition of American culture that has been influential in our present-day understanding of American literature and art.

PHOTO BY EDWARD STEICHEN
CARL SANDBURG

SANDBURG, CARL

The widespread reverence for Carl Sandburg and his international fame rest as much on his loving, scholarly biography of Lincoln as on his achievement as a poet. Born in Galesburg, Illinois, on June 6, 1878, of Swedish immigrant parents, Sandburg was forced by his family's poverty to abandon his schooling at the age of thirteen. His youth was spent vagabonding in the West, doing any work handy; it was then that he developed his close feeling and abiding admiration for "the common man." With the outbreak of the Spanish-American War, Sandburg enlisted in the Army, and served eight months in Puerto Rico. Following his discharge he attended Lombard College briefly, and there published his first book, *In Reckless Ecstasy*. With the type set by hand, and the sheets of all fifty copies printed and bound in a professor's basement, this book is now extremely rare, but its contents bear only faint promise of the achievement yet to come. In the years following, Sandburg worked mostly as journalist, and was long a reporter for the Chicago *Daily News*. Meanwhile, his poems began to appear in Harriet Monroe's *Poetry* magazine, drawing attention to a "new school" of poets, of which he was the acknowledged leader, who wrote in free, often explosive, verse of the glory and power of industrial America. Taking a cue from Whitman, Sandburg sang of the sprawling, dynamic wonder of America, and of the natural wisdom of ordinary people. The popularity of his early collections, *Chicago Poems* (1916) and *Cornhuskers* (1918) enabled him to give up journalism and devote himself to more serious writing. For many years he labored on the now definitive biography of Lincoln. *Abraham Lincoln: The Prairie Years* appeared in two volumes in 1926; the four volumes of *Abraham Lincoln: The War Years* were published in 1939.

During these years, Sandburg toured the country, reading his poems and singing American folk-songs, accompanying himself on the guitar. His collection, *American Songbag* (1927), remains an important contribution to our knowledge of American folklore. *Rootabaga Stories* (1922), a book for children, also utilized folk materials.

Sandburg achieved new popularity and recognition during the depression years of the '30s, when widespread social consciousness provoked a taste for "proletarian" literature, and with *The People, Yes* (1936) he became a sort of folk hero to America's leftist intelligentsia. In more recent years he has written a long, dull novel, *Remembrance Rock* (1948), and a lively, engaging first volume of autobiography, *Always The Young Stranger* (1952).

SANTAYANA, GEORGE

Although he did not come to the United States until he was nine years old, and spent the last forty years of his life in Europe, the work of Jorge Augustin Nicolas de Santayana was preeminently American and it is a cruel irony that his books, highly regarded abroad, are little-read in his adopted homeland.

Santayana was born in Madrid on December 16, 1863, and brought to America in 1872 by his mother, then resident in Boston. He attended the Boston Latin School and then Harvard, graduating in 1886 with a fellowship to study in Europe. For two years he attended the University of Berlin, returning to Harvard to conclude his studies. In June, 1889, he received both his M. A. and Ph. D. from Harvard, and in September, aged 26, joined the faculty of philosophy. Living in virtual seclusion, he was seldom seen on campus except when hurrying to and from his lectures, which are remembered by his students (e.g., T. S. Eliot, Walter Lippmann) as much for their style as for their content.

Santayana's first published work was poetry, *Sonnets and Other Verses* (1894), poorly received by critics and soon eclipsed by his own philosophical writings. Re-evaluation by a less sentimental age has revived much of Santayana's poetry, but his reputation still rests mainly on his philosophy and criticism. Such books as *The Sense of Beauty* (1896), *The Life Of Reason* (1905-06), *Three Philosophical Poets* (1910), and *Character And Opinion in the United*

States (1920) remain basic texts in any study of the development of American thought. The analysis of Lucretius in *Three Philosophical Poets* (plus the surprising defense of Shelley), and the essay on the "Genteel Tradition" in *Character and Opinion* are milestones in American literary criticism.

In 1912, falling heir to a small private income, Santayana resigned his position at Harvard and departed for Europe, living for a while in Oxford, and then in Rome. *The Last Puritan,* his only novel, was a surprise best-seller in 1936. Largely autobiographical, it traced the growth of one man's intellect in the turbulent America of the turn of the century. The book's success gave Santayana a new, wide audience unfamiliar with his more specialized writings, an unexpected popularity that made a best-seller of his autobiography, *Persons and Places* (1944).

Santayana lived in a convent in Rome through the war, where he wrote, read, and received callers. He remained lucid and in good health until his death at eighty-nine, on September 26, 1952. He was buried in unconsecrated ground at his own request.

SCHWARTZ, DELMORE

Delmore Schwartz was born in Brooklyn, New York, on December 8, 1913. He was educated at the University of Wisconsin, New York University, and Harvard, and at the age of 26 displayed on the literary scene an already mature talent with *In Dreams Begin Responsibilities* (1939). This first book contained poetry, a play, and a short story, demonstrating Schwartz's mastery of each genre. In 1941, following the publication of *Shenandoah,* a play, Schwartz was awarded a Guggenheim Fellowship and was offered a teaching position at Harvard. In 1943 he became editor of *Partisan Review;* that same year he published a long poem, *Genesis: Book I,* a brilliantly sustained work that secured his position at the vanguard of young American poets. Resigning from his post at Harvard and his job on *Par-*

tisan Review in 1947, Schwartz devoted himself more exclusively to his writing. *The World Is A Wedding,* a collection of short stories, was published in 1948. *Vaudeville For A Princess* (1950) contained poetry and prose interspersed. In the ensuing years, Schwartz was briefly connected with *Perspectives* and the *New Republic.* Since 1955, he has been associate editor at New Directions, his publisher.

A comprehensive collection of Schwartz's poetry, together with new work, was published in *Summer Knowledge* (1959), for which he received the Bollingen Prize for Poetry.

SHAPIRO, KARL

Karl Jay Shapiro, born in Baltimore on November 10, 1913, published his first book, *Poems* (1935), when he was only 21 years old. The book, however, escaped general attention, and it was not until the war years that Shapiro's reputation began to grow. *Person, Place and Thing* (1942), and *The Place of Love* (1943), written during his wartime military service, showed that he was one of the finer poets of his generation, and the Pulitzer Prize-winning *V-Letter and Other Poems* confirmed his position as *the* American poet of the war. His direct, declarative style was perfectly suited to the didactic purpose of *An Essay on Rime* (1945), a disquisition in verse on the theory and practice of modern poetry.

Following his discharge from the Army, Shapiro served as poetry consultant to the Library of Congress for a year, and then, from 1947-50, taught creative writing at Johns Hopkins University, where he had himself studied in the late '30s. From 1950 to 1956 he was editor of *Poetry;* since 1956 he has edited the University of Nebraska's *Prairie Schooner* and has taught there as a professor of English.

Shapiro's straightforward, colloquial diction has been attacked as prosy and unaesthetic; but the collection of his *Poems: 1942-1953* and his more recent

Poems of a Jew (1958) reveal a supple linguistic skill applied by a sensitive and imaginative intelligence to the engrossing complexities of modern life.

SHERWOOD, ROBERT E.

Although primarily connected with the theater, Robert Emmet Sherwood's wide interests and talents won him fame in several different fields. He was born in New Rochelle, New York, on April 4, 1896, and educated at Harvard, where he wrote his first play, *Barnum Was Right*. His career at Harvard was interrupted when he enlisted in the Canadian Black Guards. Wounded and gassed in Europe, Sherwood was deeply embittered by the war experience and became a vocal pacifist, dramatizing this philosophy in some of his best plays (e.g., *Idiot's Delight*). During the early twenties he worked as a writer and editor for *Life, Vanity Fair*, and *Scribner's;* but with the first Broadway production of his work (*The Road To Rome*, 1927), he devoted himself entirely to his plays. During the '30s and early '40s, Sherwood dominated the Broadway stage, and three times won the Pulitzer Prize (for *Idiot's Delight*, 1936; *Abe Lincoln in Illinois*, 1939; and *There Shall Be No Night*, 1941). As Hitlerism grew, threatening the ultimate destruction of civilization, Sherwood's determined pacifism gave way to a fierce and vociferous militarism. He was an early agitator for support of England and for intervention, and was named special consultant to the Secretaries of War and the Navy when this became official policy. During the war, he served with the Office for War Information, and worked as an advisor and speech-writer for President Roosevelt. Following the death of Harry Hopkins, Sherwood fell heir to his papers. Utilizing these, and his own memory of close association with both Hopkins and the President, he wrote the Pulitzer Prize-winning study, *Roosevelt and Hopkins* (1948).

In the years before his death, on November 14, 1955, Sherwood emerged as a brilliant screen writer, winning the Academy Award for his screenplay, *The Best Years of Our Lives;* as a librettist, working with Irving Berlin on *Miss Liberty;* and as an early and prolific writer of original television plays.

SIMMS, WILLIAM GILMORE

William Gilmore Simms was born in Charleston, South Carolina, on April 17, 1806. Two years later his mother died, and his father set out for the Tennessee frontier, leaving the boy with his grandmother. When he was 18, Simms visited his father briefly, and the experience of frontier life was to be the main theme of his later novels. But he was not in the wilderness long, for his grandmother won a lawsuit for the boy's guardianship and brought him back to Charleston, where he read law. In 1826, he was admitted to the bar, but never practiced; instead, he married, and became editor of the *City Gazette*. During the next four years, Simms published several books of poetry in Charleston, but when his wife died in 1832, he set out for New York, where he began writing fiction. Three years later he was back in South Carolina for good, marrying again in 1836. "Woodlands," his wife's ancestral estate, was the center of his activity until the Civil War, except for the two years (1844-46) he served in the state legislature. Because Simms was the best-known Carolinian author, "Woodlands" was also the center for all authors and would-be authors of the region.

Simms was an active and vocal secessionist, but the Civil War brought him total ruin. His wife died, "Woodlands" was twice burned, and finally his property in Columbia was destroyed. He died on June 11, 1870, a broken man.

Few of his works survive today, although he was extremely popular in his own time, hailed as the "southern Cooper." He wrote lurid romances of the frontier, of which *The Yemassee* (1835) is the best remembered. He had an early understanding that the romance was the form of fiction most adaptable to the American experience, and perceived the epic quality of the American frontier. The tone of his work and some of its themes foreshadow Faulkner, and his writing has probably been influential on the modern Southern novelists.

SMITH, LOGAN PEARSALL

Lloyd Logan Pearsall Smith was born in Millville, New Jersey, on October 18, 1865; he died in his beloved England on March 2, 1946. The intervening eighty years were devoted to self-cultivation and the writing of short, precise essays in impeccable English. Long considered an expert on English usage, Smith was often consulted by authorities in this field. Although he wrote a number of books on a variety of subjects, including Wotton, Milton, Shakespeare, and the English language, he is best remembered for *Trivia* (1902), *More Trivia* (1921) and their successors which were collected in *All Trivia* (1934). These essays revealed his erudition, his love of money, his preference for aristocrats, and, most important of all, his love of the English language.

STEIN, GERTRUDE

Born to a well-to-do Jewish family in Allegheny, Pennsylvania, on February 3, 1874, Gertrude Stein early exhibited both the brilliance and eccentricity for which she is best remembered. As a student at Radcliffe she became interested in psychology, chiefly through the influence of William James, and there wrote an essay on automatic writing that gives a clue to the sources of her literary theories. For four years she studied medicine at Johns Hopkins, specializing in brain anatomy, but never took a degree because examinations bored her. She left soon thereafter for Europe, settling in 1903 in Paris with her confidante and constant companion, Alice B. Toklas. (During World War II they took refuge in the village of Culoz.) Of independent means, she never had to write "for a living," she herself financed the publication of her earlier works and rarely collected royalties even after she had made her repu-

tation. This financial independence allowed her to write as she pleased, and her works display an appealing lack of concern for pleasing the general public. However, if all bear the stamp of originality and intelligence, many are deliberately obscure. Her first book, *Three Lives* (1909), is easily her most widely read and most readily understood work; it contains three beautifully written short novels. Her next, *Tender Buttons* (1914), is more characteristic and more usually praised by her avowed admirers. Most of her subsequent writing was devoted to her "solution of language," amplification through constant repetition. She believed in simplifying communication by simplifying language, ordering it in a close resemblance to the associative and repetitive patterns of thought. A world-famous example of the style is her dictum, "A rose is a rose is a rose," which strikes most readers (particularly out of context) as merely whimsical. The effectiveness of her method is more easily illustrated with another famous line: "In the United States there is more space where nobody is than where anybody is. This is what makes America what it is."

In her early days in Paris, Miss Stein distinguished herself as a patroness of modern art, giving encouragement to the quality she saw in such then obscure painters as Picasso, Matisse, and Braque. During the period between wars, she was a fixture among the American expatriates; every serious American writer in France felt duty-bound to visit her. Her influence on some of them, notably on Ernest Hemingway, extended her theories far beyond the reach of her own work.

Her writing for the stage, bound by the same peculiarities as her books, has achieved notable success. *Four Saints in Three Acts*, set to music by Virgil Thomson, was produced in 1934; *The Mother of Us All*, also set by Thomson, was staged in 1947; *In Savoy or "Yes" is For Yes is For A Very Young Man* (1946) appeared on Broadway in 1949 as *Yes Is For A Very Young Man*. Her other plays, like *Doctor Faustus*

Lights the Lights, are perennial favorites for college or experimental productions. Before her death on July 27, 1946, Miss Stein returned to the United States only once, for a lecture tour in 1934, recorded in *Lectures In America* (1935). A representative sampling of her work was published shortly after her death in *Selected Writings of Gertrude Stein* (1946), and Yale University has undertaken the publication of her unpublished writings, several volumes of which have already appeared.

PHOTO BY PHILIPPE HALSMAN

JOHN STEINBECK

STEINBECK, JOHN

John Ernst Steinbeck was born in Salinas, California, on February 27, 1902. He attended Stanford University as a special student for four years, earning no degree. Then, determined to make his way as a writer, he deliberately traveled widely, working at a variety of jobs in search of experience. During these years he was, at one time or another, bricklayer, house painter, chemist, news reporter, and estate caretaker. He settled in Monterey in 1930 to pursue a literary career. His early writings attracted little attention, but with *Tortilla Flat* (1935), a warm, candid portrait of low life in sunny California, he scored an immediate success. Each of his subsequent novels met with similar acclaim: *In Dubious Battle* (1936), a penetrating study of social turmoil during the depression; *Of Mice and Men* (1937), a chilling tale of

symbiosis between a pathetic, simpleminded brute and a wily, intelligent friend; and *The Grapes of Wrath* (1939), an angry account of the plight of the "Okies," dust bowl refugees seeking migrant work in California. For *The Grapes of Wrath,* Steinbeck received the Pulitzer Prize.

The successful stage adaptation of *Of Mice and Men* led Steinbeck to experiment with a new form—the play-novel, minimizing the narrative to little more than stage directions. The result was the wartime drama, *The Moon Is Down* (1942), which, being neither fish nor fowl, succeeded as neither. Following the war, he returned to the scene and light-hearted vein of *Tortilla Flat* in *Cannery Row* (1945), *The Wayward Bus* (1947), and *Sweet Thursday* (1954) His more serious fiction, the allegorical novella *The Pearl* (1948), the semi-surrealistic play-novel *Burning Bright* (1950), and the rambling pseudo-epic *East of Eden* (1952) provoked mixed reactions from the critics. Although clearly indicative of Steinbeck's heightened conceptual power, these books betrayed a waning of artistic control and a troubling inconsistency of theme. Steinbeck's more recent works include the satirical *The Short Reign of Pippin IV* (1957); *Once There Was a War* (1958), taken from his writings as a war correspondent; and a novel, *Winter of Our Discontent* (1961).

STEVENS, WALLACE

Against the traditional image of the sensitive, impractical poet, alienated and bewildered in a world of pragmatic and hard-headed philistines, the example of Wallace Stevens is usually contrasted. Born in Reading, Pennsylvania, on October 2, 1879, Stevens worked for many years as an executive for a Hartford insurance company, while producing some of the most exquisite and difficult poetry of the twentieth century. It was not until 1923, when the poet-businessman was already 44, that his first book, *Harmonium,* appeared. Unlike most first books, which are usually mere youthful promises of work to come, *Harmonium* revealed not only an understandable maturity of vision, but an astonishing maturity of technique. These early Stevens poems demonstrate all the skill and subtlety with which his later work is associated, all the hard brilliance of language and style. *Harmonium* was revised, expanded, and re-published in 1931, after which began a steady stream of Stevens books, including *Ideas of Order* (1935), *The Man With The Blue Guitar* (1937), *Parts Of A World* (1942), *Notes Toward A Supreme Fiction* (1942), etc., all gathered in his *Collected Poems* (1954). In the earlier poems, *Stevens* drew much of his imagery from the exotic opulence of the Caribbean, turning to New England for the increased pessimism of his later work. But his essential subject matter was non-geographical and remained constant throughout his writings: the artistic vision and the tools of expression. He died in his seventies on August 2, 1955, and the publication of *Opus Posthumous* in 1957 confirmed his position as a leading poet of the 20th century.

TABB, JOHN BANISTER

John Banister Tabb was born in Amelia County, Virginia, on March 22, 1845, eighth in a direct line from Humphrey Tabb, a 1637 Virginia settler. An ardent Confederate, Tabb tried to enlist in the rebel Army when war broke out; he was rejected, not because of his youth (he was 16), but because of poor eyesight. Instead, he served as a courier and agent aboard some of the more notorious blockade runners. In June, 1864, he was captured aboard the *Siren*, court-martialed, and imprisoned. It was while he lay in prison with the fever that Tabb met Sidney Lanier, whom he came to admire, and who inspired a revival of his interest in poetry and music. Following the war, Tabb studied and taught, first music and then religion. In 1872 he was converted to Catholicism and in 1884 was ordained as a priest. After his ordination he taught English at Saint Charles' Boys' School in Richmond until his death on November 19, 1909.

Tabb began writing poetry while still a boy, but none was published until 1882. In 1893 he published *An Octave to Mary* and the following year *Poems* appeared, a volume that was to see seventeen editions. Despite his popularity, Tabb never fulfilled the promise of his best poems, intense religious lyrics that recall both Emily Dickinson and the English metaphysical poets; but those few brilliant flashes of wit and poetic power have rescued him from the neglect and obscurity into which merely popular writers inevitably fall.

TATE, ALLEN

Allen John Orley Tate was born in Winchester, Kentucky, on November 19, 1899, and attended Vanderbilt University, where he was a member of the "Fugitive" group (see J. C. Ransom), graduating in 1922. Like other of the "Fugitives," he has since pursued a brilliant career as teacher, critic, and poet. Tate has taught at Southwestern College, the University of North Carolina, Columbia, Princeton, and, since 1951, the University of Minnesota.

As an essayist, Tate has an inclination for subjective evaluation, tempered by careful scholarship and intensive reading. He labels himself a reactionary (*Reactionary Essays on Poetry and Ideas*, 1936), justified to some extent by his defense of Poe and Pound against "liberal" criticism; but his close reasoning usually prevails against immoderate attack, and he has been instrumental, not only in restoring unpopular writers of the past, but in focusing attention on all that is best in modern poetry. Other books of criticism include *Reason in Madness* (1941), and *The Forlorn Demon* (1953), written after his conversion to Roman Catholicism.

Tate's poetry is precise, fiercely symbolic, and classically formal. Motivated often by religious feeling, he is able to impart a sense of multiple significance to every line, building a rich and varied experience into the entire poem. Most of them were printed in the collected edition, *Poems: 1922-1947* (1948).

TAYLOR, BAYARD

Although he longed throughout his life for an enduring literary reputation, Bayard Taylor was best-known as the American Marco Polo. Born January 11, 1825, of a Quaker family in the Quaker milieu of Chester County, Pennsylvania, Taylor sought his way out into the great world beyond his provincial confines at an early age. His youthful poetry attracted the attention of Rufus Griswold, editor of *Graham's Magazine,* who published *Ximena* in 1844 and provided Taylor with the means to escape his apprenticeship to a printer. Taylor was advanced money by several magazines for letters which he promised to send from abroad, and in 1844 he sailed for Europe, destined to become the century's most famous traveler. Journeying mainly afoot, he covered most of Europe, sending home the breathless, excited reports that were collected in *Views Afoot* (1846), which ran to twenty editions. *Eldorado* (1850) described his adventures in California and Mexico and created a sensation. In the decade that followed, Taylor's reputation rested on travels in Africa, Asia, Russia, and the Near East. In later years he published a number of trashy novels and an incredible quantity of mediocre poems, of which only a handful have stood the test of time. A new reputation came in 1870-1871, with the publication of his translation of *Faust,* faithful and accurate, but pedestrian in its language, which was nevertheless long the standard translation. He died December 19, 1878, in Germany. High repute was always in his grasp, but enduring fame eluded him.

TAYLOR, EDWARD

A chance discovery in 1937 by T. H. Johnson brought to light the work of one of America's finest poets, which had fortunately been preserved in manuscript for nearly two and a half centuries. With the publication in 1939 of *The Poetical Works of Edward Taylor* recognition finally came to this great Puritan poet, who had forbidden publication of his work during his lifetime.

Edward Taylor was born about 1645 in Leicestershire, England, but nothing is known about his life before his arrival in America in 1668. He had letters of introduction to Increase Mather and John Hull, both prominent in Colonial Massachusetts. He attended Harvard, probably with advanced standing, where he formed his life-long friendship with Samuel Sewall, the famous diarist, and graduated in 1671. He accepted the pulpit offered him by the congregation at Westfield, Connecticut, serving as minister until his death in 1729. He thrived in the quiet of his relatively isolated rural community, but maintained correspondence with his famous friends, who never lost their regard for him, and frequently visited him.

His poems are cast in the vigorous metaphysical mode of John Donne, but reflect the religious piety and homely reverence of George Herbert. Comparison with these giants of the 17th century in no way pales his achievement, for, though he wrote in a similar manner, he was scarcely imitative. Taylor's fresh and startling imagery and his incisive vision of God's hand in everything place his poems among the finest in all literature. Ironically, his work would probably have been neglected if published because it ran counter to the prevailing tastes of the 18th and 19th centuries; it was fortuitously rescued from oblivion in an era when metaphysical poetry was once again in favor.

Since Dr. Johnson's pioneering work, more Taylor manuscripts have been uncovered. In 1960, a fuller, though by no means complete, edition by Donald E. Stanford *(Poems of Edward Taylor)* was published.

THOREAU, HENRY DAVID

"Methinks I should be content," wrote Thoreau to his mother in 1843, "to sit at the back door in Concord, under the poplar tree, henceforth forever." Although he journeyed through New England north to the border and on into Canada, and later as far west as the Sioux country in Minnesota, Thoreau spent most of his life in his beloved Concord. He was born on July 12, 1817, named David Henry (he reversed the order twenty years later without explanation) for an uncle who died the following month. Except for brief sojourns in Boston and Chelmsford, he was raised in Concord and prepared at the Academy for his education at Harvard.

Thoreau's biography is not so much a succession of events as it is a recital of people and places. His uneventful and relatively undistinguished career at Harvard is thus characterized by the influential tutorship of Edward T. Channing, Jones Very, and, between terms, of Orestes A. Brownson. Following his graduation in 1837, Thoreau taught at Concord's town school for two weeks, but resigned rather than submit to parental pressure to whip the boys. The following year he and his brother John opened a school in their father's house, where moral suasion was the rule and where revolutionary new methods like "field trips" for nature study were initiated. Despite its success, the school was closed in 1841 owing to John Thoreau's ill health. Following his brother's death some months later, Thoreau went to live at Emerson's house where the two soon became fast friends. In 1843 he went to New York and became a tutor in the home of Emerson's brother on Staten Island for a year. Upon his return to Concord he prepared for the two-year residence at Walden Pond that was to prove the central experience of his life.

From July 4, 1845, to September 6, 1847, Thoreau lived in a small hut at the edge of Walden Pond. Popular misconceptions of his stay see him as a solitary hermit, living off the land and disdaining the comfort of civilization. Actually, Thoreau spent much of this time in Concord, and was dependent on the Emerson pantry for food, the tradesmen for supplies. The sojourn at Walden was not so much a self-reliant "return to nature" as it was an essay in simplification, and, despite the criticism of Concord life in *Walden* (1854), Thoreau clearly had no objection to so-

HENRY DAVID THOREAU

ciety as such, but protested against the meaningless complexity upon which his society relied.

While at Walden Pond, Thoreau prepared the manuscript of *A Week on the Concord and Merrimack Rivers*, a compilation from his early journals threaded around the chronicle of a vacation he spent with his brother in the summer of 1839. Afterward, he traveled afoot in Cape Cod, visited the Maine woods again, and spent a week in Canada. Each of these expeditions was recorded in later books.

During the '50s he became an active and articulate abolitionist and, at the end of the decade, a defender of his friend John Brown. His circle of acquaintances became ever wider, and during these years he formed friendships with the poets Ellery Channing and Walt Whitman, and with the most prominent writers, scholars, and philosophers of New England. In 1860 a neglected cold led to an aggravated bronchial condition ending in tuberculosis. In 1861, feeble though he was, Thoreau voyaged to Minnesota to witness a gathering of the Sioux. His health failing, he returned to his Concord bedroom with the lingering illness, and, on May 6, 1862, he died.

The standard edition of Thoreau's works runs to twenty volumes, though he published little while he was alive.

On this mass of work, Thoreau has developed two reputations, neither of which is entirely accurate, as a naturalist and as a social philosopher. Although he spent much time in his later years on exact "scientific" observation of nature, his best nature writing is that which re-creates the sense of awe and wonder with which he beheld the natural world, and is seldom scientific. In the same way, his social thought is never really programmatic, though he is claimed as a prophet by socialists, anarchists, and non-violent activists. His ultimate reputation is literary, both as a minor poet and as a major prose stylist. Seldom in literature is style, form, and content so effectively welded. Thoreau's nature observations, though infrequently as precise and accurate as those of more scholarly naturalists, are somehow always more cogent and meaningful, conveying the tension and breath of man in nature. *Walden,* his supreme achievement, is not a call to the woods, but an essay on man's condition and a speculation of his possibilities within the natural world of which he is part. Seen in this light, even the essay on civil disobedience is not so much a program of political action as an appeal to the nobler instincts of man. From his small world of Concord, Thoreau enlarged his experience to cosmic proportions, enlarged the entire American experience, and, with Yankee particularity, brought Transcendental mysticism down from its ethereal heights to the very soil on which men stand.

TIMROD, HENRY

Henry Timrod, the "poet-laureate of the Confederacy," was born in Charleston, South Carolina, on December 8, 1828, and was even more neglected in his lifetime than he has been since. In 1844 he entered Franklin College (later the University of Georgia) to prepare for an academic appointment he was never able to find. Working as a tutor on a Carolina plantation for over ten years, he wrote poems for magazines like *The Southern Literary Messenger,* and often journeyed to Charleston to join the literary circle around William Gilmore Simms. A slim collection of poems was published in 1860, but was quickly buried, despite favorable reception among critics, by the focus of interest on North-South hostility.

The war that followed, however, proved the necessary inspiration to his undeniable talents, and during the first years of the war he produced some of his best poems. Recognition was slow in coming, however, and from 1862 to 1867 Timrod was dogged by ill-health, personal misfortune, and poverty. In the summer of 1867, following a painful operation, he composed "Magnolia Cemetery," probably his finest poem. Several weeks later, on October 6, he died.

The sincere attempts by Simms and others to resurrect his reputation was briefly successful in 1899, when a collection of his poems was published and interest was revived. But the revival was short-lived and to this day Timrod is little anthologized, and only obscurely remembered, compounding the injury of this fine poet's tragic life.

TRILLING, LIONEL

Except for his continued recognition of the validity of Freudian insights in our understanding of literature, Lionel Trilling cannot be identified as a member of any "school" of criticism. His guiding critical principles are his own keen perception and fine taste.

He was born in New York City on July 4, 1905, educated in the public schools and at Columbia University, where he is now a professor of literature. His first book, *Matthew Arnold* (1939), is already a classic of critical biography, rescuing the reputation of the great Victorian poet-critic from severe and undeserved decline. *E. M. Forster* (1943) brilliantly interpreted for American readers a novelist, who, before Trilling's study, was chiefly known as the author of *A Passage to India.* Essays by Trilling have been instrumental in reviving critical interest in surprisingly neglected classics, like Henry James's *The Princess Casamassima,* and in introducing the work of unknown writers like Isaac Babel. He has been connected editorially with *Kenyon Review* and *Partisan Review* and may be regarded as partially responsible for the high standard these magazines have maintained. His essays have been collected in *The Liberal Imagination* (1950), *The Opposing Self* (1955) and *A Gathering of Fugitives* (1956). Trilling's only novel, *The Middle of the Journey* (1949), although too static and self-consciously literary, remains one of the few novels to deal seriously with an American leftist confronted with Communist treason.

TWAIN, MARK

A. F. BRADLEY

MARK TWAIN

The famous pseudonym "Mark Twain" was attached in 1865 to *The Celebrated Jumping Frog of Calaveras County,* a sketch which made its author famous overnight. That young man was Samuel Langhorne Clemens, who was born in Florida, Missouri, on November 30, 1835. Clemens was reared in Hannibal, Missouri, where his father moved when the boy was only four; but the father died when he was eight, and young Clemens was apprenticed to his brother, a printer and journalist. In 1851, he left his trade to become a pilot on the Mississippi, at which exacting job he worked for ten years. At the outbreak of the Civil War, Clemens joined his brother in Nevada, then drifted as an itinerant journalist and gold prospector to various parts of the west. In California, he became friendly with Artemus Ward and Bret Harte, who delighted in his humorous sketches and urged their publication. With the appearance of *The Jumping Frog,* Clemens became forever Mark Twain.

In 1869, Twain's first book, *The Innocents Abroad,* was published. In its confrontation of "greenhorns" and polite (European) society it foreshadowed one of Twain's basic themes. The following year he married Olivia Langdon, and settled permanently in the East. *Roughing It,* a loosely autobiographical account of his western adventures, appeared in 1872. With the publication of

Adventures of Tom Sawyer (1875), a perennial boys' favorite, the stage was set for Twain's masterpiece. He had written of the rough life on the frontier; he had contrasted it with "sivilization"; and he had returned to the scenes of his childhood, on the pre-war Mississippi. He started on the new book immediately, but it eluded him. He frittered away time on such minor efforts as *A Tramp Abroad* (1870) and *The Prince and The Pauper* (1882) still circling around the theme. *Life On The Mississippi* (1883) gave a hint of what was to come. Finally, in 1884, he completed *The Adventures of Huckleberry Finn.* This book contained all the humor of his early sketches, all the outdoor vigor of his frontier tales, a deft, subtle contrast between natural freedom and the confinements of society, and all the rich lore and color of the river. And more: it gave America a new style and a living myth. Some critics claim that the book escaped Twain's intentions, some that it fails, some that it is great in spite of itself and its author. In any case, the book endures as a classic of American literature.

In later years Twain wrote prolifically but never quite recaptured the spirit of fluency of *Huck Finn.* The best works of the last period were pessimistic in outlook and seldom achieved the popularity of more pedestrian efforts like *A Connecticut Yankee In King Arthur's Court* (1889). Those that receive serious attention today include the puzzling *Pudd'nhead Wilson* (1894), the bitter short novel *The Man That Corrupted Hadleyburg*, and (posthumously published) *The Mysterious Stranger* (1916).

Twain was born in the year of Halley's Comet, and predicted his death for the year of its return. On April 2, 1910, the prophecy was fulfilled.

TYLER, ROYALL

Christened William Clark Tyler (later changed by court order), Royall Tyler was born in Boston on July 18, 1757. He entered Harvard three days before his fifteenth birthday, and upon his graduation in 1776 was awarded a degree by Yale as well, an early tribute to his intellectual ability. Two years later he served as a major in the Independent Company of Boston, but was forced to withdraw from military service when his father's death left his mother dependent on him. In 1780 he was admitted to the bar, practicing first in Maine, then in Braintree, Massachusetts. By 1787, however, he was again in uniform, engaged in the suppression of Shays' Rebellion. In the course of this service he was sent on a mission to New York, where he attended the theatre and became friendly with the well-known comedian, Thomas Wignell. Within a month he wrote his first play, *The Contrast*, the first native American comedy produced by a professional company. The "contrast" of the title—between honest American modes and the artificial manners of Europe (in this case, of an Englishman)—has remained one of the enduring themes of American literature. The character Jonathan became the prototype for generations of stage Yankees. Although Tyler wrote many plays after this, few survived and none matched this first pioneering achievement.

Tyler also penned a good deal of poetry, remembered, if at all, mostly for its careful depiction of everyday life in the early days of the republic. His novel,

The Algerine Captive (1797), a Swiftian satire on Northern quackery and Southern slavery, is an important landmark in the history of American fiction. Meanwhile, Tyler pursued his law career in Vermont, serving in a variety of judicial positions, including Chief Justice of the Supreme Court (1807-13). Both his literary and judicial careers were cut short by a cancer that led to blindness and, on August 26, 1826, to death.

VERY, JONES

Never widely known during his lifetime, though an intimate of Emerson and other New England Transcendentalists, Jones Very has fallen into nearly total obscurity since his death. He was born in Salem, Massachusetts, on August 28, 1813, descended from six generations of seafarers. At the age of ten Very sailed with his father aboard the *Aurelia*, his father's ship, to Russia, and the following year to New Orleans, snatching what education he could while in port. In 1824 his father died and Very's seagoing career ended. For the next ten years he pursued an assortment of jobs while he continued his education, and in 1834 he entered Harvard as a sophomore. A prizewinning though relatively friendless student, Very earned an appointment as freshman Greek tutor, providing the funds for study at Harvard Divinity School. While here he began to write religious sonnets which he claimed were verbatim records of "communications" from the Holy Ghost. His sincerity and apparent spiritual exaltation drew Emerson's enthusiasm when they met in Concord, inspiring Very to even greater heights upon his return to Cambridge. His colleagues, however, did not share Emerson's delight and doubted Very's sanity. Resigning in 1838, Very spent a month in an asylum, but the experience only intensified his religious conviction.

Essays and Poems (1839), published with Emerson's help, stated Very's quietistic philosophy of total submission to God's will and enjoyed some popularity in the Transcendentalist circle. But as the interest in his theories waned, his own powers decreased. Few of his later poems have the same power as those of his first volume. His last forty years were spent in awaiting the eternity of which he had had visions in his youth, and he died on May 8, 1880, a self-pronounced "failure." The recent revival of interest in the intellectual background of the "American Renaissance" has brought about a rediscovery of these quiet, profound visions of a higher truth, mystical revelations clad in a poetry of a very high order.

VIERECK, PETER

Peter Robert Edwin Viereck was born in New York City on August 5, 1916. He was educated at Harvard, receiving his B. S. in 1937, and returning after a year as a Henry fellow at Oxford to take his advanced degrees. Viereck has taught history at a series of well-known women's colleges: Radcliffe, Smith, and, since 1948, at Mt. Holyoke. His first book, *Metapolitics* (1941) is an historical study pleading Viereck's pet political viewpoint, "liberal conservatism." He has written numerous books and essays in this vein, notably *Conservatism Revisited* (1949), *The Shame and Glory of the Intellectuals* (1953), and *Conservatism: From John Adams to Churchill* (1956).

His special political bias lends animus to much of his poetry, often marring its effect. But since the publication of his first volume of poems, *Terror and Decorum* (1948), which won the Pulitzer Prize, Viereck has established himself as an important young lyricist of remarkable sensitivity. Other books of his poetry include *Strike Through the Mask!* (1950), *The First Morning* (1952), *The Persimmon Tree* (1956), and, most recently, *The Tree Witch: A Poem and a Play* (1960).

WARREN, ROBERT PENN

One of the more gifted and prolific of the "Fugitive" group (see J. C. Ransom), Robert Penn Warren has pursued successful careers in several fields —as teacher, poet, novelist, and critic. He was born in Guthrie, Kentucky, on

UPI PHOTO

ROBERT PENN WARREN

April 24, 1905, and educated at Vanderbilt University, where he joined the "Fugitives." Further studies took him to the University of California, Yale, and Oxford. In 1935, after accepting a post at Louisiana State University, he founded the *Southern Review*, which he edited until his departure for the University of Minnesota seven years later. Not only was he active in fostering "the Southern renascence," but he was its chief ornament. That *XXXVI Poems* (1935) heralded a bright and imaginative poet was amply proved by *Eleven Poems on The Same Theme* (1942); the brilliantly sustained long poems, *Brother To Dragons* (1953); and the Pulitzer Prize-winning *Promises* (1957). His career as a writer of fiction began with *Night Rider* (1938), a dark, violent tale of Southern mores. His fictional account of a demogogue's career, *All The King's Men* (1946), won the Pulitzer Prize and was adapted into an Academy Award-winning film. A collection of short stories, *The Circus In The Attic*, appeared in 1948, and an historical novel, *World Enough And Time* (based on the "Kentucky Tragedy") in 1950. Warren's best critical writing was assembled in *Selected Essays* (1958). Other books include a number of college textbooks (mostly in collaboration with Cleanth Brooks); two novels, *Band of Angels* (1955), and

The Cave (1959), and his most recent collections of poems, *You, Emperors and Others* (1960).

UPI PHOTO

EUDORA WELTY

WELTY, EUDORA

Eudora Welty was born in Jackson, Mississippi, on April 13, 1909, and has lived there for most of her life. After two years at the Mississippi State College for Women, she went to the University of Wisconsin, where she took her B. A. in 1929. In 1930 she studied advertising at Columbia University and worked as a copy-writer for a year or so; but, disturbed at the prospect of spending her life talking people into buying things they didn't want, she gave it up and returned to Jackson. She published her first story in 1936, and was surprised at its acceptance. She has published dozens more since. Her personal ingenuousness is an asset in her writing, which depends on economy and simplicity for its effect. At her best, she writes in a spare, sincere style that can be incisive and powerful. *Delta Wedding*, her first novel which appeared in 1946, demonstrated that she could extend the same graceful clarity and vigor through a longer work. The delightful novelette, *The Ponder Heart* (1953) was even more successful, and it remains a masterpiece of that form. Her most recent novel is *Bride of the Innisfallen* (1955).

WHITMAN, WALT

"The good, gray poet," open-collared and open-hearted, a kind of cross between Johnny Appleseed and Moses: this is the popular image of Walt Whitman, created by the poet himself and cultivated for more than half his lifetime.

Although Emerson, presented with a copy of the first edition of *Leaves of Grass,* envisioned "a long foreground, for such a start," there is little in Whitman's early life to indicate the great achievement of his poetry. He was born near Huntington, Long Island, on May 31, 1819. In 1823 his father, failing as a carpenter, moved to Brooklyn, where young Whitman attended the public schools briefly, quitting at the age of twelve to become an apprentice printer. Except for two years spent as a teacher in Long Island's country schools, he worked for the next twenty years as a printer and journalist. In the early 1840s he worked for several New York newspapers. For two years he edited the Brooklyn *Eagle,* and, following the loss of that position, departed on the long and perilous overland journey to New Orleans, where he worked three months on the *Crescent* before returning to New York. It is thought that the experiences he must have had on this trip, the close contact with the wild variety of America in that day, inspired his poetic ambitions. A love affair in New Orleans is conjectured; but in fact, little is known except that he found journalistic work hard to come by when he returned. Therefore, he joined his father in the building trades, which in the early '50s were experiencing a small boom in Brooklyn. Whitman showed a keen business sense—in a short while he had become a contractor and speculated in real estate. But somewhere he had developed the ambition to write poetry, and the next few years were devoted to producing the first edition of *Leaves Of Grass* (1855). The book was violently attacked, as Whitman did not hesitate to trade on Emerson's supposed enthusiasm, revising and expanding the book in ever-larger editions. In spite of all the excitement pro and con, however, the book did not sell well. In 1861, visiting a wounded brother in Virginia, Whitman became aware of the need for male nurses, and voluntarily served in this capacity until the end of the Civil War. Exposed in this way to all the brutal horror of combat, and at the same time to the grim courage of the soldiers, most of them farmers, laborers, and artisans, Whitman was moved to write *Drum-Taps* (1865) his sequence of war poems, which were later incorporated into *Leaves of Grass*. When Lincoln was assassinated, it was Whitman who composed the most eloquent and enduring elegy, *When Lilacs Last in the Dooryard Bloom'd*, which was also later incorporated, together with a number of other Lincoln poems, into *Leaves of Grass*. In fact, all his later life is inevitably bound with the history of his book, not only because most of his energy was devoted to its continual revision, but also because he deliberately fitted himself to his public image as exposed in his book until, in the end, they were congruent. An appointment in the Bureau of Indian Affairs was lost when the Secretary of the Interior read some of Whitman's poetry. It was then that William Douglas O'Connor wrote the rhapsodic *Good Gray Poet* in his defense, which influenced his appointment as a clerk in the Treasury Department. He resigned in 1873 following a paralytic stroke, and retired to Camden, New Jersey. There he continued to revise *Leaves of Grass,* establishing the eighth and final order of the poems for a publication in 1881 by a reputable publisher. Ironically, the book was now banned. This resulted in a tremendous demand, which Whitman gladly filled from Camden, and made the book finally successful. From that point on Whitman made frequent additions to the text, appending the new material at the end. The final edition was authorized by the poet just before his death, on March 27, 1892.

From the very beginning, *Leaves of Grass* was a revolutionary departure from the conventional verse of the day, but sources for the long lines and the expansive imagery can be found in the Bible, epic poetry, and the opera, for which Whitman had a great fondness. More radical are the ideas that the book embodied, for which the style proved the perfect vehicle. The key to Whitman is his great capacity: he loved everything, all objects, all places, and above all, people. He pleaded for a natural acceptance of life as it is; he celebrated the body and bodily functions; he called for a straightforward attitude toward sex, devoid of shame. (His own emotional bent was homosexual.) He was the great apostle of democracy, of the equality of peoples and the dignity of simple occupations. He was a prophet of social and economic progress, and particularly of future American glory.

To express this grandiose vision, he hit upon a bardic style, a capricious gesture in words. Many of his poems are nothing more than the stringing-together of place names; the names of rivers flow together into an ocean of sound. Others are a series of vignettes; still others are conventional lyrics, jewels all the brighter owing to their lavish, extravagant setting. The style and the message jarred America into wakefulness, and much of the sentiment of *Leaves of Grass* entered the national consciousness as myth, the great American dream.

Whitman was not without his excesses, either in style or sentiment; but they are the excesses allowed the innovator. In the conscious way he cultivated his public image there are indications that he may have been aware of his myth-making role, an indication borne out by some of the material in *Specimen Days* (1882). There is little doubt as to the sincerity of his convictions, either. In *Democratic Vistas* (1871) he presented a more sober and realistic image of democracy than in his poems; but, in the last analysis, he voted for it.

WHITTIER, JOHN GREENLEAF

Modern standards of taste have somewhat dimmed the reputation of John Greenleaf Whittier among critics

JOHN GREENLEAF WHITTIER

and scholars, but he remains one of America's most familiar and popular poets. He was born on December 17, 1807, in Haverhill, Massachusetts, and grew up on his father's farm. When his older sister, Mary, sent off his poem "The Exile's Departure" to the *Newburyport Free Press*, the editor, William Lloyd Garrison, not only gladly published it, but came to call on the lad. Despite Garrison's urging, Whittier's father would not allow him to go to school, dubbing education "foolishness." Encouraged by Garrison, however, Whittier continued writing poems, publishing them in the *Free Press* and in the *Haverhill Gazette*. In 1827 his father relented, and Whittier studied for a year at Haverhill Academy. During the next four years he worked as editor of several small newspapers, publishing his first book, *Legends of New England in Prose and Verse*, in 1831. The following year, under Garrison's tutelage, Whittier became an active abolitionist, writing anti-slavery tracts, participating in runaway slave escapes, and devoting much of his poetry to this political objective for thirty years. Most of his best-known poems, like *The Barefoot Boy* and *Snow-Bound; a Winter Idyl*, were not written until after the Civil War, when Whittier settled into a less active life in rural new England. Present-day

readers tend to return, however, to those early *Legends of New England*, to such poems as *Ichabod* and *Skipper Ireson's Ride*. Until his death, Whittier was active and vocal in Republican circles, but in contrast to his ante-bellum radicalism, he became an arch-conservative. Vigorously opposed to agrarian and labor reform, he actually wrote poems extolling poverty and urging the working classes to be happy with their lot. He died on September 7, 1892, in Hampton Falls, Massachusetts.

WHITE, E. B.

Since 1925, when he began writing for *The New Yorker*, Elwyn Brooks White has been regarded as one of America's foremost essayists. He was born in Mount Vernon, New York, on July 11, 1899. Delayed by a year in the army, he graduated from Cornell University in 1921. Uncertain about his vocation, White traveled westward, working in Seattle, Washington, for a year as a newspaper reporter, then continuing onward to the Aleutians and the Arctic. In 1925 *The New Yorker* was founded, and White contributed occasional pieces to the new magazine. His lean, lively style and his clear view of the American scene impressed Harold Ross, the editor, who invited White to join the staff. From 1925 to 1938, E. B. White's unsigned "Notes and Comment" was one of the magazine's most distinguished features.

White's gentle satire appeared in book form first in 1929, with the publication of *Is Sex Necessary?* (in collaboration with James Thurber). In 1938, White began a column in *Harper's Magazine* called "One Man's Meat," which he continued until 1943. Since then, he has been a frequent contributor of prose and verse to *The New Yorker*. *The Second Tree From The Corner* (1954) collected some of his best essays. In 1959, prompted by a decline in good writing in America and nostalgia for his own days at Cornell, he revised and published *Elements of Style*, by his former teacher, William Strunk, which proved a surprise best-seller.

UPI PHOTO

RICHARD WILBUR

WILBUR, RICHARD

Anyone who saw the Broadway production of Leonard Bernstein's delightful operetta *Candide* (1957), or who has heard the recording, is familiar with the work of Richard Wilbur. In collaboration with Lillian Hellman, he wrote the libretto for the show.

Wilbur was born in New York City on March 1, 1921, and educated at Amherst. Following the war, he pursued an academic career, teaching at Harvard, Wellesley College, and, since 1957, at Wesleyan University. His first book of poems, *The Beautiful Changes,* was published in 1947, followed by *Ceremony* (1950) *and Poems* (1957). Characteristically witty and urbane, many of his poems tend to be slick turns of phrase, skimming on the surface of experience. At his best, Wilbur turns his confident technical skill to superb lyric expression, always guided by a wry and lively sense of humor. The interest in classical French literature revealed by his work on *Candide* also prompted a first-rate translation of Molière's *Misanthrope* (1955).

WILDER, THORNTON

A continuously striking freshness of viewpoint, combined with meticulous craftsmanship, characterize Thornton Niven Wilder as novelist and playwright. He was born on April 17, 1897,
in Madison, Wisconsin, but moved at an early age to China, where his father, Amos Parker Wilder, editor of the *Wisconsin State Journal,* served as American consul-general, first in Hong Kong, then in Shanghai. It was in China that Wilder received his early education. After his return to the United States in 1914 he studied at Oberlin, Yale, and Princeton, and in Rome. His first book, *The Cabala,* appeared in 1925, but it was in 1927, with the publication of *The Bridge of San Luis Rey,* that Wilder burst upon the American literary scene. This Pulitzer Prize-winning novel, based on an actual event, was an investigation into the meaning of the lives of several victims of a disaster in colonial Peru.

From 1930 to 1936, Wilder taught at the University of Chicago and began writing plays. *The Long Christmas Dinner* was published in 1931. Production of each of his subsequent plays has been considered an important theatrical event, particularly *Our Town* (1938), *The Skin Of Our Teeth* (1942), and *The Matchmaker* (1954). *Our Town* has received innumerable performances in many languages. Wilder's witty, economical style, developed in his writing for the stage, is evident in his most recent novel, *The Ides Of March* (1948), a fanciful recreation of the time of Caesar's fall.

WILLIAMS, TENNESSEE

Thomas Lanier Williams was born in Columbus, Mississippi on March 26, 1914. His father was a traveling shoe salesman, and the family lived in the rectory with the boy's grandfather, who was the town's Episcopal minister. In 1926, when his father was offered an office job with the company, Williams moved with his family to St. Louis. He turned college age during the depression and, although he made a beginning try at attending, economic necessity forced him to work instead. Williams worked for several years in the factory of his father's company; but the combination of hard work by day and long hours of trying to write by night was too much for Williams' health, and he

TENNESSEE WILLIAMS

suffered a breakdown. Following his recovery, he alternated a series of odd
jobs with attendance at school and finally, in 1938, received his B. A. at the
University of Iowa. It was while there
that he wrote his first play and changed
his name because, as he explains, he
had already published a quantity of bad
poetry under his real name and wanted
to disassociate it from the work that was
to follow. A Rockefeller Fellowship in
1940 enabled him to write *Battle of
Angels.* Although the play failed when
it was produced in 1941, it drew attention to him as a promising young playwright. This promise was fulfilled in
1945, with the production of *The Glass
Menagerie,* one of the finest plays of the
modern American theatre, and the first
in a succession of Williams stage triumphs. A *Streetcar Named Desire* won
the Pulitzer Prize in 1947, and was followed by *Summer and Smoke* (1948),
The Rose Tattoo (1951), *Camino Real*
(1953), and *Cat on a Hot Tin Roof*
(1955), which again won him the Pulitzer Prize. His more recent plays, *Or-
pheus Descending, Sweet Bird of Youth,*
and *Period of Adjustment* have not met
with the same critical approval as his
earlier work, but they reveal a slow
change in his point of view and are
clearly the work of a writer who knows
what he is doing.

Most of Williams' better-known
plays have been filmed, and his screenplay for *Baby Doll* demonstrated his
mastery of that genre. Several of his
shorter plays have been successfully
produced off-Broadway and on television.

As a writer of fiction, Williams does
not have that same fluidity of style and
clarity of vision which marks his best
plays. They display a tendency to be
precious and self-consciously poetic, although they treat the same problems of
violence, spiritual degeneration, and de-
spair that are his themes on the stage.
His only novel, *The Roman Spring of
Mrs. Stone* was published in 1950, and
his short stories have been collected
in *One Arm* (1948) and *Hard Candy*
(1954).

WILLIAMS, WILLIAM CARLOS

For more than half a century the
prolific writings of William Carlos Williams have influenced poets and prose
writers, have been admired by critics,
have been studied by collegians, but,
unfortunately, have not found a wide
public. Heedless of public apathy, he
has quietly published more than forty
volumes of prose and poetry, and has
achieved stature as one of America's
finest writers.

Williams was born in Rutherford,
New Jersey, on September 17, 1883.
He was educated at a variety of schools
in New York City, France, and Switzer-
land, then attended the University of
Pennsylvania Medical School where he
received his M. D. in 1906. Following
graduate study in pediatrics at the University of Leipzig and internship in New
York, he established in 1909 his long
medical practice in his home town of
Rutherford, which he ended only recently. His first book, *Poems,* appeared
in the same year.

His taut, precise style was probably
influenced in the beginning by his
friendship with Ezra Pound and "H. D."
(Hilda Doolittle), early exponents of
imagism; but his poetry, retaining imagism's insistence on the value of the
object—"no ideas but in things," Williams has pronounced—has never lapsed

into that sentimentality and preciosity to which imagism easily falls prey. The total effect of his work is a luminous, sensual experience, intensely lyrical and highly individual. Everyday objects, the hardness of actuality, are converted in his poems into emblems of deep feeling and great power. The numerous volumes of his poetry have been collected several times, most recently in *The Collected Earlier Poems* (1951) and *The Collected Later Poems* (1950). More recent publications include *Desert Music,* (1954), *Journey to Love* (1955) and *Sappho* (1957).

Williams' prose is as much to be reckoned with as his poetry. Writing mostly short stories and novelettes, he has applied the same eye for precision and ear for true speech to his fiction that he has to his poetry, lending in a somewhat satiric point of view and absolute honesty of observation. His most notable works of fiction are *The Great American Novel* (1923), *The Knife of the Times* (1932), *In The Money* (1940), and *The Build Up* (1952). He has also writen plays, an autobiography (1951), and numerous essays, including the remarkable *In The American Grain* (1925), a beautifully written account of the growth of the American mind. One of his experimental plays, *Many Loves,* began in 1959 a long and successful engagement in a small New York repertory

UPI PHOTO
WILLIAM CARLOS WILLIAMS

theater. He died March 4, 1963, in Rutherford, New Jersey.

WYLIE, ELINOR

Until 1910, Elinor Morton Hoyt lived the quiet life of a well-to-do Philadelphia "socialite." She was born September 7, 1885, in Somerville, New Jersey, and grew up in the fashionable Philadelphia suburb of Rosemont. When, in 1897, her father was named Assistant Attorney-General of the United States (he was later Solicitor-General), the family moved to Washington and the society of officialdom, In 1903, Elinor, together with her sister and uncle, spent "the season" in Paris and London; in 1905 she married Philip Hichborn, a Philadelphian—and in 1907 bore him a son. In 1910, she scandalized Philadelphia society by eloping with Horace Wylie, who was also married. They sailed for England, where Elinor began writing poetry. Philip Hichborn died a suicide in 1912, but Wylie's wife refused to grant him a divorce until 1915, at which time he and Elinor were married. They returned to Boston the following year. If the social world was closed to them, the literary world was not; and with the publication of *Nets to Catch the Wind* (1921), Elinor was set firmly in its midst. In 1923 she divorced Wylie and married William Rose Benét. That year she published a new book of poems, *Black Armour,* and her first novel, *Jennifer Lorn.* In the next five years she wrote three more novels, including *The Venetian Glass Nephew* (1925) and *The Orphan Angel,* besides several volumes of verse. Considering that she was a founder and director of the Literary Guild, and that she wrote fragile, precious poetry and prose that does not lend itself to quantitative production, this was a prodigious output. In 1928 she returned to England and wrote the 19-sonnet sequence, *One Person,* probably her best work. Partially paralyzed by a stroke, she returned in December to New York. For a few days she worked on the manuscript of her final poetic statement, *Angels and Earthly Creatures,* and when that was all in order. on December 15, she died.

INDEX TO FIRST LINES OF POEMS

DICTIONARY—INDEX
TO THE FIVE VOLUMES

American Scholar, The (1837), Ralph Waldo Emerson, E 21

Anderson, Lon (old miner in *The Great Divide*), D 107

ANDERSON, SHERWOOD (1876–1941)
I Want to Know Why, S 173
discussed in *Introduction*, S 8
discussed in *Social Themes in American Realism*, E 267
discussed in *Traditions in American Literature*, E 51–53

Andrews, Mrs. (character in *Shore Acres*), D 49

Andrews, Squire (character in *Shore Acres*), D 49

Angels at Hamburg, The (1948), Randall Jarrell, P 223

Anglo-American Difference, The (1957), W. H. Auden, E 208

Annabel Lee (1845), Edgar Allan Poe, P 61

Anne Rutledge (1915), Edgar Lee Masters, P 137

Annie (Mike Braneen's burro in *The Wind and the Snow of Winter*), S 234

Annie (subject of *For Annie*), P 61

Apology for Bad Dreams (1925), Robinson Jeffers, P 175

Architect (employed by Ghent in *The Great Divide*), D 107

Arizona, setting in *The Great Divide*, D 107

Armandy (whore in *The Wind and the Snow of Winter*), S 237

Armstrong, Louis (jazz musician), E 62

Arnold, Matthew (1822–1888, English poet, essayist, and critic), E 3, 38, 123–24

Ars Poetica (1946), Archibald MacLeish, P 187

Art and Democracy (1891), William Dean Howells, E 38

Art of Fiction, The (1888), Henry James, E 250

At Lanier's Grave (1892), John Banister Tabb, P 136

At Magnolia Cemetery (1860), Henry Timrod, P 126

Attitudes toward Henry James (1943), Philip Rahv, E 153

Auber, Lake, setting for *Ulalume—A Ballad*, P 58

AUDEN, W. H. (1907—)
The Anglo-American Difference, E 208
quoted, P 243

Aunt (of Mildred Douglas in *The Hairy Ape*), D 141

Aurelius, Marcus (121–180 A.D., Roman emperor and philosopher), P 134

Babbitt (hero, title of Sinclair Lewis novel), E 267

Bacchus (1867), Ralph Waldo Emerson, P 27

Backward Glance, A (1888), Walt Whitman, E 176

Bacon, Francis (1561–1626, English statesman, philosopher, and essayist), E 2

Bailey, Steve (character in *Shore Acres*), D 49

Baldy (Mike Braneen's burro in *The Wind and the Snow of Winter*), S 235

Ballad of Trees and the Master, A (1880), Sidney Lanier, P 134

Bar Harbor, Maine, setting for *Shore Acres*, D 49

BARRETT, WILLIAM (1913—)
We're on the Road, E 307

Barron, Homer (Miss Emily's sweetheart in *A Rose for Emily*), S 189

Bartleby the Scrivener (1853), Herman Melville, S 64

Barton, Bruce (American advertising man, author), P 188

Bartram (lime burner in *Ethan Brand*), S 31

Baudelaire, Pierre Charles (1821–1867, French poet, author of *Flowers of Evil*, a sensation in 1857), P 6

Bayard, Mother (oldest character in *The Long Christmas Dinner*), D 210

Bear, The (1930), Robert Frost, P 154

Bearded Oaks (1944), Robert Penn Warren, P 211

Because I could not stop for Death— (712) (1890), Emily Dickinson, P 130

Becker, Ed (stable owner in *I Want to Know Why*), S 174

Beckersville, Kentucky, setting for *I Want to Know Why*, S 173

Bedouin Song (1852), Bayard Taylor, P 124

Beerbohm, Max (English author, caricaturist, and "man about town" of *fin de siècle* London), E 3

Behmen, Jakob (1575–1624, German Theosophist and mystic), E 145; P 134

Belasco, David (1954–1931, American playwright and producer), D 8

Bellhouse, Lady (Mamie Cutter's friend in *Mrs. Medwin*), S 107

Bells for John Whiteside's Daughter (1945), John Crowe Ransom, P 179

Bells of San Blas, The (1882), Henry Wadsworth Longfellow, P 38

BENÉT, STEPHEN VINCENT (1898–1943)
American Names, P 194
From *John Brown's Body*:
The Song of the Breath, P 194
biography, P 244

Berg, The (1866), Herman Melville, P 122

Berni, Rosalba (heroine of *The Venetian Glass Nephew*), N 362

Bernis, Cardinal de (Rosalba's father in *The Venetian Glass Nephew*), N 368

Berry, Ann (Martin's wife in *Shore Acres*), D 49

Berry, Bob (character in *Shore Acres*), D 49

Berry, Helen (Martin's daughter in *Shore Acres*), D 49

Berry, Martin (owner of *Shore Acres*), D 49

Berry, Mary (character in *Shore Acres*), D 49

Berry, Millie (character in *Shore Acres*), D 49

Berry, Nathan'l (Uncle Nat, Martin's older brother in *Shore Acres*), D 49

Berry, Young Nat (character in *Shore Acres*), D 49

BERRYMAN, JOHN (1914—)
Homage to Mistress Bradstreet, P 225
biography, P 244

Besant, Walter (1836–1901), E 251–64

Bierce, Ambrose (American author), E 51; S 7

Bill (cowboy in *The Blue Hotel*), S 144

Billson, John Wharton (leading citizen in *The Man That Corrupted Hadleyburg*), N 80

Billy Budd (1888–1891), Herman Melville, N 18

BISHOP, ELIZABETH (1911—)
Florida, P 217
A Miracle for Breakfast, P 216
Wading at Wellfleet, P 216
biography, P 244

Bivouac on a Mountain Side (1865), Walt Whitman, P 118

Blackberry Winter (1946), Robert Penn Warren, S 204

Black Mesa, Arizona, setting for *The Petrified Forest*, D 169

BLACKMUR, R. P. (1904—)
The Craft of Herman Melville, E 102
Introduction, N 1
discussed in *Introduction*, E 8–9

Black Riders, The (1895), Stephen Crane, P 144

Blades of Grass, The (1895), Stephen Crane, P 144

Blake, Josiah (postmaster, storekeeper in *Shore Acres*), D 49

Blanc, Mr. (Easterner in *The Blue Hotel*), S 144

Blue Girls (1945), John Crowe Ransom, P 182

Blue Hotel, The (1898), Stephen Crane, P 143

Boston, Massachusetts
setting in *Portion of an Autobiography*, E 71
setting for *Where the Rainbow Ends*, P 230

Botticellian Trees, The (1938), William Carlos Williams, P 168

Boucicault, Dion (adaptor of *Rip Van Winkle* for stage, 1865), D 7

Boy (ranch hand in *The Great Divide*), D 107

Bradford, Andrew (1686–1742, American printer, son of William Bradford and friend of Benjamin Franklin), E 79–80

BRADSTREET, ANNE (1612?–1672)
The Flesh and the Spirit, P 9
A Letter to Her Husband, P 11
To My Dear and Loving Husband, P 11
Upon the Burning of Our House, P 10
biography, P 244
discussed in *What Is American Poetry?*, P 4
subject of *Homage to Mistress Bradstreet*, P 225

Bradstreet, Simon (Anne Bradstreet's husband), P 225

Brahma (1867), Ralph Waldo Emerson, P 34

Brahmin Caste of New England, The (1860), Oliver Wendell Holmes, E 147

Brain—is wider than the Sky—, The (632) (1896), Emily Dickinson, P 129

Brand, Ethan (main character in *Ethan Brand*), S 31

Brandon, Cousin (character in *The Long Christmas Dinner*), D 210

Braneen, Mike (old prospector in *The Wind and the Snow of Winter*), S 234

Brave New World (1946), Archibald MacLeish, P 189

Bray, Henry (Mike Braneen's friend in *The Wind and the Snow of Winter*), S 240

Breughel (a celebrated 16th-17th century family of Flemish painters), P 168

Bricklayer Love (1916), Carl Sandburg, P 157

Bridge, The (1930), Hart Crane, P 195

Bridgepoint, fictional setting for *Melanctha*, N 236

Bridges, Shirley (college student in *Larchmoor Is Not the World*), S 252

Brinnin, John Malcolm (American poet), E 221

Broken Circuit: Romance and the American Novel, The (1957), Richard Chase, E 270

Broken Tower, The (1930), Hart Crane, P 196

BROOKS, VAN WYCK (1886—)
  On Literature Today, E 301

Brother A (financier in *The £1,000,000 Bank-Note*), S 117

Brother B (financier in *The £1,000,000 Bank-Note*), S 117

Brown, Charles Brockden (first American novelist), E 53, 273

Brown, Faith (wife of *Young Goodman Brown*), S 41

Brown, Goodman (hero of *Young Goodman Brown*), S 41

BRYANT, WILLIAM CULLEN (1794–1878)
  The Death of Lincoln, P 25
  A Forest Hymn, P 23
  Inscription for the Entrance to a Wood, P 19
  The Prairies, P 20
  Thantatopsis, P 17
  To the Fringed Gentian, P 20
  To a Waterfowl, P 20
  biography, P 245

Budd, Billy (hero of *Billy Budd*), E 18

Buddha (563?–483? B.C., Siddhartha Gautauma, Asian religious teacher. The word Buddha means "the enlightened one."), P 133

Bully (bulldog in *Blackberry Winter*), S 207

Bumppo, Natty (character in Leather Stocking Series), E 81–83, 85, 276

Bunyan, John (1628–1688, English preacher and author of *Pilgrim's Progress*), E 71, 77

Burgess, Dave (fisherman in *Shore Acres*), D 49

Burgess, Rev. Mr. (character in *The Man That Corrupted Hadleyburg*), N 70

but mr can you (1931), E. E. Cummings, P 190

Byron, George Gordon (1788–1824, English poet), E 182

Cabell, James Branch (American novelist), E 46–47

Caedmon (c. 670, earliest English Christian poet), P 134

California
  Influence on short stories, E 242–44
  setting for *The Chrysanthemums,* S 218
  setting for *Mliss,* S 128
  topic in *The Great American Novel,* N 341-42

Cameron, Dr. (English professor in *Larchmoor Is Not the World*), S 248

Campbell, Jefferson, Dr. (friend of *Melanctha*), N 247

Capital of the World, The (1936), Ernest Hemingway, S 179

Capote, Truman (American author), E 51

Carl Hamblin (1915), Edgar Lee Masters, P 137

Carlyle, Thomas (1795–1936, Scottish essayist and historian), E 3

Carol (Harris' date in *The Hitch-Hikers*), S 229

Carrier, Martha (villager in *Young Goodman Brown*), S 47

CASSILL, R. V. (1919—)
  Larchmoor Is Not the World, S 248
  discussed in *Introduction,* S 10–11

Caterina (Rosalba's mother in *The Venetian Glass Nephew*), N 372

Cather, Willa (American novelist), E 56

Cato (hotel bellboy in *The Hitch-Hikers*), S 228

Cavalry Crossing a Ford (1865), Walt Whitman, P 118

Cecil, David (1902—, English biographer, critic), P 242–43

Chambered Nautilus, The (1858), Oliver Wendell Holmes, P 63

Channing, W. H. (1810–1884, American Unitarian clergyman, reformer), P 31

Chaplain (naval chaplain in *Billy Budd*), N 59

CHAPMAN, JOHN JAY (1862–1933)
  Emerson, E 92

Charles (son of Roderick and Lucia in *The Long Christmas Dinner*), D 210

Charleston (1860), Henry Timrod, P 125

Charlotte (Colonel Manly's sister in *The Contrast*), D 13

CHASE, RICHARD (1914—)
  The Broken Circuit: Romance and the American Novel, E 270

Chastelneuf, de, Chevalier de Langeist (aristocratic magician in *The Venetian Glass Nephew*), N 351

Chattahoochee River, subject of *Song of the Chattahoochee,* P 131

Chaucer (1873), Henry Wadsworth Longfellow, P 39

Chesterton, G. K. (English author), E 3

Children's Hour, The (1859), Henry Wadsworth Longfellow, P 37

Chingachgook (character in Leather Stocking Series), E 83

Chisholm, Mr. and Mrs. (wealthy tourists in *The Petrified Forest*), D 168

Chrysanthemums, The (1938), John Steinbeck, S 218

Churm, Miss (Cockney artist's model in *The Real Thing*), S 93

CIARDI, JOHN (1916—)
  Mystic River, P 228
  biography, P 245

Hastings, Lloyd (Henry Adams' friend in *The £1,000,000 Bank-Note*), S 122

Haunted Palace, The (1845), Edgar Allan Poe, P 54

Hawley, Jack (narrator's friend in *The Real Thing*), S 99

HAWTHORNE, NATHANIEL (1804–1864)
   Ethan Brand, S 31
   The Romance and the Novel: Four Extracts, E 231
   Young Goodman Brown, S 41
   discussed in *Attitudes toward Henry James*, E 157–58
   discussed in *The Broken Circuit: Romance and the American Novel*, E 271–74
   discussed in *Emily Dickinson*, E 119–23
   discussed in *Introduction*, S 2, 3, 9
   discussed in *Reality in America*, E 48–49
   discussed in *Traditions in American Literature*, E 51–54
   subject of *Hawthorne and His Mosses*, E 90–92

Hawthorne and His Mosses (1850), Herman Melville, E 90

Hayes, Tim (character in *Shore Acres*), D 49

Hazlitt, William (1778–1830, English critic and essayist), E 3

Hearn, Lafcadio (American author), S 7

Hecht, Anthony (American poet), E 223

Helen (subject of *To Helen*), P 53

Hellinfinger, Harry (Beckersville loafer in *I Want to Know Why*), S 175

HEMINGWAY, ERNEST (1898—1961)
   The Capital of the World, S 179
   discussed in *Introduction*, S 8–9
   discussed in *Traditions in American Literature*, E 53–54

Hemley, Cecil (American poet), E 224

Henry C. Calhoun (1915), Edgar Lee Masters, P 138

He preached upon "Breadth" till it argued him narrow— (1207) (1891), Emily Dickinson, P 131

Herb (cowboy in *The Petrified Forest*), D 168

Herbert, James (father of *Melanctha*), N 239

Herbert, Melanctha (heroine of *Melanctha*), N 236

Herbert, "Mis," (mother of *Melanctha*), N 238

Heresy of the Didactic (1849), Edgar Allan Poe, E 174

Herman, President (college president in *Larchmoor Is Not the World*), S 249

HERNE, JAMES A. (1839–1901)
   Shore Acres, D 48
   discussed in *Introduction*, D 7–8

Hertzlinger, Boze (Maple's helper in *The Petrified Forest*), D 167

Hewitt, Nancy (Goodson's sweetheart in *The Man That Corrupted Hadleyburg*), N 79

Higgins, Abe (character in *Shore Acres*), D 49

Hill, The (1915), Edgar Lee Masters, P 138

Hitch-Hikers, The (1941), Eudora Welty, S 225

Hodgekins, Bill (fisherman in *Shore Acres*), D 49

HOLMES, OLIVER WENDELL (1809–1894)
   The Brahmin Caste of New England, E 147
   The Chambered Nautilus, P 63
   The Deacon's Masterpiece, P 63
   My Aunt, P 62
   Realism in Literature, E 233
   biography, P 248
   discussed in *Introduction*, E 5

Homage to Mistress Bradstreet (1956), John Berryman, P 225

Homer (c. 850 B.C., name attributed to the author of the *Iliad* and the *Odyssey*), P 133

Homer, Scott (Mamie Cutter's half-brother in *Mrs. Medwin*), S 105

"Hope" is the thing with feathers— (254) (1891), Emily Dickinson, P 128

How Annandale Went Out (1910), Edwin Arlington Robinson, P 141

HOWELLS, WILLIAM DEAN (1837–1920)
   Art and Democracy, E 38
   Subjects for American Fiction, E 236
   discussed in *Introduction*, S 7, 8
   discussed in *Traditions in American Literature*, E 53

How happy is the little Stone (1510) (1891), Emily Dickinson, P 131

Hulme, T. E. (English essayist), P 6

Humor in America (1931), Constance Rourke, E 42

Hunt, Leigh (English poet, essayist), E 3

Hurricane, The (1930), Hart Crane, P 196

Hurt Hawks (1928), Robinson Jeffers, P 177

Huswifery (1685), Edward Taylor, P 12

Hutchins, Ben, Captain (skipper in *Shore Acres*), D 49

Hymn to the Night (1839), Henry Wadsworth Longfellow, P 35

Ianthe (character in *Al Aaraaf*), P 51

Ibsen, Henrik (1828–1906, Norwegian dramatist. His plays remolded dramatic literature), D 6, 8

Manly, Colonel (Revolutionary War officer in *The Contrast*), D 3–5, 13

Man on the wagon (itinerant worker in *The Chrysanthemums*), S 220

Man Saw a Ball of Gold in the Sky, A (1895), Stephen Crane, P 143

Mantee, Duke (gangster in *The Petrified Forest*), D 168

Man That Corrupted Hadleyburg, The (1900), Mark Twain, N 68

Man Thinking (Emersonian ideal), E 23–33

Maple, Gabby (Jason Maple's daughter in *The Petrified Forest*), D 167

Maple, Gramp (Jason Maple's father in *The Petrified Forest*), D 167

Maple, Jason (owner of the Black Mesa Filling Station and Bar-B-Q in *The Petrified Forest*), D 167

Marblehead, Massachusetts, setting for *Skipper Ireson's Ride*, P 40

March into Virginia, The (1866), Herman Melville, P 121

Maria (Dimple's fiancee in *The Contrast*), D 13

Maria (Mike Braneen's burro in *The Wind and the Snow of Winter*), S 235

Maria (Miranda's sister in *The Grave*), S 202

Marina (1936), T. S. Eliot, P 185

Marvel, Andrew (1621–1678, English poet), P 190

Mary Magdalen (nun in *The Venetian Glass Nephew*), N 373

Master, The (1910), Edwin Arlington Robinson, P 139

Master, The (village schoolmaster in *Mliss*), S 129

MASTERS, EDGAR LEE (1868–1950)
Anne Rutledge, P 137
Carl Hamblin, P 137
Fiddler Jones, P 136
Henry C. Calhoun, P 138
The Hill, P 138
The Village Atheist, P 137
biography, P 250
discussed in *What Is American Poetry?*, P 6

Mather, Cotton (1663–1728, American clergyman and author prominent in the Salem witchcraft trials of 1692), E 121, 124–26; S 15

Matthiessen, F. O., (1902–1950, American critic and biographer), P 240

Medford, Massachusetts, setting for *Mystic River*, P 228

Meditation Eight (1685), Edward Taylor, P 13

Mediterranean, The (1933), Allen Tate, P 205

Medwin, Mrs. (Mamie Cutter's client in *Mrs. Medwin*), S 105

Melanctha (1909), Gertrude Stein, N 236

Mellon, Andrew (1855–1951, American banker, Secretary of Treasury under Harding), P 188

MELVILLE, HERMAN (1819–1891)
Bartleby the Scrivener, S 64
The Berg, P 122
Billy Budd, N 18
Hawthorne and His Mosses, E 90
The Maldive Shark, P 122
The March into Virginia, P 121
Misgivings, P 121
biography, P 250
    Discussed in *The Broken Circuit: Romance and the American Novel*, E 276
discussed in *Introduction*, N 5–8; S 2, 6, 9
discussed in *Reality in America*, E 47
discussed in *Traditions in American Literature*, E 53–55
subject of *The Craft of Herman Melville*, E 103–15

MENCKEN, H. L. (1880–1956)
American Culture, E 39
Poetry in America, E 196
discussed in *Introduction*, E 8

Mending Wall (1930), Robert Frost, P 145

Merlin (1867), Ralph Waldo Emerson, P 32

Merrill, James (American poet), E 223

Merwin, W. S. (American poet), E 224

Mexican (drunken marauder in *The Great Divide*), D 107

Mexican Revolution, topic in *The Great American Novel*, N 320–321

Mexican War, sparked by the annexation of Texas in 1845, E 241

Middlestride (racehorse in *I Want to Know Why*), S 177

Mike (old collie in *The Hitch-Hikers*), S 228

Milford Corners, Massachusetts, setting in *The Great Divide*, D 129

Mill, The (1937), Edwin Arlington Robinson, P 142

MILLAY, EDNA ST. VINCENT (1892–1950)
Epitaph for the Race of Man (excerpts), P 187
First Fig, P 186
Second Fig, P 186
biography, P 250

Miller, Arthur (American playwright), D 12

Milly (granddaughter of *Wash*), S 193

Milton (1873), Henry Wadsworth Longfellow, P 39

Milton, John (1608–1674, English poet, considered second only to Shakespeare), P 134

RANSOM, JOHN CROWE (1888—)
   Bells for John Whiteside's Daughter,
    P 179
   Blue Girls, P 182
   The Equilibrists, P 180
   Janet Waking, P 181
   Philomena, P 179
   biography, P 251
Ratcliffe, Lieutenant (minor character in
   Billy Budd), E 20
Raven, The (1845), Edgar Allan Poe, P 56
Rawson, Matt (tenant farmer in *Blackberry
   Winter*), S 213
Realism in Literature (1891), Oliver Wen-
   dell Holmes, E 233
Reality in America (1940), Lionel Trilling,
   E 45
Real Thing, The (1892), Henry James,
   S 87
Red Whiskers (sailor in *Billy Budd*), N 21
Reifsneider, Henry (hero of *The Lost
   Phoebe*), S 163
Reifsneider, Phoebe (Henry's wife in *The
   Lost Phoebe*), S 164
Repetitive Heart, The (1938), Delmore
   Schwartz, P 221
Repplier, Agnes (American essayist), E 6
Rest, The (1926), Ezra Pound, P 173
Reuben Bright (1897), Edwin Arlington
   Robinson, P 141
Revolutionary War
   setting for *The Sleepers,* P 108
   subject of *Concord Hymn,* P 25
   subject of *To the Memory of Brave
    Americans,* P 14
   topic in *The Great American Novel,*
    N 324
Rhapsody on a Windy Night (1936), T.
   S. Eliot, P 183
Rich, Adrienne Cecile (American poet),
   E 224
Richard Cory (1897), Edwin Arlington
   Robinson, P 140
Richards, Edward (leading citizen in *The
   Man That Corrupted Hadleyburg*),
   N 70
Richards, Ike (character in *Shore Acres*),
   D 49
Richards, Jem (friend of *Melanctha*), N 298
Richards, Mary (Edward's wife in *The
   Man That Corrupted Hadleyburg*),
   N 69
Rieback, Henry (narrator's friend in *I Want
   to Know Why*), S 174
Riggs, Lynn (American playwright), D 11
Rise of the Short Story, The (1899),
   Bret Harte, E 239
River, The (1930), Hart Crane, P 199
River-Merchant's Wife: A Letter, The
   (1926), Ezra Pound, P 171

Rivet, Claude (artist in *The Real Thing*),
   S 87
ROBINSON, EDWIN ARLINGTON
   (1869–1935)
   Cliff Klingenhagen, P 140
   How Annandale Went Out, P 141
   Luke Havergal, P 139
   The Master, P 139
   The Mill, P 142
   Mr. Flood's Party, P 141
   New England, P 143
   Reuben Bright, P 141
   Richard Cory, P 140
   Walt Whitman, P 142
   biography, P 252
   discussed in *What Is American Poetry?,*
    P 6
   quoted in *The Anglo-American Differ-
    ence,* E 210
Rob Roy (Colonel Sutpen's horse in *Wash*),
   S 193
Roderick (Mother Bayard's son in *The
   Long Christmas Dinner*), D 210
Roderick II (son of Charles and Leonora in
   The Long Christmas Dinner), D 210
Rodman, Selden (American poet, critic),
   P 242
ROETHKE, THEODORE (1908—1963)
   Dolor, P 212
   The Dream, P 213
   Elegy for Jane, P 213
   My Papa's Waltz, P 213
   Night Crow, P 213
   The Shape of the Fire, P 214
   biography, P 252
   discussed in *The New Poetry,* E 218–20
**Romance and the Novel: Four Extracts,
   The** (1850, 1851, 1852, 1859), Na-
   thaniel Hawthorne, E 231
Romance as Epic, The (1835), William
   Gilmore Simms, E 230
Roosevelt, Franklin D. (1882–1945, thirty-
   first President of the United States),
   E 265
Rose for Emily, A (1930), William Faulk-
   ner, S 186
ROURKE, CONSTANCE (1885–1941)
   Humor in America, E 42
Rousseau, Jean Jacques (1712–1778, Swiss-
   born philosopher and author), N 1
Route of Evanescence, A (1463) (1891),
   Emily Dickinson, P 131
Ruby (gangster in *The Petrified Forest*),
   D 168
Rum Alley, slum neighborhood in *Maggie:
   A Girl of the Streets,* N 97
Ruth (Harris' friend in *The Hitch-Hikers*),
   S 229
Rush, Benjamin (American physician, pa-
   triot), E 4